Arthur W. Pink's

Eternal Punishment

&

Eternal Security

Printed in the United States of America and Australia.

Bottom of the Hill Publishing
Memphis, TN
www.BottomoftheHillPublishing.com

ISBN: 978-1-61203-543-7

Contents

Eternal Punishment

Contents

Introduction

This time we take up our pen to write on one of the most solemn truths taught in the Word. And ere we began we turned to the Lord and earnestly sought that wisdom and grace which we are conscious we sorely need; making request that we might be preserved from all error in what we shall say, and that nothing may find a place in these pages which shall be displeasing to that Holy One, "whose we are, and whom we serve." O that we may write in the spirit of One who said, "Who knoweth the power of Thine anger, even according to Thy fear, so is Thy wrath" (Ps. 90:11).

The subject before us is one that needs stressing in these days. The great majority of our pulpits are silent upon it, and the fact that it has so little place in modern preaching is one of the signs of the times, one of the many evidences that the Apostasy must be near at hand. It is true that there are not a few who are praying for a world-wide Revival, but it appears to the writer that it would be more timely, and more scriptural, for prayer to be made to the Lord of the harvest, that He would raise up and thrust forth laborers who would fearlessly and faithfully preach those truths which are calculated to bring about a revival.

While it is true that all genuine revivals come from God, yet He is not capricious in the sending of them. We are sure that God never relinquishes His sovereign rights to own and to bless where and as He pleases. But we also believe that here, as everywhere, there is a direct connection between cause and effect. And a revival is the effect of a previous cause. A revival, like a genuine conversion, is wrought of God by means of the Word—the Word applied by the Holy Spirit, of course. Therefore, there is something more needed (on our part) than prayer: the Word of God must have a place, a prominent place, the prominent place. Without that there will be no Revival, whatever excitement and activities of the emotions there may be.

It is the deepening conviction of the writer that what is most needed today is a wide proclamation of those truths which are the least acceptable to the flesh. What is needed today is a scriptural setting forth of the character of God—His absolute sovereignty, His ineffable holiness, His inflexible justice, His unchanging veracity. What is needed today is a scriptural setting forth of the condition of the natural man—his total depravity, his spiritual insensibility, his inveterate hostility to God, the fact that he is "condemned already" and that the wrath of a sin-hating God is even now abiding upon him. What is needed today is a scriptural setting forth of the alarming danger in which sinners are—the indescribably awful doom which awaits them, the fact that if they follow only a little further their present course they shall most certainly suffer the due reward of their iniquities. What is needed today is a scriptural setting forth of the nature of that punishment which awaits the lost—the awfulness of it, the hopelessness of it, the unendurableness of it, the endlessness of it. It is because of these convictions that by pen as well as by voice we are seeking to raise the alarm.

It may be thought that what we have said in the above paragraph stands in need of qualification. We can imagine some of our readers saying, Such truths as these may be needed by the lost, but surely you do not wish to be understood as saying that these subjects ought to be pressed upon the Lord's people! But that is exactly what we do mean and do say. Re-read the Epistles, dear friends, and note what place each of these subjects has in them! It is just because these truths have been withheld so much from public ministrations to the saints that we now find so many backboneless, sentimental, lop-sided Christians in our assemblies. A clearer vision of the awe-inspiring attributes of God would banish much of our levity and irreverence. A better understanding of our depravity by nature would humble us, and make us see our deep need of using the appointed means of grace. A facing of the alarming danger of the sinner would cause us to "consider our ways" and make us more diligent to make our "calling and election sure." A realization of the unspeakable misery which awaits the lost (and which each of us fully merited) would immeasurably deepen our gratitude, and bring us to thank God more fervently that we have been snatched as brands from the burning and delivered from the wrath to come; and too, it will make us far more earnest in our prayers as we supplicate God on behalf of the unsaved. Moreover, scriptural and searching addresses along these lines would, in some cases at least, lay hold of those who have a form of godliness but who deny the power thereof. They would have some effect on that vast company of professors who are "at ease in Zion." They would, if God were depended upon, arouse the indifferent, and cause some who are now careless and unconcerned to cry, "What must I do to be saved?" Remember that the ground must be plowed before it is ready to be sowed: and the truths mentioned above are needed to prepare the way for the Gospel.

Concerning the eternal punishment of the wicked there are few, it seems, who realize the vital importance of a ringing testimony to this truth, and fewer still who apprehend the deep seriousness of what is involved in a denial of it. The importance of a clear witness to this doctrine may be seen by noting what a prominent place it holds in the Word; and contrariwise, the seriousness of denying it is evidenced by the fact that such denial is a rejection of God's truth. The need of giving this solemn subject a prominent place in our witness is apparent, for it is our bounden duty to warn sinners of their fearful peril and bid them flee from the wrath to come. To remain silent is criminal; to substitute anything for it is to set before the wicked a false hope. The great importance of expounding this doctrine, freely and frequently, also appears in that, excepting the Cross of Christ, nothing else so manifests the heinousness of sin, whereas every modification of eternal punishment, only serves to minimize the evil of it.

We propose to deal with our present theme under the following divisions. First, we shall examine briefly some of the leading objections brought against the truth of eternal punishment. Second, we shall classify various passages which treat of the destiny of the lost, showing that death seals the sinner's doom, that his condition is then beyond hope, that the punishment awaiting him is interminable. Third, we shall examine those scriptures which throw light upon the nature of the punishment which awaits the lost. Finally, we shall seek to make a practical application of the whole subject.

Chapter I
Objections Considered

In taking up the objections made against the truth of eternal punishment it would be a hopeless task were we to attempt to notice every argument which the fertile mind of unbelief (under the control of Satan, as it is) has devised. We shall, however, consider those of greatest weight, and those which have received the widest acceptance among unbelievers. These we shall classify as follows: First, deductions drawn from the Divine perfections. Second, passages appealed to by Universalists. Third, passages appealed to by Annihilationists. Fourth, assertions that punishment is not penal and retributive but disciplinary and remedial.

1. DEDUCTIONS DRAWN FROM THE DIVINE PERFECTIONS.

(1) God is love, From this scriptural premise the conclusion is drawn that He will never cast any of His creatures into endless woe. But we must remember that the Bible also tells us that "God is light," and between light and darkness there can be no fellowship, Divine love is not a sentimental passion which overrides moral distinctions. God's love is a holy love, and because it is such He hates all evil; yea, it is written, "Thou hatest all workers of iniquity" (Ps. 5:5). Startling as it may sound, it is nevertheless a fact, that the Scriptures speak much more frequently of God's anger and wrath, than they do of His love and compassion. Let anyone consult Young's or Strong's Concordance and they may verify this for themselves. To argue, then, that because God is love, He will not inflict eternal torment on the wicked, is to ignore the fact that God is light, and is to asperse His holiness.

(2) God is merciful. Man may be a sinner, and holiness may require that he should be punished, but it is argued that Divine mercy will intervene, and if the punishment be not entirely revoked it is imagined that the sentence will be modified and the term of punishment be shortened. We are told that the eternal torment of the lost cannot be harmonized with a God of mercy. But if by the mercy of God be meant that He is too tenderhearted to apportion such miseries to His creatures, then we might as logically reason that seeing God's mercy, like all His attributes, is infinite, therefore, none of His creatures will be permitted to suffer at all. Yet this is manifestly erroneous. Facts deny it. His creatures do suffer, ofttimes excruciatingly, even in this life. Look out on the world today and mark the untold misery which abounds on every hand, and then remember that, however mysterious all this may be to us, nevertheless, it is all permitted by a merciful God. So, too, read in the Old Testament the accounts of the deluge, the destruction of Sodom and Gomorrah by fire and brimstone from heaven, the plagues upon Egypt, the judgments which were visited upon Israel, and then bear in mind that these were not prevented by the mercy of God! To reason, then, that because God is merciful

He will not cast into the Lake of Fire every one whose name is not found written in the book of life, is to fly in the face of all God's judgments in the past!

(3) God is just. It is often said it would be unjust for God to sentence any of His erring creatures to eternal perdition. But who are we to pass judgment upon the justice of the decisions of the All-Wise? Who are we to say what is consistent or inconsistent with God's righteousness? Who are we to determine what shall best vindicate the Divine benevolence or equity? Sin has so enfeebled our power of righteous judgment, so darkened our understanding, so dulled our conscience, so perverted our wills, so corrupted our hearts, that we are quite incompetent to decide. We are ourselves so infected and affected by sin that we are altogether incapable of estimating its due merits. Imagine a company of criminals passing judgment on the equity and goodness of the law which had condemned them! The truth of the matter is—and how often is it lost sight of!—that God is not to be measured by human standards.

But have we realized that to deny the justice of eternal punishment is also to repudiate the grace of God? If endless misery be unjust, then exemption from it must be the sinner's right, and if so, his salvation could never be attributed to grace, which is unmerited favor! Moreover, to deny the justice of eternal punishment is to fly in the face of Christian consciousness, which universally witnesses to the fact that punishment, and only punishment, is all that each of us deserves. Moreover, if the sinner has despised and rejected eternal happiness, is there any reason why he should complain against the justice of eternal misery? Finally, if there is an infinite evil in sin—as there is—then infinite punishment is its due reward.

(4) God is holy. Because God is infinitely holy, He regards sin with infinite abhorrence. From this scriptural premise it has been erroneously concluded that, therefore, God will ultimately triumph over evil by banishing every last trace of it from the universe; otherwise, it is said, His moral character is gone. But against this sophistry we reply; God's holiness did not prevent sin entering His universe, and He has permitted it to remain all these thousands of years, therefore a holy God can and does coexist with a world of sin! To this it may be answered: There are good and sufficient reasons why sin should be allowed now. Quite so, is our rejoinder; and who knows what these reasons are? Conjecture we may; but who knows? God has not told us in His Word. Who, then, is in the position to say that there may not be eternal reasons—necessities— for the continued existence of sin? That God will triumph over evil is most certainly true. His triumph will be manifested by incarcerating every one of His foes in a place where they can do no more damage, and where in their torments His holy hatred of sin will shine for ever and ever. The Lake of Fire so far from witnessing to Satan's victory, will be the crowning proof of his utter defeat.

2. THE PASSAGES APPEALED TO BY UNIVERSALISTS.

Universalists may be divided, broadly, into two classes: those who teach the ultimate salvation of every member of Adam's race, and those who affirm the ultimate salvation of all creatures, including the Devil, the fallen angels, and the demons. The class of passages to which both appeal are verses where the words "all," "all men," "all things," "the world" are to be found. The simplest way to refute their contentions on these passages is to show that such terms are restricted usually modified by what is said in the immediate context.

The issue raised by Universalists narrows itself down to the question of whether "all men" and "all things" are employed, in passages which speak of salvation, in a limited or unlimited sense. Let us, then, point to a number of passages where these general terms occur, but where it is impossible to give them an absolute force or meaning:

"And there went out unto him all the land of Judea, and they of Jerusalem, and were all baptized of him in the river of Jordan, confessing their sins" (Mark 1:5). "And as the people were in expectation, and all men mused in their hearts of John, whether he were the Christ or not" (Luke 3:15). "And they came unto John, and said unto him, Rabbi, He that was with thee beyond Jordan, to whom thou barest witness, behold the same baptizeth, and all come to Him" (John 3:26). "And early in the morning He came again into the temple," and "all the people came unto Him; and He sat down, and taught them" (John 8:2). "For thou shalt be His witness unto all men of what thou hast seen and heard (Acts 22:15). "Ye are our epistle written in our hearts, known and read of all men" (2 Cor. 3:2).

In none of the above passages has "all," "all men," "all the people" an unlimited scope. In each of those passages these general terms have only a relative meaning. In Scripture "all" is used in two ways: meaning "all without exception" (occurring infrequently), and "all without distinction" (its general significance), that is, all classes and kinds—old and young, men and women, rich and poor, educated and illiterate, and in many in-stances Jews and Gentiles, men of all nations. Very frequently the "all" has reference to all believers, all in Christ.

What we have just said concerning the relative use and restricted meaning of the terms "all" and "all men" applies with equal force to "all things." In Scripture this is another expression which often has a very limited meaning. We give a few examples of this: "For one believeth that he may eat all things: another, who is weak, eateth herbs" (Rom. 14:2). "For meat destroy not the work of God. All things indeed are pure" (Rom. 14.20). "I am made all things to all, that I might by all means save some" (1 Cor. 9:22). "All things are lawful for me, but all things are not expedient" (1 Cor. 10:23). "Tychicus, a beloved brother and faithful minister in the Lord, shall make known to you all things" (Eph. 6:2 1). I can do all things through Christ which strengtheneth me" (Phil. 4:13). In each of these passages "all things" has a restricted force.

Another class of passages appealed to by Universalists are verses where "the world" is mentioned. But a careful examination of every passage where this term occurs in the New Testament will show that we are not obliged to understand it as referring to the entire human race, because in a number of instances it means far less. Take the following examples. "For the bread of God is He which cometh down from heaven and giveth life unto the world" (John 6:33). Mark that here it is not a matter of proffering "life" to the world, but of giving "life." Does Christ "give life"—spiritual and eternal life, for that is what is in view—to every member of the human family? "If thou do these things, show Thyself to the world" (John 7.4). Here it is plain that "the world" is an indefinite expression—show Thyself in public, to men in general, is its obvious meaning here. "The Pharisees therefore said among themselves, Perceive ye how we prevail nothing? Behold, the world is gone after Him" (John 12:19). Did the Pharisees mean that the entire human race had "gone after" Christ? Surely not. "First, I thank my God through Jesus Christ for you all, that your faith is spoken of throughout the whole world" (Rom. 1:8). Must this mean that the faith of the Roman saints was known and spoken of by all the race of mankind? Did all men everywhere "speak" of it? Did one man out of every ten thousand in the Roman Empire know anything about it? "The word of the truth of the Gospel, which is come unto you, as it is in all the world" (Col. 1:5, 6). Does "all the world" here mean, absolutely and unqualifiedly, all mankind? Had all men everywhere heard the Gospel? Surely the meaning of this verse is, that the Gospel, instead of being confined to the land of Judea and the lost sheep of the house of Israel, had gone forth abroad without restraint, into many places. "And all the world wondered after the beast" (Rev. 13:3). That the reference here cannot be to all men without exception we know from other scriptures.

It will be seen, then, from the passages cited above that there is nothing in the words themselves which compel us to give an unlimited meaning to "all men," "all things," "the world." Therefore when we insist that "the world" which is saved, and the "all men" who are redeemed, are the world of believers and the all men who receive Christ as their personal Savior, instead of interpreting the Scriptures to suit ourselves we are explaining them in strict harmony with other passages. On the other hand, to give to these terms unlimited scope and to make them mean all without exception is to interpret them in a way which manifestly clashes with the many passages which plainly teach there are those who will be finally lost.

One other remark may be made upon Universalism before turning to our next subdivision, and that is, the very fact that Universalism is so popular with the wicked, is proof irresistible, that it is not the system taught in the Bible. 1 Corinthians 2:14 tells us "the natural man receiveth not the things of the Spirit of God: for they are foolishness unto him: neither can he know them, because they are spiritually discerned." That the natural man does receive the teaching that everyone will ultimately be saved, is a sure sign it does not belong to "the things of the Spirit of God." The wicked hate the light, but love the darkness; hence, while they deem as "foolishness" the truth of God and reject it, they esteem as reasonable the Devil's lies, and greedily devour them.

3. PASSAGES APPEALED TO BY THE ANNIHILATIONISTS.

Truth is one: consistent: eternally unchanged. Error is hydra-headed, inconsistent and contradictory, ever wavering in its forms. So determined are men to persuade themselves that the eternal punishment of the wicked is a myth, the enmity of the carnal mind has devised a variety of ways of ridding themselves of this truth which is so hateful to them. "God hath made man upright; but they have sought out many inventions" (Eccl. 7:29). One of these inventions is the theory that at death the wicked pass into oblivion, and that after their resurrection and judgment at the Great White Throne, they are annihilated in the Lake of Fire. Incredible as this view appears, nevertheless it has had and still has many advocates and adherents; and what is even more unthinkable, the Word of God is appealed to in support of it. It is because of this that we make a brief notice of it here.

The first class of passages to which they appeal are verses where "death" is mentioned. Death is regarded in the most absolute sense. Death they take to mean the passing from existence into non-existence; an utter extinction of being. Death is applied to the soul as well as the body. How, then, is this error to be met? We answer, By an appeal to God's Word. The meaning of a word is to be defined not from its derivation, not from its employment by heathen writers, not from the definition supplied by a standard English dictionary, nor from the lexicons, but from its usage in the Holy Scriptures. What, then, does death mean as used by the Holy Spirit?

Let us turn first to 1 Corinthians 15:36: "Thou fool, that which thou sowest is not quickened, except it die." Here is the Holy Spirit's illustration and type of the death and resurrection of a believer. Now, does the living germ in the seed sown become extinct before it brings forth fruit? Surely not. There is a decaying, of course, of its outer shell— and therein lies the analogy with the death of man—but the living germ within dies not, otherwise there could be no harvest. Death, then, according to this illustration of the Holy Spirit is not annihilation. The same illustration was used by our Lord. Said He, "Except a corn of wheat fall into the ground and die, it abideth alone: but if it die, it bringeth forth much fruit" (John 12:24). The stalk and ear of corn in harvest time are but the life-germ fully developed. So it is with man. The body dies; the soul lives on. Note how this comes out, unmistakably, in the Savior's words as recorded in Matt. 10:28: "And fear not them which kill the body, but are not able to kill the soul: but rather fear Him which is able to destroy both soul and body in hell." The "soul" man is unable to kill! But God is able—and mark carefully the distinction—"to destroy (not kill) both soul and body in hell." As the word "destroy" is another word misused and erroneously defined by the Annihilationists, a few words must be said upon it.

As used in Scripture the words "destroy," "destruction," "perish" etc. never signify cessation of existence. In Matthew 10:7 one of the principal Greek words for "destroyed" is rendered "the lost sheep of the house of Israel." Those Israelites had not ceased to be, but were away from God! In Mark 2:22 the same word is translated "marred" in connection with "bottles" of skins which the new wine burst. So, too, the word "perish" never signifies annihilation in Scripture. In 2 Peter 3:6 we read, "The world" that then was, being overflowed with water, perished." The "world" that perished, whether the reference be to the pre-Adamic earth or the world destroyed by the Flood, was not reduced to nothing. When, then, Scripture speaks of the wicked as perishing and as being destroyed, it is in order to expose the error of those who assert that they have a gospel for those who die unsaved, That the wicked have "perished" excludes all hope of their subsequent salvation. 1 Timothy 5:6 tells us there is a living-death even now—"She that liveth in pleasure is dead while she liveth"—so will there be in eternity.

The absurdity and unscripturalness of Annihilationism are easily exposed. If at death the sinner passes out of existence, why resurrect him in order to annihilate him again? Scripture speaks of the "punishment" and "torment" of the wicked; but anyone can see that annihilation is not these! If annihilation were all that awaits the wicked, they would never know that they had received their just deserts and the "due reward" of their iniquities! Scripture speaks of degrees of punishment for the lost; but annihilation would make this impossible; annihilation would level all distinctions and ignore all degrees of guilt. In Isaiah 33:14 we are told, "Who among us shall dwell with the devouring fire? Who among us shall dwell with everlasting burnings?" So far from sinners being annihilated they shall dwell with the devouring fire! Scripture speaks again and again of the "wailing and gnashing of teeth" of those who are cast into hell, and this, at once, gives the lie to those who affirm extinction of being.

4. THE THEORY THAT THE PUNISHMENT OF THE WICKED IS DISCIPLINARY AND REMEDIAL.

There are those who allow that the wicked will be cast into hell, and yet they insist that the punishment is corrective rather than retributive. A sort of Protestant Purgatory is invented, the fires of which are to be purifying rather than penal. Such a conception is grossly dishonoring to God. Some who hold this view make a great pretense of honoring Christ, yet in reality they greatly dishonor Him. If men who died rejecting the Savior are yet to be saved, if the fires of hell are to do for men what the blood of the Cross failed to effect, then why was the Divine Sacrifice needed at all—all might have been saved by the disciplinary sufferings of hell, and so God could have spared His Son. Again; if God compassionates His enemies and cherishes nothing but gracious designs of infinite pity toward those who have despised and rejected His Son, we may well ask, Then why does He take such dreadful measures with them? If loving discipline be all that they need, cannot Divine wisdom devise some gentler measure than consigning them to the "torment" of the Lake of Fire for "the ages of the ages?" This is an insuperable difficulty in the way of the theory we are now refuting. But once we see that the Lake of Fire is the place of punishment, not discipline, and that it is Divine wrath and not love that casts the reprobate into it, then the difficulty entirely disappears.

Utterly inconsistent though it be, there are those who argue that the fires of hell owe their disciplinary efficacy to the blood of Christ. These enemies of the truth have been well answered by Sir Robert Anderson: "Such punishment, therefore, must be the penalty due to their sins; else it were unrighteous to impose it. If, then, the lost are ultimately to be saved, it must be either because they shall have satisfied the penalty; or else through redemption—that is, because Christ has borne that penalty for them. But if sinners can be saved by satisfying Divine justice in enduring the penalty due to sin, Christ need not have died. If, on the other hand, the redeemed may yet be doomed, though ordained to eternal life in Christ, themselves to endure the penalty for sin, the foundations of our faith are destroyed. It is not, I repeat, the providential or disciplinary, but the penal consequences of sin, which follow the judgment. We can therefore understand how the sinner may escape his doom through his debt being paid vicariously, or we can (in theory, at all events) admit that he may be discharged on payment personally of "the uttermost farthing;" but that the sinner should be made to pay a portion of his debt, and then released because someone else had paid the whole before he was remitted to punishment at all—this is absolutely inconsistent with both righteousness and grace" ("Human Destiny").

Again; if it be true that the damned in the Lake of Fire are still the objects of Divine benevolence; that as the creatures of His hand, the Lord still looks upon them with the most benign regard, and the unquenchable fire is nothing more than a rod in the hand of a wise and loving Father, we ask, How can this be harmonized with the manner in which Scripture uniformly speaks of unbelievers? God has not left us in ignorance of how He regards those who have openly and persistently defied Him. Again and again the Bible makes known to us the solemn fact that God looks upon the wicked as cumberers of the earth, as repugnant to Him. They are represented as "dross" not gold (Ps. 119:119); as worthless "chaff (Matt. 3:12); as "vipers" (Matt. 12:34); as "vessels unto dishonor" and "vessels of wrath" (Rom. 9:21, 22); as those who are to be made the Lord's footstool (1 Cor. 15:2 7) as "trees whose fruit withereth, without fruit, twice dead, plucked up by the roots" (Jude 12) and therefore fit for nothing but the fire; as those who will be "spewed out of the Lord's mouth" (Rev. 3:16), that is, as objects of revulsion. Some of these passages describe Jewish reprobates, others sinners of the Gentiles; some refer to those who lived in a by-gone dispensation, others belong to the present; some speak of men this side of the grave, some of those on the other side. One purpose in calling attention to them is to show how God regards his enemies. The estimate expressed in the above passages (and they might easily be multiplied) cannot be harmonized with the view that God still looks upon them in love and entertains only the most tender regards for them.

Another class of passages may be referred to in this connection. "For I lift up My hand to heaven, and say, I live forever. If I whet My glittering sword, and Mine hand take hold on judgment; I will render vengeance to Mine enemies, and will reward them that hate Me. I will make Mine arrows drunk with blood, and my sword shall devour flesh; and that with the blood of the slain and of the captives, from the beginning of revenges upon the enemy" (Deut. 32:40-42). Can this be made to square with the theory that God has naught but compassion toward those who have despised and defied Him?

"Because I have called, and ye have refused; I have stretched out My hand, and no man regarded; But ye have set at nought all My counsel, and would none of My reproof; I also will laugh at your calamity; I will mock when your fear cometh; When your fear cometh as desolation, and your destruction cometh as a whirlwind; when distress and anguish cometh upon you. Then shall they call upon Me, but I will not answer; they shall seek Me early, but they shall not find Me" (Prov. 1:24-28). Is this the language of One who still has designs of mercy toward His enemies?

"I have trodden the winepress alone; and of the people there was none with Me; for I will tread them in Mine anger, and trample them in My fury; and their blood shall be sprinkled upon My garments, and I will stain all My raiment" (Isa. 63:3). Weigh this carefully, and then ask if such treatment is meted out toward those unto whom the Lord cherishes nought but compassion.

Should it be said, Each of these passages is from the Old Testament, it would be sufficient to say, True, but it is the same God as the New Testament reveals that is there speaking. But consider one verse from the New Testament also. The Christ of God is yet going to say to men, "Depart from Me, ye cursed into everlasting fire" (Matt. 25:41). Is it thinkable that the Son of God would pronounce this awful malediction upon those who are merely appointed to a season of disciplinary chastisement, after which they will be forever with him in perfect bliss!

Thus we have sought to show that the various objections brought against eternal punishment will not stand the test of Holy Writ; that, though often presented in a plausible form, and with the avowed intention of vindicating the Divine character. yet, in reality, they are nothing more than the reasonings of that carnal mind which is enmity against God.

Having disposed of the principal objections brought against the truth of Eternal Punishment, we now turn to consider:

Chapter II
The Destiny Of The Wicked

There is deep need for us to approach this solemn subject impartially and dispassionately. Let writer and reader cry earnestly to God that all prejudices and preconceptions may be removed from our minds. It ill becomes us to sit at the feet of Infinite Wisdom determined to hold fast to our foregone conclusions. Nothing can be more insulting to God than to presume to examine His Word, professing a desire to learn His mind, when we have already settled to our own satisfaction what it will say. Someone has said that we ought to bring our minds to the Scriptures as blank paper is brought to the printing press, that it may receive only the impress of the type. May such grace be vouchsafed to us all that we may ever present our minds to the Holy Spirit's teaching that only the impress may be left which God has designed. May our only desire be to hear "What saith the Lord?"

1. THE CERTAINTY OF THEIR JUDGMENT.

It is written "It is appointed unto men once to die, but after this the judgment" (Heb. 9:27). This is one of the many verses which refute the errors of the Annihilationists, who make the judgment of the sinner to be, itself, death. But here death and judgment are clearly distinguished. The one follows the other.

The fact of a future judgment for sinners is established by numerous passages. In Ecclesiastes 11:9 we read, "Rejoice, O young man, in thy youth; and let thy heart cheer thee in the days of thy youth, and walk in the ways of thine heart, and in the sight of thine eyes: but know thou, that for all these things God will bring thee into judgment." Again, in Ecclesiastes 12:14, we are told, For God shall bring every work into judgment, with every secret thing, whether it be good, or whether it be evil." The New Testament witnesses to the same truth: "He hath appointed a day, in the which He will judge the world in righteousness by that man whom He hath ordained" (Acts 17:31). The judgment itself is described in Revelation 20:11-15.

Of the certainty of this coming judgment we are left in no doubt—"The Lord knoweth how to deliver the godly out of temptations, and to reserve the unjust unto the day of judgment to be punished" (2 Pet. 2:9). It will be impossible for the sinner to evade it. Escape there will be none—"How can ye escape the damnation of hell?" (Matt. 23.33). Resistance, individually or collectively, will be futile—"Though hand join in hand, the wicked shall not be unpunished" (Prov. 11:2 1). No confederacy of His foes shall hinder God from taking vengeance upon them.

2. DEATH SEALS THE SINNER'S FATE.

Scripture teaches plainly that man's opportunity for salvation is limited to the period of his earthly life. If he dies unsaved his fate is sealed inexorably. There are two passages in the New Testament most generally relied upon by those who affirm that there is for the lost a hope beyond death. These are both found in the 1st Epistle of Peter. A brief notice then shall be taken of them.

"For Christ also hath once suffered for sins, the just for the unjust, that He might bring us to God, being put to death in the flesh, but quickened by the Spirit: By which also He went and preached unto the spirits in prison; Which sometime were disobedient, when once the long-suffering of God waited in the days of Noah, while the ark was a preparing" (3:18-20). But these verses make no reference whatever to any preaching heard by those who had already passed out of this life. They simply tell us that the Spirit of God preached through Noah, while the ark was being built, to those who were disobedient; and because they refused to respond to that preaching they are now "spirits in prison." It was not Christ Himself who "preached," but the Holy Spirit, as is plain from the opening words of v. 19—"By which also:" the "by which" points back to "the Spirit" at the end of v. 18. That the Holy Spirit did address Himself to the antediluvians we know from Genesis 6:3—"My Spirit shall not always strive with man." The Spirit strove through Noah's preaching. That Noah was a "preacher" we learn from 2 Peter 2:5.

The second passage is found in 1 Peter 4:6, "For this cause was the Gospel preached also to them that are dead." But this need not detain us. The Gospel was preached, not is now being preached, or, will again be preached to them! That such passages as these are appealed to only serves to show how untenable and impossible is the contention they are supposed to support.

That death seals the doom of the lost, we may prove negatively by the fact—and this is conclusive of itself—that we have not a single instance described in either the Old Testament or the New of a sinner being saved after death. Nor is there a single passage which holds out any promise of this in the future. But there are passages which contain positive teaching to the contrary. Several of these are now submitted.

We turn first to Proverbs 29:1: "He, that being often reproved hardeneth his neck, shall suddenly be destroyed, and that without remedy." This is so explicit and unequivocal it needs no words of ours either to expound or enforce it. Once the rebellious sinner is "cut off" he is "without remedy." Nothing could be clearer: at death his doom is sealed.

Again, in Matthew 9:6 we read, "But that ye may know that the Son of Man hath power on earth to forgive sins, (then saith He to the sick of the palsy) Arise, take up thy bed, and go unto thine house." Why did not the Lord simply say, "The Son of Man hath power to forgive sins," and then stop? That would have been sufficient reply to His critics. The only reason that we can suggest why the Savior should have added the qualifying words—"The Son of Man hath power on earth to forgive sins—was because He would give us to understand that after a sinner leaves the "earth" the Son of Man (Christ in His mediatonal character) has not the "power" (or "authority" as exousia really means) to forgive sins!

A similar instance to the above is found in John 12:25: "He that loveth his life shall lose it; and he that hateth his life in this world shall keep it unto life eternal." Notice that the antithesis would be complete without the restricting words "in this world"

—"He that loveth his life shall lose it; and he that hateth his life shall keep it unto life eternal." Again, we say, that the only reason we can see why Christ added the qualifying clause, "He that hateth his life in this world shall keep it unto life eternal" was in order to show that destiny is fixed once we leave this world.

In 2 Corinthians 5:10, which speaks of believers, we have another example of this careful employment of qualifying language: "We must all appear before the judgment seat of Christ; that every one may receive the things done in his body." The saints are to be dealt with not merely according to what they have done, but that they may receive "the things done in the body." What they have done after they left the body and prior to the resurrection is not taken into account.

In John 8:21 it is recorded how that Christ said to His enemies, "I go My way, and ye shall seek Me, and shall die in your sins; whither I go, ye cannot come." Observe carefully the order of the last two clauses. Once they died in their sins, it was impossible for them to go to heaven. The solemn force of this verse comes out even more clearly if we contrast with it John 13:36: "Simon Peter said unto Him, Lord, whither goest Thou? Jesus answered him, Whither I go, thou canst not follow Me now; but thou shalt follow Me afterwards." Mark the absence of the qualifying "now" in John 8:21. To Peter it was said, as to a representative saint, "Thou shalt follow Me (to heaven) afterwards;" but to the wicked, Christ declared, "Whither I go, ye cannot come!"

3. WHAT AWAITS THE SINNER AT DEATH

We naturally turn for light on this to the teaching of the Lord, for more was said through Him than through any other concerning the future of the wicked. Nor shall we turn in vain to the record of His words. In Luke 16 we find Him drawing aside the veil which hides from us what lies beyond death. He tells us of a rich man who died "and was buried" (v. 22). But he had not ceased to exist. So far from it, the Lord went on to say, "And in hell he lift up his eyes, being in torments." That Christ was here describing the actual experience of this rich man after death there is no good reason to doubt; to say otherwise, is to be guilty of blasphemously charging the Son of God with using language which He knew would mislead countless numbers of those who later would read the record of His words. No one who comes to this passage with an unprejudiced mind would ever suppose that it gave anything else than a plain and simple picture of what befalls the wicked after death. It is only those who have previously arrived at the foregone conclusion that there is no torment for the unbeliever after death, who approach this passage determined to explain away its obvious meaning, who rule out of it what is there and read into it what is not there.

"In Hades he lift up his eyes, being in torments." The Greek word here translated hell is "Hades," which is a generic term for the unseen world, into which the souls of all pass at death. No doubt it is due to the fact that the souls of saints as well as sinners are represented as entering Sheol at death that caused the translators to render it "grave" in many instances. But the fact that in both the Hebrew and the Greek there is an entirely different word used for "grave" ought to have prevented such a mistake. The Holy Spirit has carefully preserved the distinction between the two terms throughout. A careful examination of every passage in the Old and New Testaments where these words occur will show that many things are said of the grave" (Heb. "queber"; Gk. "mnemeion") which could never be said of "Sheol" or "Hades;" and many things are said of the latter which are never predicated of the former. For example: both the Hebrew and Greek words for "grave" occur in the plural again and again; Sheol and Hades never do so. The Hebrew and Greek words for "grave" are frequently referred to as the possession of individuals—"My grave" (Gen. 50:5); "grave of Abner" (2 Sam. 3:32); "His own (Joseph's) new tomb" (Matt. 27:60); "The sepulchers of the righteous" (Matt. 23:29); etc. In Gen. 50:5 we read, "In my grave which I have dug for me;" of "mnemeion" we read, "And he laid it in his own new tomb, which he had hewn out in the rock" (Matt. 27:60). Sheol and Hades are never so referred to. The body enters "queber" and mnemion," but it is never said to enter Sheol or Hades. Sufficient has been said to demonstrate that Sheol or Hades is not the grave. We may, therefore, confidently affirm that neither Sheol or Hades should ever be rendered "grave" or "the grave."

Hades refers to the same place as Sheol. Their identification is unequivocally established by a comparison of Psalm 16:10 with Acts 2:27; "Thou wilt not leave My soul in Sheol" (Ps. 16:10), is "Thou shalt not leave My soul in Hades" in Acts 2:27. But it is important to bear in mind that Sheol or Hades had two compartments, reserved respectively for the saved and the lost. And "between" these two, our Lord tells us there is "a great gulf fixed" (Luke 16:26). The compartment we are now considering is that which receives the souls of the wicked. In this, Christ declares, is a "flame" which torments. This is in perfect harmony with the teaching of the Old Testament concerning Sheol. In Deuteronomy 33:22 we read, "For a fire is kindled in Mine anger, and shall burn unto the lowest Sheol." Again; in the parable of the tares our Lord said, "I will say to the reapers, Gather ye together first the tares, and bind them in bundles to burn them" (Matt. 13:30). The explanation of this is found in vv. 40-42 of the same chapter: "As therefore the tares are gathered and burned in the fire; so shall it be in the end of this age. The Son of Man shall send forth His angels, and they shall gather out of His Kingdom all things that offend, and them which do iniquity; And shall cast them into a furnace of fire: there shall be wailing and gnashing of teeth." As this takes place at the end of this age and before the judgment begins, the "furnace of fire" must refer to Hades rather than the Lake of Fire.

Returning then to the teaching of Luke 16 concerning the experience of the wicked immediately after death, we read, "And in hell he lift up his eyes, being in torments." Here we have a sentient being, a conscious person, in a definite place; suffering there excruciatingly. He was in "torments." So great was his anguish he begged that one might "dip the tip of his finger in water and cool my tongue" (v. 24). But such alleviation was denied him. He was bidden to "remember" how he had lived—a worshipper of Mammon. Such, we are assured, will be the doom of every one that dies in his sins.

4. THE UTTER HOPELESSNESS OF THE LOST.

Thus far we have seen, first, that the judgment of the wicked is certain; second, that death seals their doom; third, that at death the souls of unbelievers go to Hades, into that compartment of the unseen world reserved for the lost, there to be tormented in the flame. There they remain until the judgment, when they shall be resurrected and brought before the Great White Throne to receive their final sentence. We, therefore, devote a separate section to show that after the wicked are brought out of Hades there is even then, no hope whatever of their salvation.

The first scripture we appeal to in proof of this is John 5:29: "All that are in the graves shall hear His voice, and shall come forth; they that have done good, unto the resurrection of life, and they that have done evil, unto the resurrection of damnation." This is the solemn announcement of the Son of God. Let His words be well weighed. Here He tells us briefly, what awaits the sum total of the dead. They are divided into two classes: they that have done good, and they that have done evil. For the one there is the "resurrection of life;" for the other the resurrection of damnation." For evil-doers there is no resurrection of probation, and no resurrection of salvation; but simply and solely the resurrection of damnation. How this removes the very foundation on which any might desire to build a future hope for the wicked!

In 1 Thessalonians 4:13 we read, "But I would not have you to be ignorant, brethren, concerning them which are asleep, that ye sorrow not, even as others which have no hope." Here the apostle draws a contrast between the Christian grieving over the death of believing loved ones, and the heathen who mourned the loss of their dear ones. The Christian may sorrow over the departure of a saved relative or friend, but he can also comfort himself with the blessed hope presented to him in the Scriptures, the hope of being re-united at the coming of the Lord. This hope the heathen, and the unsaved in Christendom who mourn the loss of unsaved friends, have not. Yea, they have "no hope." This is not weakened at all by the fact that in Eph. 2:12, 13 we read of those once "without hope" who had nevertheless, been "made nigh by the blood of Christ." The Ephesian scripture speaks of those alive in the world, and while here there is always a hope they may be saved; though while they remain unsaved they are "without hope," that is, without any scripturally-warranted hope. But the Thessalonian passage speaks of those who have passed out of this world unsaved, and for them there is "no hope." Whatever vain hopes the wicked may now cherish in the day to come, the very "expectation of the wicked shall perish" (Prov. 10:28)!

Another scripture which proves the hopeless state of those who have rejected God's truth is to be found in Hebrews 10:26-29: "For if we sin willfully after that we have received the knowledge of the truth, there remaineth no more sacrifice for sins, But a certain fearful looking for of judgment and fiery indignation, which shall devour the adversaries, He that despised Moses' law died without mercy under two or three witnesses: Of how much sorer punishment, suppose ye, shall he be thought worthy, who hath trodden underfoot the Son of God, and hath counted the blood of the covenant, wherewith he was sanctified, an unholy thing, and hath done despite unto the spirit of grace?" For our present purpose we need not stop to consider of whom this passage is specifically speaking. Sufficient to know that it treats of those who have willfully resisted the light. For these we are told "there remaineth no more sacrifice for sins." If there remaineth no more sacrifice for sins, then they must themselves suffer the Divine penalty for them. What that penalty is this same passage tells us; it is "fiery indignation" which shall devour them. It is a judgment "without mercy." It is a "punishment" sorer than that which befell him that despised Moses' law.

"For he shall have judgment without mercy, that hath showed no mercy; and mercy rejoiceth against judgment" (James 2:13). It is true that the apostle is here writing to saints, but in the verse we have just quoted there is a noticeable change in his language, and here he is obviously speaking of the unsaved, In the previous verse he had said "Ye," but now he changes to "he." He that hath showed no mercy (to his fellow-men) shall have "judgment without mercy" from God; and this, in spite of the fact that "mercy rejoiceth against judgment." The last clause is plainly for the purpose of adding solemnity to what precedes. Judgment "without mercy" is language which looks back to Isaiah 27:11, where we read, "It is a people of no understanding: therefore He that made them will not have mercy on them, and He that formed them will show them no favor." If, then, this judgment is "without mercy" how it closes the door against all possibility of a final reprieve, or even a modification of the dread sentence! And how it exposes the baselessness of that hope which is cherished by many, viz., that in the last great Day they think to cast themselves upon the mercy of that One whom they now despise and defy! Vain will it be to cry for mercy then. Of old God said to Israel, "Therefore will I also deal in fury: Mine eye shall not spare, neither will I have pity: and though they cry in Mine ears with a loud voice, yet will I not hear them." So it will be at the last Judgment. One other scripture may be considered in this connection: "Raging waves of the sea, foaming out their own shame; wandering stars, to whom is reserved the blackness of darkness forever" (Jude 13). Unspeakably solemn is this. This verse is referring to the future portion of those who now turn "the grace of our God into lasciviousness" and deny "the only Lord God and our Lord Jesus Christ" (Jude 4). Unto them is reserved "the blackness of darkness forever." The endless night of their doom shall never be relieved by a single star of hope. Thus have we sought to show that the Word of God by a variety of expressions, each of which is unambiguous and conclusive, reveals the utter hopelessness of those taking part in "the resurrection of damnation." We shall next consider:

5. THE LAST ABODE OF THE LOST.

This is given at least two different names in the New Testament: "Gehenna" and "Lake of Fire." Let us now examine the teaching of Scripture concerning them.

First, "Gehenna" is the Grecianized form of the Hebrew for "valley of Hinnom," which was a deep gorge on the east of Jerusalem. This valley of Hinnom was first used in connection with idolatrous rites (2 Chron. 28:3). Later it became a burial ground (Jer. 7:31), or more probably a crematorium. Still later it became the place where the garbage of Jerusalem was thrown and burned (Josephus). Its fires were kept constantly alight so as to consume the filth and rubbish deposited therein.

Second, this valley of Hinnom foreshadowed the great garbage-receptacle of the universe—Hell, just as other places and persons in the Old Testament Scriptures adumbrated other objects more vile—for example, the "king of Tyre" in Ezekiel 28. Just as what is there said of this king has in view one more sinister than he, so what is said of the valley of Hinnom symbolized that which was far more awful. We can no more limit

Gehenna to the valley outside of Jerusalem than we can restrict "the king of Tyre" to a mere man of the past.

Third, the valley of Hinnom our Lord used as an emblem of Hell, and stamped with the hall-mark of His authority the wider and more solemn scope of the word. It should be carefully noted that when speaking of Gehenna He never referred to the mere literal valley outside of Jerusalem, but employed it to designate the place of eternal torments.

Fourth, Gehenna, in its New Testament usage, refers to a place. "And if thy right eye offend thee, pluck it out, and cast it from thee: for it is profitable for thee that one of thy members should perish. and not that thy whole body should be cast into Gehenna" (Matt. 5:29. See also Matt. 18:9).

Fifth. the fire of Gehenna is eternal. "And if thy hand offend thee, cut it off: it is better for thee to enter into life maimed, than having two hands to go into Gehenna, into the fire that never shall be quenched: where their worm dieth not, and the fire is not quenched" (Mark 9:43, 44).

Sixth, Gehenna is the place in which both soul and body are destroyed. "And fear not them which kill the body, but are not able to kill the soul: but rather fear Him which is able to destroy both soul and body in Gehenna" (Matt. 19:28). This passage is most important, for more than any other it enables us to gather the real scope of this term. The fact that the "soul" as well as the body is destroyed there, is proof positive that our Lord was not referring to the valley of Hinnom. So, too, the fact that the "body" is destroyed there, makes it certain that "Gehenna"is not another name for "Hades." In pondering this solemn verse we should remember that "destroy" does not mean to annihilate. Some have raised a quibble over the fact that Christ did not here expressly say that God would "destroy both soul and body in hell," but merely said "Fear Him which is able to." This admits of a simple and conclusive reply. Surely it is apparent on the surface that Christ is not here predicating of God a power which none can deny, but which, notwithstanding, He will never exert! He was not simply affirming the omnipotence of God, but uttering a solemn threat which will yet be executed. That such was His meaning is established beyond the shadow of doubt when we compare Matthew 10:28 with the parallel passage in Luke 12:5: "But I will forewarn you whom ye shall fear: fear Him, which after He hath killed hath power to cast into hell; yea, I say unto you, fear him." This threat we know will be fulfilled.

Seventh, Gehenna is identical with the Lake of Fire. There are four things which indicate this, and taken together they constitute a cumulative but clear proof. First, the fact that in Gehenna God "destroys" both soul and body (Matt. 10:28). This shows the wicked who are there destroyed have already received their resurrection bodies. Second, the fact that the fire of Gehenna is eternal: it will "never be quenched" (Mark 9:43). This is nowhere said of the fires of sheol or hades. Third, in Isaiah 30:33 we learn that "Tophet" is ordained for "the king"—it is "the king" of Daniel 11:36, that is the Antichrist, "the Assyrian" of Isaiah 30:30. Now "Tophet" is another name for the valley of Hinnom, as may be seen by a reference to Jeremiah 7:31, 32. In Rev. 19:20 we are told that the Beast (the Antichrist) together with the False Prophet will be "cast alive into a lake of fire burning with brimstone." Thus by comparing Isaiah 30:33 with Revelation 19:20 we learn that

Gehenna and the Lake of Fire are one and the same. Finally, notice the absence of "Gehenna" in Revelation 20:14, "And death and hades were cast into the lake of fire." The meaning of this is the people whom death and hades had seized

—"death" capturing the body; "hades" claiming the soul. That the casting of "death and hades" into the Lake of Fire refer to their captives is clear from the concluding words of the verse

—"This is the second death," i.e. for their victims. Note then that we are not told that "Gehenna" was cast into the Lake of Fire because Gehenna and the Lake of Fire and one and the same place.

We shall now offer a few remarks upon the Lake of fire and brimstone. The following analysis indicates the teaching of Scripture concerning it.

First, it is the place which finally receives the Beast and the False Prophet: Revelation 19:20.

Second, it is the place which finally receives the Devil: Revelation 20:10.

Third, it is the place which finally receives all whose names are not found written in the book of life: Revelation 20:15 and cf. 21:8.

Fourth, it is a place of "torment;" Revelation 20:10.

Fifth, it is a place whose torment is ceaseless and interminable, "day and night for ever and ever:" Revelation 20:10 and cf. 14:11.

Sixth, it is also termed "The Second Death:" Revelation 20:14; 21:8, etc.

Seventh, it has "no power" on the people of God: Revelation 20:6 and cf. 2:11.

In the sixth item above we have pointed out that the Lake of Fire is also denominated "The Second Death." At least three reasons may be suggested for this. First, this designation intimates that the endless torments of the Lake of Fire are the penalty and wages of sin. "The wages of sin is death." Second, the use of this appellation calls attention to the fact that all who are cast into the Lake of Fire will be eternally separated from God. As the first death is the separation of the soul from the body, so the second death will be the eternal separation of the soul from God—"Punished with everlasting destruction from the presence of the Lord" (2 Thess. 1:9). Third, such a title emphasizes the dreadfulness of the Lake of Fire. To the normal man death is the object he fears above all others. It is that from which he naturally shrinks, It is that which he most dreads. When, then, the Holy Spirit designates the Lake of Fire the "Second Death" He is emphasizing the fact that it is an object of horror from which the sinner should flee.

6. THE ETERNALITY OF THE SUFFERINGS OF THE LOST.

Upon this point the language of Scripture is most explicit. In Matthew 25:41 we read of "everlasting fire." In Matthew 25:46 of "everlasting punishment." In Mark 6:29 of "eternal damnation." And in 2 Thessalonians 1:9 of "everlasting destruction." We are aware that the enemies of God's truth have sought to tamper with this word rendered everlasting and eternal. But their efforts have been entirely futile. The impossibility of rendering the Greek word by any other English equivalent appears from the following evidence:

The Greek word is "aionios" and its meaning and scope has been definitely defined for us by the Holy Spirit in at least two passages. "While we look not at the things which are seen: but at the things which are not seen: for the things which are seen are temporal; but the things which are not seen are eternal" (2 Cor. 4:18). Here a contrast is drawn between things "seen" and things "not seen," between things "temporal" and things "eternal." Now it is obvious that if the things "temporal" should last forever, there would be no antithesis between them and the things "eternal." It is equally obvious that if the things "eternal" are merely "age-long," then they cannot be properly contrasted with things that are temporal. The difference between things temporal and things eternal in this verse is as great as the difference between the things "seen" and the things "not seen."

The second example, which is of the same character as the one furnished in 2 Corinthians 4:18, is equally conclusive. In Philemon 15 we read, "For perhaps he therefore departed for a season, that thou shouldest receive him forever." Here the Greek for "forever" is aionios. The apostle is beseeching Philemon to receive Onesimus, who had left his master, and whom Paul had sent back to him. When the apostle says "receive him forever," his evident meaning is, never banish him, never sell him, never again send him away. "Aionios" is here contrasted with "for a season," showing that it means just the opposite of what that expression signifies.

Eternal or everlasting is the one and unvaried meaning of aionios in the New Testament. The same word translated "everlasting destruction," "everlasting punishment," "everlasting fire," is rendered "everlasting life" in John 3:16; "the everlasting God" in Romans 16:26; "eternal salvation" in Hebrews 5:9; "His eternal glory" in 1 Peter 5:10. No argument needs to be made to prove that in these passages it is impossible to fairly substitute any other alternative for everlasting and eternal, And it is thus with the other class of passages. The "everlasting fire" will synchronize with the existence of "the everlasting God." The "everlasting punishment" of the lost will continue as long as the "everlasting life" of believers. The "eternal damnation" of the wicked will no more have an end than will the "eternal salvation" of the redeemed. The "everlasting destruction" of unbelievers will prove as interminable as the "everlasting glory" of God. To deny the former is to deny the latter. To affirm the everlastingness of God is to prove the endlessness of the misery of His enemies.

7. THE FINALITY OF THEIR STATE.

The doom of those who shall be cast into the Lake of Fire is irrevocable and final. Many independent considerations prove this. Forgiveness of sins is limited to life on this earth. Once the sinner passes out of this world there remaineth "no more sacrifice for sins." The fact that at death the soul of the wicked goes at once into the "furnace of fire" (Matt. 12:42) witnesses to the fixity of his future state. The fact that, later, his resurrection is one "of damnation" (John 5:29) excludes all possibility of a last-hour reprieve. The fact that he is cast soul and body into a lake of fire argues that then he receives his final portion. The fact that the Lake of Fire is denominated the "Second Death" denotes the hopelessness of his situation. Just as the first death cuts him off forever from this world, so the second death cuts him off forever from God.

In Philemon 3 the apostle Paul speaks of the enemies of the Cross of Christ, and moved by the Holy Spirit he tells us that their "end is destruction" (v. 19). Stronger and more unequivocal language could not be used. There is nothing beyond the "end." And the end of the enemies of the Cross of Christ is "destruction" not salvation. The Greek word here translated "end" is "telos." It is found in the following passages: "Of His Kingdom there shall be no end" (Luke 1:33); "Christ is the end of the law for righteousness to everyone that believeth" (Rom. 10:4); "Having neither beginning of days nor end of life" (Heb. 7:3); "I am ... the Beginning and the End, the First and the Last" (Rev. 22:13).

As we have already seen, the twentieth chapter of Revelation describes the final judgment of the wicked before the Great White Throne, after which they are cast into the Lake of Fire. The chapters which follow—the last two in the Bible—may be read carefully and searched diligently, but they will not be found to contain so much as a single hint that those cast into the Lake of Fire shall ever be delivered from it. Instead, we find in the very last chapter of God's Word the solemn statement, "He that is unjust, let him be unjust still: and he which is filthy, let him be filthy still" (Rev. 22:11). Thus the finality of their condition is expressly affirmed on the closing page of Holy Writ.

In the last two articles we have considered some of the principal sophistries which unbelief has brought against the truth of eternal punishment, and have also examined the teaching of Scripture concerning the Destiny of the wicked. We approach now the most solemn aspect of our subject, namely:

Chapter III
The Nature Of Punishment Awaiting The Lost

1. THE PORTION OF THE WICKED IMMEDIATELY AFTER DEATH.

We turn first to the teaching of our Lord found in Luke 16. Here, we learn the following facts; First, that in Hades the lost are in full possession of all their faculties and sensibilities. They see, for the rich man saw Abraham afar off, and Lazarus in his bosom (v. 23). They feel, for he was in "torments" (v. 24). They cry for mercy, for he asked—but in vain—for a drop of water to cool his tongue (v. 24). They are in possession of memory, for the rich man was bidden to "remember" what he had received during his lifetime on earth (v. 25). It is impossible for them to join the redeemed: there is "a great gulf fixed" between them (v. 26).

Unspeakably solemn is all this. Not only will the lost be tormented in flames, but their anguish will be immeasurably increased by a sight of the redeemed being "comforted." Then shall they see the happy portion of the blest which they despised, preferring as they did the pleasures of sin for a season. And how the retention of "memory" will further augment their sufferings! With what unfathomable sorrows will they recall the opportunities wasted, the expostulations of parents and friends slighted, the warnings of God's servants disregarded, the proclamations of God's Gospel spurned. And then to know there is no way of escape, no means of relief, no hope of a reprieve! Their lot will be unbearable; their awful portion, beyond endurance. The Son of God has faithfully forewarned that "there shall be wailing and gnashing of teeth" (Matt. 13:42). It is very significant that Christ referred to this just seven times—denoting the completeness of their misery and anguish; see Matthew 8:12; 13:42-50; 22:13; 24:51; 25:30; Luke 13:28.

2. THE FINAL PORTION OF THE WICKED.

(1) This is spoken of as being "punished with everlasting destruction from the presence of the Lord" (2 Thess. 1:9). None but one who really knows God can begin to estimate what it will mean to be eternally banished from the Lord. Forever separated from the Fount of all goodness! Never to enjoy the light of God's countenance! Never to bask in the sunshine of His presence. This, this is the most awful of all. 2 Thessalonians 1:9 furnishes clear intimation that the judgment of Matthew 25, with its eternal sentence, looks beyond the Assize. "Destruction from the presence of the Lord" is paralleled with "depart from Me ye cursed."

(2) The final portion of the wicked is spoken of as "everlasting punishment" (Matt. 25:46). In 1 John 4:18 the same Greek word is rendered "torment." This term announces the satisfying of God's justice. In the punishing of the wicked God vindicates His outraged majesty. Herein punishment differs from correction or discipline. Punishment is not designed for the good of the one who suffers it. It is intended for the enforcing of

law and order; it is necessary for the preservation of government.

(3) The final portion of the wicked is spoken of as a "tormenting. " This is proven by the fact that the everlasting fire into which the wicked depart is "prepared for the Devil and his angels" (Matt. 25:41) which emphasizes the awfulness of this punishment, rather than specifies who are going to endure. This verse sets forth the severity of the punishment of the lost. If the everlasting fire be "prepared for the Devil and his angels," then how intolerable it will be! If the place of eternal torment into which all unbelievers shall be cast is the same as that in which God's arch-enemy will suffer, how dreadful that place must be.

That this everlasting fire, prepared for the Devil and his angels, produces the most awful suffering is clear from Revelation 20:10, where we are told that Satan shall be "tormented day and night for ever and ever." No doubt this torment will be both internal and external, mental and physical. The word occurs for the first time in the New Testament in Matthew 8:6. "Lord, my servant lieth at home sick of the palsy, grievously tormented." The same word occurs again in Revelation 9:5 where we read of infernal locusts, issuing from the Pit, and which are given power to torment men, the nature of which is explained as "the torment of a scorpion, when he striketh a man." So intense will be the suffering caused therefrom "men shall seek death and shall not find it, and they shall desire to die, and death shall flee from them" (Rev. 9:6). This torment then cannot mean less than the most excruciating pain which we are now capable of conceiving. How much the pains of Hell will exceed the pains of earth we know not.

(4) The final portion of the wicked is spoken of as "suffering the vengeance of eternal fire" (Jude 7). But many say this is merely a figurative expression. We ask, How do they know that? Where has God told them so in His Word? Personally, we believe that when God says "fire" He means "fire." We refuse to blunt the sharp edge of His Word. Was the Deluge figurative? Was it figurative "fire and brimstone" which descended from heaven and destroyed Sodom and Gomorrah? Were the plagues upon Egypt figurative ones? Is it figurative fire which shall yet burn this earth, and cause the very elements to "melt with fervent heat?" No' in each of these cases we are obliged to take the words of Scripture in their literal signification. Let those who dare affirm that Hell-fire is non-literal answer to God. We are not their judges; but we refuse to accept their toning down of these solemn words. Literal fire in Hell presents no difficulty at all to the writer. The lost will have literal bodies when they are cast into Hell. The "angels" also have bodies; and for all we know to the contrary, the Devil has too.

But the question is often asked, How can the bodies of the lost be tormented eternally by literal fire? Would not the fire utterly consume them? Even though we were unable to furnish an answer to this question, we should still believe that Scripture meant what it said. But we are satisfied that God's Word answers this question. In Exodus 3 we read of the bush in the wilderness burning with fire, and yet was not consumed! In Daniel 3 we read of the three Hebrews being cast into the fiery furnace of Babylon, yet they were not consumed. Why was this? Because, m some way unknown to us, God preserved the bush, and the bodies of the three Hebrews. Is God, then, unable to preserve the bodies of the damned from being consumed? Surely not. But we are not left even to this unescapable inference. In Mark 9:47-49 we are told, "It is better for thee to enter into the kingdom of God with one eye, than having two eyes to be cast into hell fire: where their worm dieth not, and the fire is not quenched. For every one shall be salted with fire." The expression salted with fire" confirms what we have said above. Salt is a preservative; hence, when we are told that "everyone" who is cast into Gehenna shall be "salted with fire" we learn that the very fire itself so far from consuming shall preserve. If it be asked, How can this be? We answer, Because that fire is "prepared" by God (Matt. 25:41).

(5) The final portion of the wicked is described as an association with the vilest of the vile. "But the fearful, and unbelieving, and the abominable, and murderers, and whore-mongers, and sorcerers, and idolaters, and all liars, shall have their part in the lake which burneth with fire and brimstone" (Rev. 21:8). O dear reader, weigh well this solemn language. You may be a person of culture and refinement: judged by moral standards your life may be exemplary and spotless: you may pride yourself on your honesty and truthfulness: you may be very particular in your choice of friends and very careful to avoid the company of the profane and vicious: you may even be religious, and look down in scorn and pity upon the idolaters of heathendom; but God says that if you die in unbelief your portion shall be with "the fearful, and unbelieving, and the abominable, and murderers, and whoremongers, and sorcerers, and idolaters, and all liars." Think of what it will mean to spend eternity in the Prison-house of the universe with Cain, and Pharaoh, and Judas! Think of what it will mean to be shut up with the vile Sodomites! Think of being incarcerated forever with every blasphemer who has ever lived!

(6) The final portion of the wicked is described as "the blackness of darkness forever" (Jude 13). Unrelieved will be their fearful sufferings; interminable their torments. No means of escape. No possibility of a reprieve. No hope of deliverance. Not one will be found who is able to befriend them and intercede with God for them. They had the offer of a Mediator often made them in this world; but no such offer will be made them in the Lake of Fire. "There is no peace, saith my God, to the wicked." There will be no resting-place in Hell; no secret corner where they can find a little respite; no cooling fountain at which they may refresh themselves. There will be no change or variation of their lot. Day and night, forever and ever, shall they be punished. With no prospect of any improvement they will sink down into blank despair.

(7) The final portion of the wicked will be beyond the creature's power of resistance. "And whosoever shall fall on this stone shall be broken: but on whomsoever it shall fall, it will grind him to powder" (Matt. 21:44). There are many who now say, If at the end I find myself in Hell, I will bear it as well as I can, as if by strength of will and firmness of mind they shall, in measure at least, be able to support themselves. But alas! Their resolutions will count for nothing.

It is common with men in this world to shun calamities, but if they find this is impossible, they set themselves to bear it: they fortify their spirits and resolve to support themselves under it as well as they can. They muster up all their courage and resolution in the determination to keep their hearts from sinking. But it will be utterly vain for sinners to do this in the Lake of Fire. What would it help a worm which was about to be crushed by some great rock, to collect its strength and endeavor to set itself to bear up against its weight, and so seek to prevent itself from being crushed? Much less will a poor damned soul be able to support itself under the weight of the wrath of Almighty God. No matter how much the sinner may now harden himself, in order to endure the pains of Hell, the first moment he shall feel the flames, his heart will melt like wax before the furnace —"Can thine heart endure, or can thine hands be strong, in the days that I shall deal with thee? I the Lord have spoken it, and will do it" (Ezek 22:14).

If such then be the case with impenitent sinners, that they can neither escape their punishment, nor deliver themselves from it, nor bear up under it, what will become of them? I answer in the words of another:

"They will wholly sink down into eternal death. There will be that sinking of heart, of which we now cannot conceive. We see how it is with the body when in extreme pain. The nature of the body will support itself for a considerable time under very great pain, so as to keep from wholly sinking. There will be great struggles, lamentable groans and panting, and it may be convulsions. These are the strugglings of nature to support itself under the extremity of the pain. There is, as it were, a great lothness in nature to yield to it; it cannot bear wholly to sink. But yet sometimes pain of body is so very extreme and exquisite, that the nature of the body cannot support itself under it; however loth it may be to sink, yet it cannot bear the pain; there are a few struggles, and throes, and pantings, and it may be a shriek or two, and the nature yields to the violence of the torments, sinks down, and the body dies. This is the death of the body. So it will be with the soul in Hell; it will have no strength or power to deliver itself; and its torment and horror will be so great, so mighty, so vastly disproportioned to its strength, that having no strength in the least to support itself, although it be infinitely contrary to the nature and inclination of the soul utterly to sink; yet it will sink, it will utterly and totally sink, without the least degree of remaining comfort, or strength, or courage, or hope. And though it will never be annihilated, its being and perception will never be abolished: yet such will be the infinite depth of gloominess that it will sink into, that it will be in a state of death, eternal death.

"The nature of man desires happiness; it is the nature of the soul to crave and thirst after well-being; and if it be under misery, it equally pants after relief; and the greater the misery is, the more easily doth it struggle for help. But if all relief be withholden, all strength overborne, all support utterly gone; then it sinks into the darkness of death. We can conceive but little of the matter; we cannot conceive what that sinking of the soul in such a case is. But to help your conception, imagine yourself to be cast into a fiery oven, all of a glowing heat, or into the midst of a blowing brick-kiln, or of a great furnace, where your pain would be as much greater than that occasioned by accidentally touching a coal of fire, as the heat is greater. Imagine also that your body were to lie there for a quarter of an hour, full of fire, as full within and without as a bright coal of fire, all the while full of quick sense; what horror would you feel at the entrance of such a furnace! And how long would that quarter of an hour seem to you! If it were to be measured by a glass, how long would the glass seem to be running! And after you had endured it for one minute, how overbearing would it be to you to think that you had yet to endure the other fourteen.

"But what would be the effect on your soul, if you knew you must lie there enduring that torment to the full for twenty-four hours! And how much greater would be the effect, if you knew you must endure it for a whole year, and how vastly greater still, if you knew you must endure it for a thousand years! O then, how would your heart sink, if you thought, if you knew, that you must bear it forever and ever! That there would be no end! That after millions of millions of ages, your torment would be no nearer to an end, than ever it was; and that you never, never should be delivered! But your torment in Hell will be immeasurably greater than this illustration represents. How then will the heart of a poor creature sink under it! How utterly inexpressible and inconceivable must the sinking of the soul be in such a case." (Jonathan Edwards).

Such, in brief, is the portion awaiting the lost—eternal separation from the Fount of all goodness; everlasting punishment; torment of soul and body; endless existence in the Lake of Fire, in association with the vilest of the vile; every ray of hope excluded; utterly crushed and overwhelmed by the wrath of a sin-avenging God. And let us remember in Whose Word these solemn statements are found! They are found in the Word of Him who is faithful and therefore has He written in plain and positive language so that none need be deceived, They are found in the Word of Him who cannot lie, and therefore He has not employed the language of exaggeration. They are found in the Word of Him who says what He means and means what He says, and therefore the writer, for one, dares do nothing else than receive them at their face value.

Chapter IV
The Application Of The Subject

1. In what has been before us we learn HOW the character and Throne of God will be vindicated. What can be too severe a judgment upon those who have despised so great a Being as the Almighty? If he that is guilty of treason against an earthly government deserves to lose his life, what punishment can be great enough for one who has preferred his own pleasure before the will and glory of a God who is infinitely good? To despise infinite excellence merits infinite misery. God has commanded the sinner to repent, He has courted him with overtures of grace, He has bountifully supplied his every need, and He has presented before him the Son of His love—His choicest treasure —and yet men persist in their wicked course. No possible ground, then, will the sinner have to appeal against the sentence of the Judge of all the earth, seeing that He not only tendered mercy toward him, but also bore with him in so much patience when He might justly have smitten him down upon the first crime he ever committed and removed him to Hell upon the first refusal of his proffered grace.

That God shall punish every rebel against Himself is required by the very perfections of His high sovereignty, It is but meet that He should display His governmental supremacy. The creature has dared to assert its independency: the subject has risen up in arms against his King; therefore, the right of God's throne must be vindicated—"I know that the Lord is greater than all gods: for in the thing wherein they dealt proudly He is above them" (Ex. 18:11). When Pharaoh dared to pit himself against Jehovah, God manifested His authority by destroying him at the Red Sea. Another king He turned into a beast, to make him know that the Most High ruleth in the kingdom of men. So, when the history of this world is wound up, God will make a full and final manifestation of His sovereign majesty. Though He now endures (not "loves") with much long-suffering the vessels of wrath fitted to destruction; it is that, in the coming Day, He may "show His wrath and make His power known" (Rom. 9:22).

2. What has been before us serves to expose the folly and madness of the greater part of mankind in that for the sake of present momentary gratification, they run the serious risk of enduring all these eternal torments. They prefer a small pleasure, or a little wealth, or a little earthly honor and fame (which lasts but "for a season") to an escape from the Lake of Fire. If it be true that the torments of Hell are everlasting, what will it profit a man if he gain the whole world and lose his own soul? How mad men are who hear and read of these things and pretend to believe them, who are alive but a little while, a few short years at most, and yet who are careless about what becomes of themselves in the next world, where there is neither change nor end.! How mad are they who hear that if they go on in sin, they shall be eternally miserable, and yet are not moved, but hear it with as much indifference as if they were not concerned in the matter at all!

And yet for all they know to the contrary, they may be in fiery torments before another week is at an end!

How sad to note that this unconcern is shared by the great majority of our fellows. Age makes little difference. The young are occupied with pleasures, the middle-aged with worldly advancement, the aged with their attainments or lack of them; with the first it is the lust of the flesh, with the second it is the lust of the eyes, with the third it is the pride of life, which banishes from their minds all serious thoughts of the life to come. "The heart of the sons of men is full of evil, and madness is in their heart while they live, and after that they go to the dead" (Eccl. 9:3). O the blinding power of sin! O the deceitfulness of riches! O the perversity of the human heart! Nothing so reveals these things as the incredible sight of men and women enjoying themselves and being at rest, while they are suspended over the eternal burning by the frail thread of mortality, which may be snapped at any moment.

3. What has been before us ought to make every unsaved reader to tremble as he scans these pages. These things are no mere abstractions, but dread realities, as countless thousands have already discovered to their bitter cost. They may not seem real to you now, but in a short time at most—should you continue to reject the Christ of God—they will be your portion. You, too, shall lift up your eyes in Hell, and behold the saints in heaven. You, too, shall crave a drop of water to alleviate your fearful agony; but it will be in vain. You, too, shall cry for mercy; but then it will be too late. O unsaved reader, we pray you not to throw this aside and seek to dismiss the subject from your thoughts. That is how thousands before you have acted, and the very memory of their folly only accentuates their misery. Far better had you been made wretched now for a time, than that you should weep and wail and gnash your teeth forever. Far better that you have your present false peace broken, than that you should be a stranger to real peace for all eternity.

"Except ye repent, ye shall all likewise perish." Whoever you are, whether young or old, whether rich or poor, whether religious or irreligious, if you are in a Christless state, then this is what awaits you at the end of your present course. This, this is the Hell over which you now hang, and into which you are ready to drop this very moment. It is vain for you to flatter yourself with hopes that you shall avoid it, or to say in your heart, Perhaps it may not be; perhaps things have been represented worse than they really are. These things are according to the Word of Truth, and if you will not be convinced by that Word when presented to you by men in the name of God, then God Himself will yet undertake to prove to you that these things are so.

Think it not strange that God should deal so severely with you, or that the wrath you shall suffer shall be so great. For great as it is, it is no greater than the mercy which you now despise. The love of God, His marvelous grace in sending His own Son to die for sinners, is every whit as great and wonderful as this inexpressible wrath. You have refused to accept Christ as the Savior from the wrath to come, you have despised God's dying love, why then should you not suffer wrath as great as that grace and love which you have rejected? Does it still seem incredible that God should so harden His heart against a poor sinner as to bear down upon him with infinite power and merciless wrath? Then pause and ask, Is it any greater than it is for me to harden my heart against Him, against infinite mercy, against the Son of His love? O dear friends, face this question of Christ Himself, "How can ye escape the damnation of Hell?" (Matt. 23:33). There is only one way of escape, and that is to flee to the Savior. If you would not fall into the hands of the living God, then cast yourself into the arms of the Christ who died—"Kiss the Son, lest He be angry, and ye perish from the way, when His wrath is kindled but a little. Blessed are all they that put their trust in Him" (Ps. 2:12).

4. What has been before us ought to make every professing Christian diligently examine himself Weigh carefully the tremendously solemn issues which turn on whether or not you have really passed from death unto life. You cannot afford to be uncertain. There is far too much at stake. Remember that you are prejudiced in your own favor. Remember that you have a treacherous heart. Remember that the Devil is the great Deceiver of souls. Remember that "there is a way that seemeth right unto a man, but the end thereof are the ways of death" (Prov. 14:12). Remember it is written that "Many shall say unto Me in that day, Lord, Lord, have we not prophesied in Thy name? and in Thy name have cast out devils? and in Thy name done many wonderful works?" And then He will answer them, "I never knew you; depart from Me, ye that work iniquity" (Matt. 7:22, 23).

There are many who now wear the guise of saints, who appear like saints, and their state, both in their own eyes and that of their neighbors is satisfactory. And yet they have on only sheep's clothing; at heart, they are wolves. But no disguise can deceive the Judge of all. His eyes are as a flame of fire: they search the hearts and try the reins of the children of men. Wherefore, let each take earnest heed that he be not deceived. Compare yourself with the Word of God, for that is the rule by which you will be tried. Test your works, for it is by those you will be made manifest. Inquire whether you are really living a Christian life; whether or not the fear of God is upon you; whether or not you are mortifying your members which are upon the earth; whether or nor you are "denying ungodliness and worldly lusts," and whether you are living "soberly, righteously, and godly in this present world," for it is thus that "grace" teaches the saints to live. Cry unto God earnestly and frequently that He will reveal you to yourself, and discover to you whether you are building upon the Rock, or upon the sand. Make the Psalmist's prayer yours—"Search me, O God, and know my heart; try me, and know my thoughts. And see if there be any wicked way in me, and lead me in the way everlasting" (Ps. 139:23, 24). God will search you hereafter, and make fully manifest what you are, both to yourself and to others. Let each of us, then, humbly request Him to search us now. We have urgent need of Divine help in this matter, for our heart is "deceitful above all things, and desperately wicked."

5. What has been before us should cause those who really enjoy the full assurance of faith to praise God with a loud voice. To each of you we say, God has given you wonderful cause for gratitude and thanksgiving. You, too, justly deserved to suffer the full weight of the wrath of a sin-hating and sin-avenging God. It is not long since you loved darkness rather than light, It is only a short time since you turned a deaf ear to both God's commands and entreaties. It is only a few years at most since you despised and

rejected His beloved Son. What marvelous grace was it then that snatched you as a brand from the burning! What wondrous love was it that delivered you from the wrath to come! What matchless mercy it was that changed you from a child of Hell (Matt. 23:15) to a child of God! O how you should praise the Father for having ever set His love upon you. How you should praise the Son for having died to save you from the Lake of Fire. How you should praise the blessed Spirit for having quickened you into newness of life. And how your appreciation ought to be expressed now in a life that is glorifying to the triune God. How diligently ought you to seek to learn what is well-pleasing in His sight. How earnestly should you seek His will. How quick should you be to run in the way of His commandments. Let your life correspond with the praises of your lips.

6. What has been before us ought to stir up all of God's people to a deepened sense of their duty. Fellow-Christian, have you no obligations toward your godless neighbors? If God has made clear these solemn truths to you, does it not deepen your responsibility toward the unsaved? If you have no love for souls, it is greatly to be feared that your own soul is in imminent danger. If you can witness, unmoved, men and women hurrying down the broad road which leadeth to destruction, then it is seriously to be doubted if you have within you the Spirit of that One who wept over Jerusalem. It is true you have no power of your own to save a soul from death, but are you faithfully giving out that Word which is the instrument which God uses to bring souls from death unto life? Are you supplicating God as you ought and depending on Him to bless your efforts to point the lost to the Lamb of God? Are you as fervent as you should be in your cries to God on behalf of the lost? Alas, must you not join the writer as he hangs his head in shame? Is there not reason for each of us to ask God to give us a clearer vision of that indescribably awful portion which awaits every Christ rejecter, and to enable us to act in the power of such a vision!

7. What has been before us will yet be the occasion of profoundest praise to God. Whatever difficulties the eternal punishment of the wicked may present to us now—and it is freely granted that it is difficult for our reason to grasp it, and that of necessity, for we are incapable of discerning the infinite malignity of sin, and therefore unable to see what punishment it really deserves—yet, in the Day to come it will be far otherwise. When we behold God's righteous dealings with His enemies, when we hear the sentences being given according to their works, when we see how justly and thoroughly they deserve merciless wrath, and stand by as they are cast into the Lake of Fire, so far from shrinking back in horror our hearts will give vent to gladsome praise. Just as of old the overthrow of God's enemies at the Red Sea caused His people to burst forth in worshipful song, so in the coming Day we shall be moved to rejoicing when we witness the final display of God's holiness and justice in the overthrow and punishment of all who have defied Him. Remember that in the destruction of the wicked God will be glorified and this it is which will be the occasion of the rejoicing of His people. Not only will God be "clear" when He judges (Ps. 51:4), but His perfections will be magnified in the sentences pronounced.

Eternal Security

Contents

Foreword

Eternal Security is the teaching that God shall with no uncertainty bring into their eternal inheritance those who are actually justified—delivered from the curse of the law and have the righteousness of Christ reckoned to their account—and who have been begotten by the Spirit of God. And further it is the teaching that God shall do this in a way glorifying to Himself, in harmony with His nature and consistent with the teaching of Scripture concerning the nature of those who are called saints. Why is this important? Why is it important for every Christian to know that once God has taken him for His own, He will never let him go? Arthur W. Pink gives many reasons for this in this book on Eternal Security. For one thing, it is necessary in order to strengthen young and fearful Christians in their faith—by safeguarding the honor and integrity of God and His Word. And it is also necessary in order to preserve one of the grand and distinctive blessings of the Gospel, which to deny is to attack the very foundations of the believer's comfort and assurance.

But let the reader be warned right from the start. Those who think that they are opposed to what Pink finds in Scripture may be surprised to find themselves agreeing with him. And those on the other side may find that Pink has gone way beyond the mere statement and proof of a doctrine to implications that they may have to accept for their own lives. The author is no shallow student of the Word, but asks us to follow Out its teaching so as to relate it properly to God's scheme of things.

It is important for the reader to avoid wrong impressions as he begins to read. The book has been titled Eternal Security because today that is the name given to the doctrine dealt with in this book. But historically the doctrine was called Perseverance of the Saints, and Pink himself preferred that title. But whether it is called Eternal Security or Perseverance of the Saints, it is the same doctrine that has been held down through the years. We must not take issue with him because at some points he used different words from what we are accustomed to.

As he begins, the reader may also mistakenly get the impression that Pink is arguing against Eternal Security at the same time he claims to be for it. We assure the reader that this is not so. Pink is not attempting to undermine this doctrine through trickery, not in the least. If then he doesn't seem clear, we ask the reader to be patient and give him a chance to explain himself (esp. in chap. 7). We, as Pink did, should realize that many doctrines of Scripture cannot be fairly stated as simple slogans. Eternal Security is one of these. Let us endeavor to study out this doctrine to its final conclusion since it is so important to our welfare as we walk the Christian life.

It may help to know that Pink originally came out from a group of rather sectarian hyper-Calvinistic Baptists in England. He clearly reacted strongly to some of their distinctive tenets. This is especially true of their Antinomian tendencies, in which they inclined toward the view that since all of man's actions and circumstances are predestined, a Christian need not bother with his responsibilities—God will bring all that is needed into his life so that he will automatically be directed to do what He wants.

But though he rejected this kind of thinking very strongly (Pink's book Practical Christianity gives a very helpful, balanced view), he did not overreact. He remained unashamedly Calvinistic. Yet it was his desire to avoid all lopsidedness, and it is for that reason that he may truly be said to be of value to all. No matter what he wrote on, he gave careful consideration to all who in any way try to base their view on Scripture.

Pink was unusually thorough in his writings. One can read dozens of books by other writers on a subject and find that questions have been left unanswered by them all. Not so with Pink. It rarely happens that he will not deal with a pressing question. He decried superficiality and compromise. The result was a full but practical treatment of each subject he wrote on.

Yet he did not get bogged down in philosophical theology. Pink was first and foremost a careful expositor of Scripture, and this carried over in his handling of doctrine. He did not quote a text of Scripture and leave it up to the reader to make the connections. Rather, he usually took the time to deal with it positively, relating each part to the subject and establishing beyond question that the particular Scripture applies. He was also a master in showing the meaning of a text of Scripture by a careful consideration of its context. Time after time he demonstrates in this way that it cannot mean what some have claimed. Thus he avoids the proof-text method of developing a doctrine. The reader will see this for himself in this book.

Eternal Security is a doctrine that complements and completes other truths. It is the truth which establishes a Christian in assurance of salvation. The doctrine of election in itself cannot do this. Justification cannot do this. The doctrine of sanctification cannot do this. Not even the doctrine of glorification does so. Yet each of these is incomplete without Eternal Security. Election, Justification, Sanctification, and Glorification are all hypothetical—mere possibilities—until Eternal Security complements and completes them by showing how they are applied to specific individuals. And it is also practical because it brings believers to assurance of salvation, which according to many Scripture passages they are to have.

There is, however, the possibility of self-deception. Assurance of salvation must be based on a right understanding of what God's Word teaches concerning Eternal Security. D. L. Moody told a story that illustrates the danger. A drunk stopped Moody one time and said, "Don't you remember me? I'm the man you saved here two years ago." "Well," said Moody, "it must have been me, because the Lord certainly didn't do it." Too many are "saved" by men, and not saved by God. In other words, one can have assurance of salvation — like the drunk —without being saved. We must contend for Eternal Security for those who are really saved — who are born anew, and have been changed within. This is what Arthur W. Pink explains so well in this book.

The material for this book was taken from a series of 34 articles in Pink's Studies in the Scriptures (Vols. 21-23), written under the title "The Saint's Perseverance," and first published as a separate book under that title in 1972.

Chapter 1
Introduction

In previous volumes we have expounded at some length (though not in this precise order) the great truths of Divine Election or Predestination unto salvation; the Atonement or perfect Satisfaction which Christ rendered unto the Law on behalf of His people; fallen man's total impotency unto good; the miracle of Regeneration, whereby the elect (who are born into this world dead in trespasses and sins) are quickened into newness of life; Justification by faith, whereby the believing sinner is delivered from the curse of the Law, the righteousness of Christ being reckoned to his account; the believer's Sanctification, whereby he is set apart unto God, constituted a temple of the Holy Spirit, delivered from the reigning power of sin, and made meet for Heaven. It is therefore fitting that we should now take up the complementary and completing truth of the final perseverance of the saints, or the infrustrable certainty of their entrance into the Inheritance purchased for them by Christ and unto which they have been begotten by the Spirit.

This blessed subject has been an occasion for fierce strife in the theological world, and nowhere is the breach between Calvinists and Arminians more apparent than in their diverse views of this doctrine. The former regard it as the very salt of the covenant, as one of the principal mercies purchased by the redemption of Christ, as one of the richest jewels which adorns the Gospel's crown, as one of the choicest cordials for the reviving of fainting saints, as one of the greatest incentives to practical holiness. But with the latter it is the very reverse. Arminians regard this doctrine as an invention of the Devil, as highly dishonoring to God, as a poisoning of the Gospel fountain, as giving license to self-indulgence and being subversive of all real piety. In this instance it is impossible to seek a golden mean between two extremes, for one party must be extremely right and the other extremely wrong.

While we have no doubt whatever in which of those two camps the truth is to be found, yet we are far from allowing that Calvinists have always presented this doctrine in its Scriptural proportions; yea it is our firm conviction that during the last two or three generations especially it has been dealt with by many novices in such a manner as to do far more evil than good. Large numbers of men have contended for the "Security of the Saints" in such a crude and lopsided way that not a few godly souls were stumbled, and in their revolt against such extremism supposed their only safeguard was to reject the whole subject in toto. Such a course was wrong: if some amateur would-be-bakers turn out uneatable loaves, that is no reason why I should henceforth decline all bread—I should be the loser if I acted so radically.

We have no sympathy whatever with the bald and unqualified declaration "Once saved always saved." In a publication issued by a widely-known "Bible Institute" appears the following. "I went to the death cell of that condemned man in prison a few days ago. I went to tell him of a pardon from my King. I had no right to offer him a pardon from the state . . . but I could tell him of the One who took his place on Calvary's cross, offering eternal redemption from the penalty of sin, so that he could be justified before the 'Judge of all the earth' in the court of heaven, for all the endless ages. Thank God! I found that man clear on the plan of salvation, for years ago under the ministry of he had accepted Jesus as his personal Savior. But through the years he had grown cold and indifferent: he had lost his fellowship with his Lord, not his salvation. And the result was a life of sin. It took an awful experience to turn him from his self-willed way; but as I talked with him in his prison cell, I was convinced that he was born again and repentant for his crime."

While it lies entirely outside our province to form any judgment as to the eternal destiny of that murderer, yet a few comments on the preacher's account of the above incident seem to be called for. What impression is likely to be made on the mind of the average light-headed professor by the reading of such a case? What effect is it calculated to produce upon those church members who are walking arm in arm with the world? First, we are told that this murderer was "clear on the plan of salvation": so also is the Devil, but what does such mental knowledge avail him! Next it is said that years before this condemned man "had accepted Jesus as his personal Savior" under the ministry of a certain well-known "Revivalist." But before any soul can receive Christ as Savior, he must first throw down the weapons of his rebellion, repent of his sins, and surrender to Christ as Lord.

The Savior is the Holy One of God, who saves His people "from their sins" (Matt. 1:2 1) and not in their sins: who saves them from the love and dominion of their sins. How different was the preaching of Spurgeon from that of the cheapjack "evangelists" who have followed him. Said he, "Go not to God and ask for mercy with sin in thy hand. What would you think of the rebel who appeared before the face of his sovereign and asked for pardon with the dagger sticking in his belt and with the declaration of his rebellion on his breast? Surely he would deserve double doom for thus mocking his monarch while he pretended to be seeking mercy. If a wife has forsaken her husband do you think she would have the impudence, with brazen forehead, to come back and ask his pardon leaning on the arm of her paramour? Yet so it is with you—perhaps asking for mercy and going on in sin—praying to be reconciled to God and yet harboring and indulging your lusts. . . cast away your sin or He cannot hear you. If you lift up unholy hands with a lie in your right hand, prayer is worthless on your lips" (C. H. S., 1860).

Returning to the above incident. This preacher declares of the man in the condemned cell, "But through the years he had grown cold and indifferent: he had lost his fellowship with his Lord, not his salvation, and the result was a life of sin." Such a statement is a flat contradiction in terms. Salvation and sin are opposites. "If any man be in Christ he is a new creature: old things are passed away, behold all things are become new" (2 Cor. 5:17). Divine salvation is a supernatural work which produces supernatural effects. It is a miracle of grace which causes the wilderness to blossom as the rose. It is known by its fruits. It is a lie to call a tree good if it bears evil fruit. Justification is evidenced by sanctification. The new birth is made manifest by a new life. Where one makes a profession of being saved and then follows it with "a life of sin" it is a case of "the dog turning again to his vomit and the washed sow to her wallowing in the mire" (2 Pet. 2:22).

Before dismissing this case a word should be said upon the preacher's statement "I could tell him of the One who took his place on Calvary's cross" which occurs, be it noted, at the beginning of the narrative. Surely the first thing to press upon a murderer would be the awfulness of his condition: to remind him that he had not only grievously wronged a fellow-creature, but had sinned against the Holy One; to faithfully set before him the solemn fact that in a few days he would have to appear before the Divine Judge. Then he could speak of the amazing grace of God which had provided a Savior for sinners, even the very chief of sinners, and that He is freely offered to all by the Gospel, on the terms of repentance and faith. But the Scriptures nowhere warrant us to tell any indifferent, impenitent sinner that Christ 'took his place on the cross": the substitutionary work of Christ is a truth for the comfort of believers and not a sop for unbelievers. O the ignorance and confusion now obtaining in Christendom.

In the N. T. the salvation of God is presented under three tenses: past, present and future. As a work "begun" (Phil. 1:6), but not completed in a moment of time. "Who hath saved us" (2 Tim. 1:9), "work out your own salvation with fear and trembling" (Phil. 2:12), "now is our salvation nearer than when we believed" (Rom. 13:11). These verses do not refer to three different salvations, but to three distinct phases and stages of salvation: salvation as an accomplished fact, as a present process, and as a future prospect. First, God saves from the pleasure of sin, causing the heart to loathe what it formerly loved. That which is displeasing to God is made bitter to the soul, and sin becomes its greatest grief and burden. Next, faith is communicated by the Spirit and the penitent sinner is enabled to believe the Gospel, and thereby he is saved from the penalty of sin. Then it is he enters upon the Christian life, wherein he is called upon to "fight the good fight of faith", for there are enemies both within and without which seek to bring about his destruction.

For that "fight" God has provided adequate armor (Eph. 6:11), which the Christian is bidden to take unto himself. For that fight he is furnished with effective weapons, but these he must make good use of. For that fight spiritual strength is available (2 Tim. 2:1), yet it has to be diligently and trustfully sought. It is in this fight, a lifelong process, a conflict in which no furloughs are granted, the Christian is being saved from the power of sin. In it he receives many wounds, but he betakes himself to the great Physician for healing. In it he is often cast down, but by grace he is enabled to rise again. Finally, he shall be saved from the presence of sin, for at death the believer is forever rid of his evil nature.

Now it is that third aspect of salvation which concerns us in this present series of articles, namely, the believer's perseverance: his perseverance in the fight of faith. The doctrine which is to be before us relates to the Christian's being saved from the power of indwelling sin during the interval which elapses between his being saved from its penalty and the moment when he will be saved from its presence. Between his being saved from Hell and his actual entrance into Heaven he needs saving from himself, saving from this evil world in which he is still left, saving from the devil who as a roaring lion goes about seeking whom he may devour. The journey from Egypt to Canaan lies not for the most part through green pastures and by the still waters but across an arid desert with all its trials and testings, and few who left that House of Bondage reached the Land of milk and honey: the great majority fell in the wilderness through their unbelief—types of numerous professors who begin well but fail to endure unto the end. There are multitudes in Christendom to-day deluded with the idea that a mere historical faith in the Gospel ensures their reaching Heaven: who verily suppose they have "received Christ as their personal Savior" simply because they believe that He died on the cross as an atoning sacrifice for the sins of all those who repudiate their own righteousness and trust in Him. They imagine that if under the influence of religious emotion and the pressing appeals of an evangelist, and assured that "John 3:16 means what it says", they were persuaded to "become Christians", that therefore all is now well with them: that having obtained a ticket for Glory they may, like passengers on a train, relax and go to sleep, confident that in due time they shall arrive at their desired destination. By such deceptions Satan chloroforms myriads into Hell. So widespread is this deadly delusion that one who undertakes to expose its sophistry is certain to be regarded by many as a heretic.

The Christian life commences amid the throes of the new birth, under acute travail of soul. When the Spirit of God begins His work in the heart conscience is convicted, the terrors of the Law are felt, the wrath of a sin-hating God becomes real. As the requirements of Divine holiness begin to be apprehended the soul, so long accustomed to having its own way, "kicks against the pricks," and only in the day of God's power is it "made willing" (Psa. 110:3) to take the yoke of Christ upon it. And then it is that the young believer, conscious of the plague of his own heart, fearful of his own weakness and instability, aware of the enmity of the Devil against him, anxiously cries out, How shall I be able to keep from drowning in such a world as this? what provision has God made that I shall not perish on my way to everlasting bliss? The Lord has done great things for me, whereof I am glad; but unless He continues to exert His sovereign power on my behalf, I shall be lost.

Moreover, as the young Christian holds on his way he observes how many of those who took up a Christian profession walk no more in the paths of righteousness, having returned to the world. This stumbles him and makes him ask, Shall I also make shipwreck of the faith? Ah, none stand more sure and safe than those who feel they cannot stand, whose cry is "Hold Thou me up, and I shall be safe" (Psa. 119:117). "Happy is the man who feareth always" (Prov. 28:14). Happy the soul who is possessed of that holy fear which drives him to the Lord, keeps him vile in his own eyes and causes him to ever depend upon the promise and grace of a faithful God, which makes him rejoice with trembling, and tremble with hope.

In the case which we have just supposed—and it is one which is true to life—we discover an additional reason for taking up the present subject. It is necessary that the young and fearing Christian should be further strengthened in the faith, that he should be informed the good Shepherd does not leave His lambs undefended in the midst of wolves, that full provision is made for their safety. Yet it is at this stage especially that heavenly wisdom is needed by the instructor if he is to be of real help. On the one hand he must be careful not to cast pearls before swine, and on the other he must not be deterred from giving to the children of God their rightful and needful Bread. If he must be on his guard against ministering unlawful comfort to carnal professors, he must also see to it that legitimate comforts and cordials are not withheld from saints with feeble knees and whose hands hang down because of their discouragements.

Each of the dangers we have alluded to will be avoided by due attention unto the terms of our theme and an amplification thereof. It is the final perseverance of the saints we shall write about, the enduring of those who have been washed in the blood of the Lamb and not those who have been whitewashed by self-reformation. It is the final perseverance of saints along the Narrow Way, along the paths of righteousness. It is their perseverance in the fight of faith and the performance of obedience. The Word of God nowhere teaches that once a man is born again he may give free rein to the lusts of the flesh and be as worldly as he pleases, yet still be sure of getting to Heaven. Instead, Scripture says, and the words are addressed to believers, "For if ye live after the flesh, ye shall die" (Rom. 8:13). No, if a man is born again he will desire, purpose and endeavor to live as becometh a child of God.

There has been some deliberation in our mind as to which is the better title for this doctrine: the preservation or the perseverance of the saints. At first sight the former seems preferable, as being more honoring to God, throwing the emphasis on His keeping power. Yet further reflection will show that such preferableness is more seeming than real. We prefer the latter because rightly understood it includes the former, while at the same time pressing the believer's responsibility. Moreover, we believe, it to be more in accord with the general tenor of Scripture. The saints are "kept by the power of God through faith" (1 Pet. 1:5). He does not deal with them as unaccountable automatons, but as moral agents, just as their natural life is maintained through their use of means and by their avoidance of that which is inimical to their wellbeing, so it is with the maintenance and preservation of their spiritual lives.

God preserves His people in this world through their perseverance—their use of means and avoidance of what is destructive. We do not mean for a moment that the everlasting purpose of the Most High is made contingent on the actions of the creature. The saints' perseverance is a Divine gift, as truly as is health and strength of body. The two sides of this truth, the Divine and the human, are brought together in "work out your own salvation with fear and trembling, for it is God which worketh in you both to will and to do of His good pleasure" (Phil. 2:12, 13): it is God who works in the believer both the desire and performance in using the means, so that all ground for boasting is removed from him. When God begins His work of grace in a soul the heart then turns to Him in penitence and faith, and as He continues that work the soul is kept in the exercise of its graces. As we seek to unfold this theme our emphasis will change from time to time according as we have before us those who repudiate it and those who pervert it—when we shall treat of the Divine foundations on which it rests or the safeguards by which it is protected. O for wisdom to steer clear of both Arminianism and Antinomianism.

Chapter 2
Its Importance

The theme of this present series of articles is far more than a theological dogma or sectarian tenet: it is an essential portion of that Faith once for all delivered to the saints, concerning which we are exhorted to "contend earnestly". In it is displayed, respectively, the honor and glory of the Father, of the Son and of the Holy Spirit, and therefore they who repudiate this truth cast a most horrible aspersion upon the character of the triune Jehovah. The final perseverance of the saints is one of the grand and distinctive blessings proclaimed by the Gospel, being an integral part of salvation itself, and therefore any outcry against this doctrine is an attack upon the very foundations of the believer's comfort and assurance. How can I go on my way rejoicing if there be doubts in my mind whether God will continue to deal graciously with me and complete that work which He has begun in my soul? How can I sincerely thank God for having delivered me from the wrath to come if it is quite possible I may yet be cast into Hell?

Above we have said that the honor and glory of Jehovah is bound up in the final perseverance of the saints: let us now proceed to amplify that assertion. God the Father predestinated His people "to be conformed to the image of His Son" (Rom. 8:29), which conformity is not fully wrought in any of them in this life, but awaits the day of Christ's appearing (1 John 3:2). Now is the Father's eternal purpose placed in jeopardy by the human will? is its fulfillment contingent upon human conduct? or, having ordained the end will He not also make infallibly effectual all means to that end? That predestination is founded upon His love: "I have loved thee (says the Father to each of His elect) with an everlasting love, therefore with lovingkindness have I drawn thee" (Jer. 31:3). Nor is there any variation in His love, for God is not fickle like us: "I am the Lord, I change not: therefore ye sons of Jacob are not consumed" (Mal. 3:6). Were it possible for one of God's elect to totally apostatize and finally perish it would mean the Father had purposed something which He failed to effect and that His love was thwarted.

Consider God the Son in His mediatorial character. The elect were committed unto Him as a trust by the Father: said He Thine they were and Thou gayest them Me" (John 17:6). In the covenant of redemption Christ offered to act as their Surety and to serve as their Shepherd. This involved the most stupendous task which the history of the universe records: the Son's becoming incarnate, magnifying the Divine Law by rendering to it perfect obedience, pouring out His soul unto death as a sacrifice to Divine justice, overcoming death and the grave, and ultimately presenting 'faultless" before God (Jude 24) the whole of His redeemed. As the good Shepherd He died for His sheep, and as the great Shepherd it is His office to preserve them from this present evil world. If He failed in this task, if any of His sheep were lost, where would be His faithfulness to His engagement? where would be the efficacy of His atonement? how could He triumphantly exclaim at the end "Behold I and the children which God hath given Me" (Heb. 2:13)?

The person of the Holy Spirit is equally concerned in this vital matter. It is not sufficiently realized by the saints that they are as definitely indebted to the third Person of the Godhead as truly as they are to the first and second Persons. The Father ordained their salvation, the Son in His mediatorial character purchased it, and the Spirit "applies" and effectuates it. It is the blessed Spirit's work to make good the Father's purpose and the Son's atonement: "He saved us by the washing of regeneration and renewing of the Holy Spirit" (Titus 3:5). Said Christ to His disciples "I will not leave you orphans (though I leave this world): I will come to you" (John 14:18). That promise given on the eve of His death was made good in the gift of the Spirit "But the Comforter, the Holy Spirit, whom the Father will send in My name, the same shall teach you all things" (John 14:26). Christ's redeemed were thus entrusted to the love and care of the Spirit, and should any of them be lost where would be the Spirit's sufficiency? where His power? where His faithfulness?

This, then, is no trivial doctrine we are now concerned with, for the most momentous considerations are inseparably connected with it. We are satisfied it is because of their failure to realize this that so many professing Christians perceive not the seriousness of their assenting to the opposing dogma of the total apostasy of saints. If they understood more clearly what was involved in affirming that some who were truly born again fell from grace, continued in a course of sin, died impenitent and were eternally lost, they would be slower to set their seal unto that which carried such horrible implications. Nor may we regard it as a matter of indifference where such grave consequences are concerned. For any of the elect to perish would necessarily entail a defeated Father, who was balked of the realization of His purpose: a disappointed Son, who would never see the full travail of His soul and be satisfied; and a disgraced Spirit, who had failed to preserve those entrusted to His care. From such awful errors may we be delivered.

The importance of this truth further appears from the prominent place which is accorded it in the Holy Scriptures. Whether we turn to the O. T. or the New it makes no difference; whether we consult the Psalms or the Prophets, the Gospels or the Epistles, we find it occupies a conspicuous position. If we cited every reference we should have to transcribe literally hundreds of verses. Instead, we will quote only a few of the lesser known ones. Here is one from the Pentateuch:

"He loved the people, all His saints are in Thy hand" (Deut. 33:3). One from the Historical books: "He will keep the feet of His saints" (1 Sam. 2:8). One from Job: "When he hath tried me I shall come forth as gold" (23:10). One from the Psalms: "The Lord will perfect that which concerneth me" (138:8). One from the Proverbs: "The root of the righteous shall not be moved" (12:3 contrast Matt. 13:2 1). One from the Prophets: "I will put My fear in their hearts that they shall not depart from Me" (Jer. 32:40). These are fair samples of the Divine promises throughout the O. T.

Observe the place given to this truth in the teaching of Christ. "Upon this Rock I will build My Church, and the gates of Hell shall not prevail against it" (Matt. 16:18). "False Christs and false prophets shall rise, and shall show signs and wonders, to seduce, if possible, even the elect" (Mark 14:22)—it is not possible for Satan to fatally deceive any of the elect. "Whosoever cometh to Me and heareth My sayings, and doeth them, I will show you to whom he is like: he is like a man which built a house and dUG deep, and laid the foundation on a rock; and when the flood arose, the storm beat vehemently upon that house, and could not shake it; for it was founded upon a rock" (Luke 6:47-48). "This is the Father's will which hath sent Me, that of all which He hath given Me I should lose nothing" (John 6:39). The writings of the apostles are full of it. "For if when we were enemies, we were reconciled to God by the death of His Son; much more, being reconciled, we shall be saved by His life" (Rom. 5:10). "Hath not God chosen the poor of this world rich in faith, and heirs of the kingdom which He hath promised to them that love Him" (James 2:5). "Kept by the power of God through faith unto salvation" (1 Pet. 1:5). "They went out from us, but they were not of us; for ~f they had been of us, they would have continued with us" (1 John 2:19). "Now unto Him that is able to keep you from falling" (Jude 24).

The tremendous importance of this doctrine is further evidenced by the fact that it involves the very integrity of the Scriptures. There is no mistaking their teaching on this subject: the passages quoted above make it unmistakably plain that every section of them affirms the security of the saints. He then who declares the saints are insecure so long as they remain in this evil world, who insists that they may be eternally lost, yea that some of them—like king Saul and Judas—have perished, repudiates the reliability of Holy Writ and signifies that the Divine promises are worthless. 0 my reader, weigh this well: the very veracity of the Lord God is concerned therein. He has promised to keep the feet of His saints, to deliver them from evil, to preserve them unto His heavenly kingdom, and "God is not a man that He should lie, neither the son of man that He should repent: hath He said, and shall He not do it? Or hath He spoken, and shall He not make it good? (Num. 23:19).

Elisha Coles the Puritan used a forcible argument from the less to the greater, the substance of which shall here be given. Since the Lord made good His word in things of a lower consideration, how much more will He in the eternal salvation of His people. If certain persons were destined by Him to eminent service in this world, notwithstanding the greatest of difficulties and natural impossibilities which stood in the way to obstruct it, how much more certain is the accomplishment of His purpose concerning those vessels of mercy which He has ordained for heavenly glory! God promised Abraham that his seed should have the land of Canaan (Gen. 12:7). Years passed and when little short of a century his wife was still barren, but a miracle was wrought and Isaac was born. Isaac married and for twenty years his wife remained childless, when in answer to prayer the Lord gave her conception (25:21). They had two children but the Lord rejected the elder, and the younger to whom the promise belonged was in daily danger of being killed by Esau (27:41), and to save his life he fled to Padanaram.

While in Padanaram Laban dealt harshly with him, and when he decided to return home his father-in-law followed him with evil intentions, but the Lord interposed and warned him in a dream (Gen. 31:23, 24). But no sooner had Jacob escaped from Laban than Esau comes against him with four hundred men, determined to revenge his old grudge (32:6), but the Lord melted his heart in a moment and caused him to receive Jacob with affection. When Simeon and Levi so highly provoked the Canaanites there appeared to be every prospect that Jacob and his family would be exterminated (34:25), but the Lord caused such a terror to fall on them that they touched not a single one (35:5). When a seven years famine came on the land, threatening to consume them, by a strange providence the Lord provided for them in Egypt. There, later, Pharaoh sought their destruction; but in vain. By His mighty power Jehovah brought them forth from the house of bondage, opened a way through the Red Sea, conducted them across the wilderness and brought them into Canaan. Shall He do less for the spiritual seed of Abraham to whom He has promised the heavenly Canaan for an everlasting heritage?

Joseph was one whom the Lord would honor, and in several dreams intimated he should be exalted to a position of dignity and preeminence (Gen. 37). Because of that his brethren hated him, determined to frustrate those predictions and slay him (v. 18). And how shall Joseph escape? for they are ten to one and he the least. In due course they cast him into a pit, where it seemed likely he must perish; but in the good providence of God some Midianites passed that way ere any wild beast had found him. He is delivered into their hands and they bring him to Egypt and sell him to the captain of Pharaoh's guard — a man not at all likely to show kindness to him. But the Lord is pleased to give him favor in his master's eyes (39:3, 4), yet if Joseph's hopes now rose how quickly were they disappointed. Through the lies of his mistress he was cast into prison, where he spent not a few days but many years. What prospect now of preferment? Nevertheless the counsel of the Lord was made good and he became lord over Egypt!

God promised the kingdom of Israel unto David and while yet a youth he was anointed to it (1 Sam. 16:13). What! notwithstanding all interveniences? Yes, for the Lord had said it and shall He not do it! Therefore if Saul cast a javelin at him, unsuspected, to nail him to the wall, a sharpness of eye and agility of body shall be given him to discern and avoid it (18:11). If he determined evil against him, Jonathan is moved to inform him (19:7). If he send messengers to Naioth to arrest him, they shall forget their errand and fall a prophesying (2 0-24). If he be in a city that will betray him, and no friend there to acquaint him of his peril, the Lord Himself is his intelligencer and sends him out (23:12). If Saul's army encompasses him about and no way to escape is left, the Philistines invade his land and the king turns away to meet them (vv. 26, 27). Though there were not on earth to deliver "He (said David) shall send from heaven and save me" (Ps. 57:3). Shortly after Saul was slain and David came to the throne!

"And, behold, there came a man of God out of Judah by the word of the Lord unto Bethel; and Jeroboam stood by the altar to burn incense. And he cried against the altar in the word of the Lord, and said 0 altar, altar, thus saith the Lord: Behold, a child shall be born unto the house of David, Josiah by name; and upon thee shall he offer the priests of the high places that burn incense, and men's bones shall be burnt upon thee" (1 Kings 13:1, 2). Most remarkable was this prophecy. The kingdom of Judah had been despised and deserted by the ten tribes, yet a day will come when the house of David should so recover its power that a member of it would demolish that altar. Nothing seems more contingent and arbitrary than the giving of names to persons, yet here the name of this man is foretold centuries before his birth, and in due time he was called Josiah. During the interval of three hundred and fifty years between this prediction and its fulfillment (2 Kings 23:15, 16) things transpired which made dead against its accomplishment. Athaliah determined to destroy all the royal seed of David, but Joash is stolen from the rest and preserved (2 Kings 11:2). Hezekiah falls sick unto death, but fifteen years is added to his life rather than Manasseh, who must be Josiah's grandfather, should be unborn (20:6, 21).

"Paul was a chosen vessel, appointed to preach Christ to the Gentiles (Acts 9: 15) and at last to bear witness of Him at Rome (23:11). This must be done although bonds, imprisonment and death itself do attend him in every place. If, therefore they lie in wait for him at Damascus and watch the gates night and day to kill him, he shall be let down by the wall in a basket and so escape them (Acts 9:24, 25). If all Jerusalem be in an uproar to kill him the chief captain shall come in with an army and rescue him (21:31, 32) though no friend to Paul nor to his cause. If more than forty men had bound themselves with an oath that they will neither eat nor drink until they have killed him, his kinsmen shall hear of it, and by his means the chief captain shall be his friend again and grant him a sufficient convoy (23:14-23). . .not his being once stoned, nor his thrice suffering shipwreck, nor anything else, shall make void the purpose of God for bearing witness of Christ at Rome" (Elisha Coles).

Now my reader, why, think you, are such instances as the above recorded in the sacred Scriptures? Is it not for our instruction and consolation? Is it not to assure us that the promises of God are unimpeachable, that His counsel shall stand, that once the word has gone forth from His mouth all earth and hell combined is powerless to negative it? If the Lord was so exact in carrying out His word in these lesser things, which related only to time and earth, executing His purpose despite all outward oppositions, working miracles in order to accomplish His pleasure, how much more will He be punctilious in securing the eternal welfare of those whom He has appointed to Heavenly glory! If He bore His people of old "upon eagles wings" (Ex. 19:17), above the reach of danger, if He kept them as "the apple of His eye" (Deut. 32:10)—with all possible care and tenderness—till He brought them to Himself, think you that He will now do less for any for whom Christ died!

One of the outstanding glories of the Gospel is its promise of eternal security to all who truly believe it. The Gospel presents no third-rate Physician who is competent to treat only the milder cases, but One who heals "all manner of sickness" who is capable of curing the most desperate cases. It proclaims no feeble Redeemer, but One who is "mighty to save": though the world, the flesh and the Devil, combine against Him, He cannot be frustrated. He who triumphed over the grave cannot be thwarted by any feebleness or fickleness in His people. "He is able (which would not be true if their unwillingness could balk Him) to save unto the uttermost them that come unto God by Him" (Heb. 7:25). Those whom He pardons He preserves. Therefore each one who trusts in Him, though conscious of his own weakness and wickedness, may confidently exclaim "I know whom I have believed, and am persuaded that He is able to keep that which I have committed unto Him against that day."

The importance of this truth appears clearly if we suppose the opposite. Assume that those who flee to Christ for refuge should finally end in the regions of woe: then what? Why, to what purpose would be the proclamation of a Gospel which announced "so-great salvation" only for its participants to be eventually disappointed?— it would be no better than a beautiful mirage seen by parched travelers in the desert: presenting to their view a life-giving stream, only to mock those who sought it. Why, to what purpose did Christ offer Himself as a sacrifice to God if His blood avails not for those who trust in it? Why, to what purpose is the Holy Spirit given to God's children if He is unable to subdue the flesh in them and overcome their proclivities to wander? To what purpose is the Divine gift of faith if it fails its possessor in the ultimate outcome? If the final perseverance of the saints be a delusion, then one must close his Bible and sit down in despair.

Chapter 3
Its Nature

We purpose dealing with this theme, and particularly with that aspect of it which is now to be before us, in rather a different manner than that which was followed by most of the Calvinistic divines in the past; or rather, we propose to throw most of our emphasis upon another angle of it than what they did. Their principal object was to establish this truth, by rebutting the error of Arminians, who insist that those who have been redeemed by Christ and regenerated by the Holy Spirit may nevertheless totally and finally apostatize from the Faith, and so eternally perish. Our chief aim will rather be to counteract the crude manner in which this doctrine has been only too often handled in more recent times and the evil use to which an adulterous generation has put it. While Arminianism has by no means disappeared from Christendom, yet it is the more recent inroads of Antinomianism (the repudiation of the Divine Law and the turning of God's grace into lasciviousness) which have wrought the most damage in our own lifetime.

It is not sufficiently realized by many of the Lord's own people that far more harm than good is likely to be done by immature "Gospellers", who have more zeal than knowledge, and who expect to reap a harvest (secure "results") before the ground is ploughed and harrowed. Many an ignorant evangelist has given his hearers the impression that once they "accept Christ as their personal Savior" they need have no concern about the future, and thousands have been lulled into a fatal sleep by the soothing lullaby "once saved, always saved". To imagine that if I commit my soul and its eternal interests into the hands of the Lord henceforth relieves me of all obligation, is to accept sugar-coated poison from the father of lies. When I deposit my money in the bank for safe custody, then my responsibility is at an end: it is now their duty to protect the same. But it is far otherwise with the soul at conversion—the Christian's responsibility to avoid temptation and shun evil, to use the means of grace and seek after good, lasts as long as he is left in this world.

If our ancestors erred on the side of prolixity their descendants have often injured the cause of Christ by their brevity. Bare statements, without qualification or amplification, are frequently most misleading. Brief generalizations may content the superficial, who lack both the incentive and the patience to make a thorough examination of any subject, but those who value the Truth sufficiently to be willing to "buy" it (Prov. 23:23) appreciate a detailed analysis, if so be that their contemplation thereof enables them to obtain an intelligent and balanced grasp of an important Scriptural theme. The man who accepts a piece of money—be it of paper or metal—after a cursory glance, is far more likely to be deceived with a counterfeit than he who scrutinizes it closely. And they who give assent to a mere summarized declaration of this doctrine are in far greater danger of being deluded than the ones who are prepared to carefully and prayerfully examine a systematic exposition thereof. It is, of course, for the latter we write.

Much confusion and misunderstanding has been caused through failure to clearly define terms. Those who assail this doctrine usually set up a "man of straw" and then suppose they have achieved a notable victory because so little difficulty was experienced in demolishing so feeble an object; and it must be confessed that only too often those who have posed as the champions of the Truth are largely to blame for this. It needs little argument to demonstrate that one who is in love with sin and drinks in iniquity like water does not have his face Heavenwards, no matter what experience of grace he claims to have had in the past. Yet it must not be concluded that the Arminian has gained the day when he appeals to the Christian's spiritual instincts and asks: Does it comport with God's holiness for Him to own as His dear child one who is trampling upon His commandments? The Calvinist would return a negative reply to such an iniquity as promptly and emphatically as would his opponent.

"The righteous shall hold on his way" (Job 17:9). As Spurgeon pertinently pointed out, "The Scripture does not teach that a man will reach his journey's end without continuing to travel along the road; it is not true that one act of faith is all, and that nothing is needed of daily faith, prayer and watchfulness. Our doctrine is the very opposite, namely, that the righteous shall hold on his way: or, in other words, shall continue in faith, in repentance, in prayer, and under the influence of the grace of God. We do not believe in salvation by a physical force which treats a man as a dead log, and carries him whether he will it or not towards heaven. No, 'he holds on his way', he is personally active about the matter, and plods on uphill and down dale till he reaches his journey's end. We never thought that merely because a man supposes that he once entered on this way he may therefore conclude that he is certain of salvation, even if he leaves the way immediately. No, but we say that he who truly receives the Holy Spirit, so that he believes in the. Lord Jesus Christ, shall not go back, but persevere in the way of faith. . .We detest the doctrine that a man who has once believed in Jesus will be saved even if he altogether forsook the path of obedience."

In order to define our terms we must make it quite clear who it is that perseveres and what it is in which he perseveres. It is the saints, and none other. This is evident from many passages of Scripture. "He will keep the feet of His saints" (1 Sam. 2:9). "For the Lord loveth judgment and forsaketh not His saints: they are preserved forever" (Ps. 37:28). "He preserveth the souls of His saints: He delivereth them out of the hand of the enemy" (Ps. 87:10). "He maketh intercession for the saints" (Rom. 8:27). "He shall come to be glorified in His saints" (2 Thess. 1:10). All such are preserved in God's love and favor, and accordingly they persevere in the Faith, eschewing all damnable errors; they persevere in a life of faith, clinging to Christ like a drowning man to a life-buoy; they persevere in the path of holiness and obedience, walking by the light of God's Word and being directed by His precepts—not perfectly so, nor without wandering, but in the general tenor of their lives.

Now a "saint" is a sanctified or separated one. First, he is one of those who were chosen by the Father before the foundation of the world and predestinated to be conformed unto the image of His Son. Second, he is one of those who were redeemed by Christ, who gave His life a ransom for them. Third, he is one who has been regenerated by a miracle of grace, brought from death unto life, and thereby set apart from those who are dead in sin. Fourth, he is indwelt by the Holy Spirit, whereby he is sealed unto the day of redemption. But how may I know whether or not I am a saint? By impartially examining myself in the light of Holy Writ to see if I possess the character and conduct of one. A "saint" is one whose back is toward the world and his face toward God; whose affections are drawn unto things above, who yearns for communion with his Beloved, who grieves over that in himself which displeases God, who makes conscience of his sins and confesses them to God, who prayerfully endeavors to walk as becometh a Christian, but who daily mourns his many offences.

Only those persevere unto the end who have experienced the saving grace of God. Now grace is not only a Divine attribute inherent in His character, it is also a Divine principle which He imparts to His people. It is both objective and subjective. Objectively, it is that free favor with which God eternally and unchangingly regards His people. Subjectively, it is that which He communicates to their souls, which resists their native depravity and enables them to hold on their way. A saint is one who not only has "found grace in the eyes of the Lord" (Gen. 6:8), but who has also received "abundance of grace" (Rom. 5:17) —"unto every one of us is grace given" (Eph. 4:7). The Lord "giveth grace unto the humble" Games 4:6), and His grace is an operative, influential, and transforming thing. The Lord Jesus is "full of grace and truth," and of His fullness do all His people receive, "and grace for grace" (John 1:14,16). That grace teaches its recipients "to deny ungodliness and worldly lusts, and to live soberly, righteously and godly in this present world" (Titus 2:11, 12). They come to the Throne of Grace and "find grace to help in time of need" (Heb. 4:16) and thereby prove the Divine declaration "My grace is sufficient for thee" (2 Cor. 12:9).

From all that has been pointed Out above it follows that when we affirm the final perseverance of the saints we do not mean,

1. That every professing Christian will reach Heaven. The sprinkling of a few drops of water on the head of an infant does not qualify it for the inheritance of the saints in light, for in a few years' time that child is seen to be no different than others who received not this ordinance. Nor does an avowal of faith on the part of an adult demonstrate him to be a new creature in Christ. Many born of Papish parents have been convinced of the folly of bowing before idols, confessing their sins to a priest and other such absurdities, but conversion to Protestantism is not the same as regeneration, as many evidenced in the days of Luther. Many a Jew has been convinced of the Messianic claims of Jesus Christ and has believed on Him as such, yet this is no proof of saving grace, as John 2:23, 24; 6:66 plainly shows. Thousands more have been emotionally stirred under the hypnotic appeals of evangelists and have "taken their stand for Christ" and "joined the church", but their interest quickly evaporated and they soon returned to their wallowing in the mire.

2. Nor do we mean that seeming grace cannot be lost. Satan is a clever imitator so that his tares are indistinguishable by men from the wheat. By reading theological

works and sitting under the preaching of the Word an attentive mind can soon acquire an intellectual acquaintance with the Truth and be able to discuss the mysteries of the Gospel more readily and fluently than can an unlettered child of God. Keen mentality may also be accompanied by a naturally religious disposition which expresses itself in fervent devotions, self-sacrificing effort and proselytizing zeal. But if such an one relapse and repudiates the Truth, that does not overthrow our doctrine: it simply shows he was never born of God. "They went out from us, but they were not of us; for of they had been of us, they would have continued with us" (1 John 2:19). Such characters had never been received into the fellowship of apostolic assemblies unless they gave credible appearance of possessing real grace, yet their subsequent departure was proof they had it not. "Whosoever hath not (in reality) from him shall be taken away even that which he seemeth to have" (Luke 8:18).

3. Nor do we mean that initial and preparatory grace is a guarantee of glorification. What percentage of blossoms on the apple and plum trees mature and bear fruit? And that is an adumbration in the natural of what is found in the spiritual realm. Many a promising bud is nipped by the frosts of spring and never develops into a flower. In like manner there is a large number who so far from despising and rejecting it, "receive the Word with joy, yet hath not root in himself, but dureth from a while" (Matt. 13:20, 21). That was the case when Christ Himself sowed the Seed, and many a faithful servant of His has found the same thing duplicated in his own ministerial labors. How often has he seen the buds of promise appearing in the lives of some of his young people, only to be saddened later by the discovery that their "goodness was as a morning cloud and as the early dew it went away" (Hos. 6:4). "Ye were willing for a season to rejoice in his light" (John 5:35) said Christ of certain ones who sat under the preaching of His forerunner; but observe He declared not that they had "sorrowed unto repentance".

Blazing comets and meteors are soon spent and fall from heaven like lightning, but the stars keep their orbits and stations—as do the spiritual "stars" held fast in Christ's right hand (Rev. 2:1). There is an initial grace which produces a real but transient effect, and there is a saving grace which secures a permanent result. Hebrews 6:4, 5 supplies a solemn illustration of the former. There we read of those "who were once enlightened", that is, whose minds were illumined from on high, so that they perceived clearly the excellence of Divine things. They "tasted of the heavenly gift," so that for a season they lost their relish for the things of the world. They "were made partakers of the Holy Spirit," being convicted by Him of their sins and brought to say with Balaam "let me die the death of the righteous" (Num. 23:10); but thorns sprang up and choked the good Seed, so that they "bring (forth) no fruit to perfection" (Luke 8:14). Such are cast forth "like an untimely birth."

4. Nor do we mean that true grace if left in our hands would not be lost. If Adam and Eve when left to themselves lost their innocence, how much more would those who are still affected by indwelling sin destroy themselves, did not the Lord renew them in the inner man "day by day" (2 Cor. 4:16). Regeneration does not make the Christian a God—independent and self-sufficient. No, it unites him as a branch to the true Vine, as a member of Christ's mystical body; and just as a bough detached from the tree imme-

diately withers and as an arm or leg cut off from its body is a lifeless thing, so would the saint perish if it were possible to sever him from the Savior. But the believer is not his own keeper: "your life is hid with Christ in God" (Col. 3:3) declares the apostle. At the new birth our self-righteousness received its death-wound, so that we were glad to look outside of ourselves to the righteousness of Another, and the more we grow in grace the more conscious are we of our weakness and the more are we made "strong in the Lord and in the power of His might."

5. Nor do we mean that true grace may not be hindered in its operations and suffer a relapse. "The flesh lusteth against the spirit" (Gal. 5:17): being contrary the one to the other, there is ever a warfare going on between them, one being uppermost to-day and the other so tomorrow. Christian perseverance is to be gauged not so much from single actions as by the more regular habits of the soul. As the functions of the body may be hindered by a swoon or fit, as the activities of the mind are impaired by delirium, so the stirrings of indwelling grace may be interrupted by the power of our natural corruptions. The more the saint yields to the solicitations of the flesh, the feebler become the workings of the principle of grace. That true grace may suffer a serious, though not a fatal, relapse, appears in the cases of Noah, Abraham, David and Peter, which are recorded for our warning and not for our imitation. The health of the soul varies as does that of the body, and as the latter is frequently the consequence of our own carelessness and folly, such is always the case in connection with the former.

6. Nor do we mean that the comforts of true grace cannot be eclipsed. We may indeed lose the sense of it though not the substance. Communion with Christ is lost when we experience a fall by the way, yet union with Him is not severed thereby. Mutual comforts may be suspended between man and wife though the conjugal knot be not dissolved. Believers may be separated from Christ's smile yet not so from His heart. If they wander from the Sun of righteousness how can they expect to enjoy His light and warmth. Sin and wretchedness, holiness and happiness are inseparably joined together. The way of the transgressor is hard, but peace and joy are the portion of the upright. As a parent suffers his child to scorch his fingers at the flame that he may learn to dread the fire, so God permits His people to lose their comforts for a season that they may prove the bitterness of sin, but He draws them back again unto Himself before they are destroyed thereby.

7. Nor do we mean that the presence of indwelling grace renders it unnecessary that its possessor should persevere. Yet this is one of the silly inferences which Arminians are fond of drawing. They say, "If it is absolutely certain that God will preserve His people from total apostasy, then there is no real need why they must persevere" - as well might we argue that it is unnecessary for us to breathe because God gives us breath, or that Hezekiah needed no longer to eat and drink because God had promised he should live another fifteen years. Wherever saving grace is bestowed it is accompanied by "the spirit of a sound mind" (2 Tim. 1:6) so that the soul is preserved from trifling with God or reasoning like a madman. Christians are called upon to work out their own salvation "with fear and trembling," not to conduct themselves recklessly, and to enable them thereto God worketh in them "both to will and to do of His good pleasure" (Phil 2:12,

13). Grace does not annul our responsibility but fits us to discharge it; it relieves from no duties, but equips for the performance of them.

We turn now to the positive side: having dwelt upon what is not signified or implied by the final perseverance of the saints, let us now endeavor to show whereof it consists. And here it should be duly noted that the Holy Spirit has not restricted Himself to a single expression but has used a great variety of words to describe this duty and blessing. In matters of great spiritual importance God has employed many different terms in His Word, for the instruction, comfort and support of His people. Out of the scores which set forth the believer's perseverance we may cite these. It is to "continue following the Lord our God" (1 Sam. 2:14), to "walk in the paths of righteousness" (Ps. 23:5), to be "steadfast in the Covenant" (Ps. 78:37), to "endure unto the end" (Matt. 24:13), to "deny self and take up the cross daily" (Luke 9:23), to "abide in Christ" (John 15:4), to "cleave unto the Lord" (Acts 1 11:23), to "press toward the mark" (Phil. 3:14), to "continue in the faith grounded and settled" (Col. 1:13), to "hold faith and a good conscience" (1 Tim. 1:19), to "hold fast the confidence and rejoicing of the hope firm unto the end" (Heb. 3:6), to "run with patience the race that is set before us" (Heb. 12:1), to "stablish our hearts" (James 5:8), to "be faithful unto death" (Rev. 2:10).

In the limited space at our disposal it is advisable to epitomize the main branches of this subject under a few heads.

1. Spiritual perseverance is the maintaining of a holy profession or a continuance in the word and doctrine of Christ. Wherever saving faith is imparted the soul receives the Scriptures as a Divine revelation, as the very Word of God. Faith is the visive faculty of the heart, by which the majesty and excellency of the Truth is perceived and by which such conviction and certainty is conveyed that the soul knows it is none other than the living God speaking to him. Faith "hath received His testimony" and thereby "hath set to his seal that God is true" (John 3:33). Henceforth he takes his stand on the impregnable rock of Holy Writ and neither man nor Devil can move him therefrom: "the voice of a stranger he will not follow" (John 10:5). While one who is not regenerated may intellectually believe and verbally profess his faith in the whole of revealed Truth, yet no regenerated person will repudiate the same.

"Some shall depart from the Faith, giving heed to seducing spirits and doctrines of demons" (1 Tim. 4:1). How many have done so within the memory of our older readers! Those who were looked upon as towers of orthodoxy succumbed to "evolutionism" and the "higher criticism." Those who were regarded as staunch Protestants became ensnared by Romanism. Multitudes of the rank and file who were once members of evangelical churches and teachers in the Sunday Schools, have been poisoned by infidelity and repudiated their former beliefs. But all such cases were merely the chaff being separated from the wheat, thereby causing the true to stand out more plainly from the false: "For there must be also heresies among you, that they which are approved may be made manifest" (1 Cor. 11:19). When many of Christ's disciples went back and walked no more with Him the apostles were not shaken, for when He asked them "Will ye also go away?" their spokesman answered "Lord, to whom shall we go? Thou hast the words of eternal life" (John 6:66, 68).

"Then said Jesus to those Jews which believed on Him, If ye continue in My Word, then are ye My disciples indeed" (John 8:31). That is one of the marks of those who are disciples of Christ in reality and not only in appearance. They are all "taught of the Lord" (Isa. 54:13) and not merely by men, and "I know that whatsoever God doeth it shall be forever: nothing can be put to it, nor anything taken from it" (Eccl. 3:14). False Christs and false prophets may seek to beguile them, but it is not possible to deceive the elect (Matt. 24:24). Hymeneus and Philetus may err concerning the Truth, even denying the resurrection, and in consequence "overthrow the faith of some," yet we are at once assured "Nevertheless the foundation of God standeth sure, having this seal, the Lord knoweth them that are His" (2 Tim. 2:17-19)—none with a saving faith can be overthrown. And why? Because they are enabled to continue in God's Word. Uninfluenced by "current opinion" or "modern thought," the child o-f God even though the last one left on earth, would "hold fast the profession of faith without wavering" (Heb. 10:23).

2. The maintaining of holy affections and principles. It should be clearly understood that perseverance is not a distinct and particular grace, separate from all others, rather is it a virtue which crowns all virtues, a grace which sets a glory on every other grace. The first stirrings of the new life are seen in conviction of sin and contrition for the same, yet repentance is not an act to be performed once for all, but a grace to be exercised constantly. Faith is that which lays hold of Christ and obtains from Him pardon and cleansing, yet so far from that being something which needs not to be repeated, it is an experience which requires to be renewed day by day. The same holds good of love, of hope, of zeal. Perseverance is the continued exercise of holy affections and principles so that we do not merely trust for a while, love for a while, obey for a while, and then cease; but forgetting those things which are behind we press forward to those before. "These all died in faith" (Heb. 11:13): they not only lived by faith, but they continued doing so to the very end of their earthly pilgrimage.

"Blessed are they that mourn" (Matt. 5:4). Mark well the tense: not they that mourned in the past, but who still do so. Even Pharaoh and Ahab, yea Judas also, had transient qualms of conscience, but those were nothing more than the stirrings of nature. But the child of God has within him a deeper principle, a principle of holiness which is contrary to evil, and this makes its possessor grieve over his sinfulness. "Blessed are they which do hunger and thirst after righteousness"; not only who once hungered after righteousness, but who long ardently for it now. "Blessed is the man that endureth temptation" (James 1:12): how much theology is to be found in the grammar of Scripture! "To whom coming as unto a living Stone, disallowed indeed of men, but chosen of God, precious" (1 Pet. 2:4): yes "coming" for fresh supplies of grace, for further counsel and instruction, for heart-reviving communion. "Blessed is he that watcheth and keepeth his garments" (Rev. 16:15): they upon whom the benediction of God rests are not those who once ran well, but whose graces continue in exercise.

Christians are "kept by the power of God through faith unto salvation ready to be revealed in the last time" (1 Pet. 1:5). God does not preserve His people by the mere putting forth of physical power, but by renewing their graces, particularly their faith. It is through their continued reliance upon Christ, their trusting in the Divine promises and on God's perfections as engaged to fulfill them, their keeping of His commands and their overcoming the world (1 John 5:4) that the saints are secured from fatality. And their faith is maintained by Christ's constant intercession — "I have prayed for thee that thy faith fail not"—and God's response thereto, who fulfills "all the good pleasure of His goodness in them and the work of faith with power" (2 Thess. 1:11). This does not mean that the Christian's faith continues in unabated exercise all his days, for as the most fruitful tree passes through a wintertime of non-bearing so it often is in the experience of the believer, yet as the life is still in the tree though leafless so faith remains and bursts forth afresh. "Lord I believe, help Thou mine unbelief" expresses his general course.

3. The maintaining of holy conduct or good works. When a person s understanding has been supernaturally enlightened and his affections Divinely renewed there cannot but follow a radical change of conduct, though this is made more prominent and radical in some cases than in others. The difference is much more apparent in one who was thoroughly irreligious and guilty of gross outward sins before his new birth than another who was regulated by the training of pious parents and preserved from debauchery. Yet even with the latter a "new creation" must express itself in a new life: the Word will be read and meditated upon not so much as a duty but a delight, prayer will be engaged in not perfunctorily but heartily, the Lord's people will not only be respected but loved for whatever of Christ may be seen in them, honesty and truthfulness will mark his dealings with his fellows not only because this is right but because he would not grieve the Spirit, while daily work is performed not as an irksome task which must be done but as a service gladly rendered unto Him whose providence has wisely and graciously ordered his lot.

At regeneration God imparts spiritual life to the soul, and all life is followed by motion and operation. Before the new birth the soul was spiritually dead, and at the new birth it was entirely passive, being wrought upon by God; but after the new birth the soul becomes active. Perseverance then is the endeavors of the soul to concur with God's quickening of it. Hence it is that the Christian life is often described under the figure of walking: "for we are His workmanship, created in Christ Jesus unto good works, which God hath before ordained that we should walk in them" (Eph. 2:10). The motions of the body are transferred to the soul, which by faith and love is conducted along the way of God's statutes (Ezek. 36:2 7). Walking is a voluntary action and the renewed soul has pleasure in the path of godliness. Walking is a steady and continuous action, and not a spasmodic and irregular one: so the Christian pursues an obedient course not by fits and starts but steadily and steadfastly. Walking is a progressive motion, moving onwards to a goal: so the Christian normally goes on "from strength to strength" (Ps. 84:7). Walking as such is incessant, for it ceases as soon as we sit down by the wayside: so the Christian life is a walking to the very end of his pilgrimage and until Heaven is reached perfect rest is not entered into.

"But ye, beloved, building up yourselves on your most holy faith, praying in the Holy Spirit, keep yourselves in the love of God, looking for the mercy of our Lord Jesus Christ unto eternal life" (Jude 20, 21). It is by such exhortations that the Christian is stirred to use the means that make for constancy. Care has to be taken if there is to be spiritual growth. It is not sufficient to be established in the faith, we must daily increase therein: the foundation is laid that a house may be erected thereon, and that is built steadily, bit by bit. For this, prayer is required: this is the channel through which health and strength is obtained. Neglect of prayer is followed by arrested growth, nay by decay of graces, for if we go not forward we backslide. To pray aright the assistance of the Holy Spirit has to be sought. Further, we must keep ourselves in God's love by avoiding everything which displeases Him and by maintaining close and regular communion with Him. Should we leave our first love, then we must repent and do the first works (Rev. 2:4). Finally, hope must be kept in exercise: the heart fixed upon the glorious prospect and consummation awaiting us.

4. Such maintaining of a holy profession, holy affections and holy action is necessary in order to salvation. The very term "salvation" clearly implies danger, and of none can it be said that they are completely saved until they are completely delivered from danger, and certainly the Christian is not so while sin remains in him and he is left in a wicked world and exposed to the assaults of the Evil One. "See that ye refuse not Him that speaketh: for if they escaped not who refused Him that spoke on earth, much more shall not we escape if we turn away from Him that speaketh from heaven" (Heb. 12:25). Multitudes of those who came out of Egypt, crossed the Red Sea, fed on the manna and drank of the water from the smitten rock, afterward perished in the wilderness, and we are told "Now all these things happened unto them for ensamples, and they are written for our admonition.. .wherefore let him that thinketh he standeth take heed lest he fall" (1 Cor. 12:10, 11), for a holy God will no more be mocked now than He would be then.

As we have seen in an earlier paragraph 1 Pet. 1:5 places salvation in the future—as also does Rom. 13:11; 1 Tim. 4:16 — unto which the saints are kept by the power of God through faith. Heaven can only be reached by continuing along the sole path that leads thither, namely, the "Narrow Way." Those who persevere not in faith and holiness, love and obedience, will assuredly perish. Whatever temporal faith, natural love, goodly attainments, and confident assurance may appear for a while, they are a bed shorter than a man can stretch himself upon and a covering narrower than the soul can wrap itself in (Isa. 28:20). "Many false prophets shall arise and shall deceive many, and because iniquity shall abound the love of many shall (not merely wane or cool off, but) wax cold. But he that shall endure unto the end, the same shall be saved" (Matt. 24:13). All temptations to deny the Faith, to forsake Christ, to go back unto the world, to give free rein to the lusts of the flesh, must be resisted to our last breath, or our profession will prove worthless.

5. Enablement for this perseverance is wrought in the saints by God. Their deliverance from a total and final falling away is not owing to any power or sufficiency in themselves. Though their moral agency be not impaired and though continuance in well doing be required of them, yet their enduring unto the end is not to be attributed unto their fidelity nor to the strength of the new nature which they received at regeneration. No, Christian perseverance depends wholly and entirely on the will and fidelity, the influence and energy of God, working in them both to will and to do of His good pleasure, making them perfect in every good work to do His will, working in them that which is well pleasing in

His sight, through Jesus Christ (Heb. 13:21). It is God, who having begun a good work in them, will carry it on until the day of Jesus Christ (Phil. 1:6). If the Holy Spirit were taken from the believer, and he left to himself to stand or fall, he would immediately cease to be a believer and fall totally from a state of grace" (S. Hopkins).

Freely will any renewed person subscribe to the following lines:—

> "If ever it should come to pass
> That any sheep of Christ should fall away,
> My feeble, fickle soul, alas!
> Would fall a thousand times a day;
> Were not Thy love as firm as free,
> Thou soon would'st take it Lord, from me".

6. Christian perseverance is consistent with being sanctified but in part. It is most important that this be clearly stated, lest the Lord's people conclude they are outside the pale of the Covenant. At the new birth a holy principle or nature is imparted to them, but the old and sinful nature is not eradicated, nor is it to the slightest degree improved. Indwelling corruptions are as much opposed to God as they were before conversion, and just as active. Pray against them as he may, strive against them as he will, yet the believer is constantly overcome by them: frequently does he have to exclaim with David "iniquities prevail against me (Ps. 65:3). The experience described in Romans 7:14-25 is that of every genuine Christian. God gives no man such a measure of grace in this life as to make him sinless. "In many things we all offend" (James 3:2), and by sudden surprises and under great temptations believers may fall into particular gross outward acts of sin, yet they will not become totally corrupt and sinful as the unregenerate are, nor do they sin with their whole heart. Christian sanctification then is the maintaining of holy affections and actions in the midst of native depravity and all its out-flows. Despite great discouragements their faith and grace never wholly fail. Sanctified but in part now, glorified in the future.

7. From all that has been before us it will thus be seen that perseverance can be predicated only of those who "know the grace of God in truth" (Col. 1:6), who experience its supernatural operations in their own souls. Not a suppositionary grace which may be held in reckless abandonment, but a spiritual grace which causes its possessor to walk cautiously. What Scripture teaches is that, there never was, never will be, and never can be such a thing as the total and final falling away of one who has really repented and trusted on Christ; that in every instance where a Divine miracle of grace has been wrought that soul shall stand when this world and all its works shall be burned up. Rightly has it been said, "The question of the perpetuity of grace is the question of a genuine Gospel. Is grace permanent, then the Gospel is a reality. Is grace temporary, then the Gospel is a will o' the wisp, a phantom benediction, a dream of blessedness from which one may awake, to find himself bereft of all that raptured him" (G. S. Bishop).

Chapter 4
Its Marvel

This is an aspect of our subject which has received far too little attention from those who have written and preached thereon. Amid all the dust which controversy has raised up, only too often one of the grandest wonders of Divine grace has been hidden from the sight of the theological contestants: alas, how frequently is this the case, that being so occupied with the shell we reach not the kernel. Even those who have sought to defend this truth against the assault of Papish and Arminian antagonists did not sufficiently hold up to view the glorious miracle which it embodies. The security of the saint concerns not only the Divine veracity and faithfulness but it also exemplifies the workings of Divine power. The believer's cleaving unto the Lord, despite all hindrances and temptations to the contrary, not only manifests the efficacy of God's so-great salvation but displays the marvels of His workmanship therein. That the gates of Hell shall not prevail against the Church of Christ, that Satan is unable to destroy a single member of it, that the weakest shall be more than conqueror through Him that loved them, should fill us with admiration and adoration.

All the blessings of the Christian's life may be summed up in two eminent ones, for they include all the others of which he is the recipient from the moment of the new birth to his arrival in Heaven, namely, regeneration or instating him into life and the preservation of that life through all the difficulties and dangers of his pilgrimage to the safe conducting him unto glory. Hence it is we so often find them linked together in Scripture. Just as the work of creation at the first and then the upholding of all things by Divine power and providence are yoked together as works of like wonder (Heb. 1:2, 3) so we find regeneration and preservation joined together as the sum of the operations of grace. "Hath He not made thee and established thee" (Deut. 32:6); "I have made and will bear, even I will carry and deliver you" (Isa. 46:4). In Psalm 66:9 both are comprehended in one word "who putteth (margin) thy soul in life" and "who holdeth thy soul in life," first imparting life and then sustaining it. So also in the N. T.: "I give unto them eternal life and they shall never perish" (John 10:28); "begotten us again unto a living hope. . . kept by the power of God through faith" (1 Pet. 1:3, 5): "sanctified by God the Father and preserved in Jesus Christ" (Jude 1).

This great marvel of Divine preservation is enlarged upon and celebrated in Psalm 66. After saying "O bless our God, ye people, and make the voice of His praise to be heard: which holdeth our soul in life, and suffereth not our feet to be moved" (vv. 8, 9) the Psalmist pointed out first, they had been proved and tried "as silver is tried" (v. 10), which denotes the sorest of trials (Ezek. 22:22). Second, God had brought them "into the net" and had "lain affliction upon their loins" (v. 11): that is, He had so encompassed them roundabout with afflictions that there was no way of escaping out of them (cf. Isa. 5 1:20). Third, God had caused men to "ride over their heads" (v. 12): that is, they were delivered to the will of cruel enemies, who treated them as slaves. Fourth, they had gone "through fire and water" (v. 12), which denotes the extremity of evils. Nor were these various dangers perils to their outward man only, but tryings and testings of their faith, as "Thou, Lord, hast proved us" (v. 10) intimates. Yet through all of them they had been sustained and preserved. God had supported their faith and upheld them under His sorest chastenings.

Having blessed God on behalf of other saints and invited his readers to do the same, the Psalmist added a personal testimony, recounting the Lord's goodness unto himself. "Come and hear, all ye that fear God, and I will declare what He hath done for my soul" (v. 16), which confession continues to the end of the Psalm. That testimony is not to be divorced from its context but regarded as the continuation of what he had affirmed in the preceding verses. It was as though he said, what I ask you to praise the Lord for is not something with which I have had no firsthand acquaintance but rather of that I have experienced in my own checkered history. The Lord put and held my soul in life during the many buffetings I have passed through. He did not suffer the waters to completely submerge me but kept my head above them. Give me an audience, ye fellow pilgrims, while I recount to you the wonder workings of the God of all grace with me. Let me review the whole of my wilderness journey and tell of God's failing not to show Himself strong on my behalf: "I cried unto Him. . . blessed be God who hath not turned away my prayer nor His mercy from me" (v. 20).

Ah, could not each child of God emulate the Psalmist in that. We are greatly interested and delighted when we read or hear of how different ones were brought Out of darkness into God's marvelous light. We marvel at and admire the variety of the means and methods employed by Him in convicting of sin and discovering Christ to different ones. We are awed and rejoiced when we learn of how some notorious rebel was brought to the foot of the Cross. But equally interesting, equally wonderful, equally blessed is the story of each Christian's life after conversion. If the mature believer looks back at the whole of his journey and reviews all God's gracious dealings with him, what a tale he could unfold! Let him describe the strange twistings and windings of his path, all ordered by infinite Wisdom, as he now perceives. Let him tell of the tempests and tossings. through which his frail craft has come and how often the Lord said to the winds and waves "be still." Let him narrate the providential help which came when he was in sore straits, the deliverances from temptation when he was almost overcome, the recoveries from backslidings, the revivings after deadness of heart, the comfortings in sorrow, the upliftings when borne down by difficulties and discouragements, the answers to prayer when things appeared hopeless, the patience which has borne with dullness, the grace with unbelief, the joys of communion with the Lord when cut off from public means of grace. What a series of miracles the Christian has experienced.

The saint is indeed a marvel of marvels: without strength yet continuing to plod along his uphill course. Think of a tree flourishing in the midst of a sandy desert, where there is neither soil nor water; imagine a house suspended in mid-air, with no visible means of support above or below; conceive of a man living week after week and year after year in a morgue, yet maintaining his vigor; suppose a lone lamb secure in the midst of hungry wolves, or a maid keeping her garments white as she ploughs her way through deep mud and mire, and in such figures you have an image of the Christian life. The new nature is kept alive between the very jaws of death. Health of soul is preserved while breathing a fetid atmosphere and surrounded by those with the most contagious and fatal diseases. It is like a defenseless dove successfully eluding droves of hawks bent on her destruction. It is like a man subsisting on a barren wilderness where there is neither food nor drink. It is like a traveler on some icy summit, with unfathomable precipices on either side, where a false step means certain destruction. 0 the wonder of Christian perseverance in the face of such handicaps and obstacles.

1. This is seen in the character of those who are chosen by God. We would naturally conclude that if He determined to have a people in this world through whom He would show forth His praises, that He will select the most promising and excellent: those of strong intellectual power, those of noble birth, those of sweet disposition, those of outstanding moral character. But His ways are different from ours. He singles out the most unlikely and unworthy ones to be the vessels of mercy. Thus it was in the O. T. era. Why were the Hebrews taken to be the most favored of all nations? Had they a stronger natural claim than others? Assuredly not. The Egyptians were a more intelligent race, as the monuments of their industry attest to this day. The Chaldeans were more ancient, more numerous, more civilized, and albeit exerted a much greater influence on the rest of the world. Was it then because the Israelites were more spiritual, more likely to prove amenable to the Divine government? No, for ere they set foot upon Canaan it was expressly declared unto them "Understand therefore that the Lord thy God giveth thee not this good land to possess it for thy righteousness, for thou art a stiffnecked people" (Deut. 9:6).

It is the same thing in the N. T. dispensation. "For ye see your calling, brethren, how that not many wise men after the flesh, not many mighty, not many noble, are called: But God hath chosen the foolish things of the world to confound the wise, and God hath chosen the weak things of the world to confound the things which are mighty; and base things of the world, and things which are despised, hath God chosen, and things which are not to bring to nought things that are" (1 Cor. 1:26-28). How remarkable is this: the ones chosen to successfully resist Satan, overcome the world, persevere in the difficult path of faith and obedience and finally win through to Heaven, are the feeble, the weak, the base, the despised, and the mere nobodies. This has ever presented a stumblingblock to the proud Pharisee: "have any of the rulers believed on Him?" (John 7:48). That the priests and scribes be passed by and publicans and harlots called to feast with Christ, that heavenly things should be hidden from the wise and prudent and revealed to babes, evokes the sneer of the learned "Christianity is only suited to old women and children." And why is this God's way? "That no flesh should glory in His presence" (1 Cor. 1:29), that the crown of honor should he placed on the head of Him who alone is entitled to wear it, that we may learn the marvel of perseverance is the result of sovereign and miraculous grace.

2. This is seen in the fewness of them. There is but "a remnant according to the election of grace" (Rom. 11:5) even among those who bear the name of the Lord, and in comparison with the hundreds of millions in heathendom who worship false gods and the vast multitudes in Christendom who make no profession at all, the real people of God constitute such an insignificant handful as to be almost lost to view. One had naturally thought that if the Lord purposed to have a people on earth who should glorify His name that they would be conspicuous in size, commanding attention and respect. Is it not a maxim of worldly wisdom that "there is strength in numbers" and did not Napoleon give expression thereto in his satirical dictum "God is always on the side of the biggest battalions"? Ah, but here too God's thoughts and ways are the very opposite of the world's, for His strength is "made perfect in weakness" (2 Cor. 12:9) and the things which are highly esteemed among men are "abomination in the sight of God" (Luke 16:15). Turn, my reader, to Judges 7:2 and ponder anew the lesson Jehovah taught Gideon when He said, "The people that are with thee are too many for Me to give the Midianites into their hands, lest Israel vaunt themselves!"

Not only have the Lord's people always been in the minority but they have never included more than a fractional percentage of earth's population. Only eight were delivered from the flood. From the days of Noah unto Moses — a period of roughly eight and a half centuries — we may count upon our fingers those recorded in Holy Writ who gave evidence of spiritual life. It requires no courage or resolution to follow the tide of popular opinion, for one is likely to encounter less opposition when he is on the side of the majority. What a miracle that Abraham, Isaac and Jacob preserved their piety in Canaan when surrounded by the heathen! The principle which we are now engaged in illustrating was emphasized by Moses when he said unto Israel "The Lord did not set His love upon you, nor choose you, because ye were more in number than any people; for ye are the fewest of all people" (Deut. 7:7). It is the same in this N. T. dispensation. Near the close of Paul's life Christians were referred to as a sect "everywhere spoken against" (Acts 28:22). The Lord Jesus declared that His flock was a "little" one (Luke 12:32), which increases the wonder of its survival, and though in recent years the membership of the "churches" swelled to huge proportions, more and more it is now becoming apparent that with rare exceptions they were but nominal professors and that only a "few" tread that Way which leadeth unto Life (Matt. 7:14).

3. This is seen in God's leaving them in this world. We might well suppose that since the Father hath set His heart upon them He would take them Home as soon as they are brought from death unto life. Instead they are left down here, most of them for many years, in a hostile country in the Enemy's territory, for "the whole world lieth in the Wicked one" (1 John 5:19). And why? that they may have opportunity to manifest their love for Him, that despite ceaseless opposition and innumerable temptations to cast off their allegiance they will, by His grace, remain faithful unto death. We marvel that Noah was preserved in the ark, when the devastating flood without swept away the entire human race from the earth and when he was surrounded by all manner of wild beasts within. Why was he not torn to pieces by the lions and tigers? or poisoned by the stench from the dung of all the animals? Though he remained there no less than a year, yet at

the end thereof he and all his household stepped forth alive and well. Not less wonderful is the survival of the Christian in a world where there is nothing to help spiritually but everything to the contrary.

The believer may be compared to an individual who has thrown off allegiance to his king, has disowned his country, and refuses obedience to its laws, yet continues to dwell in the land he has renounced and hard by the sovereign he has forsworn. The grace of God has called us out of the world, but the providence of God has sent us into the world. We may therefore expect nothing but hatred and hostility from it. The world will never forgive the act by which we broke from its thralldom, renounced its sway, relinquished its pleasures and resigned its friendship. Nor can it look with complacency upon the godly, self-denying and unworldly life of the Christian, which is a constant rebuke of its own carnality and folly. First it will veil its opposition and conceal its malignity beneath smiles and flattery, seeking to win back the one it has lost. But when that effort proves unavailing it changes its course and with venomed tongue, tireless zeal and devilish tactics seeks by detraction and falsehood to wound and injure the people of God. We marvel at the three Hebrews not being destroyed in Babylon's fiery furnace, but it is not less a miracle for a believer to persevere in the path of holiness amid the contagious sinfulness, seductive allurements and relentless persecutions of an evil world.

4. This is seen in the old nature being left in the saint. Since God is pleased to leave His people in this howling wilderness for a season, where everything seems to be dead against them, surely He will rid them of that which is most of all calculated to lead to their fatal undoing. If He requires them to be "holy in all manner of conversation" (1 Pet. 1:15), will He not purge them of all inward corruptions? If the sons of God are to be "without rebuke in the midst of a crooked and perverse generation," among whom they are to "shine as lights in the world" (Phil. 2:15), will He not remove all darkness from their understanding? And again we are made to realize how worthless is all human reasoning upon spiritual matters. Indwelling sin remains in the believer: the flesh is neither eradicated nor transformed. But how can we expect those with a sink of iniquity still within them to maintain a godly walk? Ah, therein we are brought to see again the marvel of the saint's perseverance. If a lorry has to pass down a street where the buildings on either side are burning fiercely, would it not greatly augment the wonder of its journeying through successfully when we learned that the lorry was laden with barrels of gunpowder and dynamite?

This is precisely the case of the believer: there is that in him which is responsive to the evil without him. The world and his heart are in a confederacy against the good of his soul, so that he can neither eat nor drink, work nor sleep in safety because of enemies without and treacherous lusts within. For a holy angel to dwell here would involve him in no danger, for in freedom from all inward corruptions there would be nothing in him to which the allurements of the world could appeal. But the Christian has a stack of dry tinder ready to ignite as soon as the sparks of temptation alight thereon. 0 the policy and power, the strength and prevalence, the nearness and treachery of indwelling sin. It is something which cleaves to all the faculties: not only in us but part and parcel of us. It dwells there (Rom. 7:17) ever seeking our overthrow. Such is our native depravity that it is capable of transmuting blessings into cursings, making things lawful into snares and entangling us with everything we meet with. Ah, my reader, if it was a miracle when Elisha caused iron to swim (2 Kings 2), not less so is it when our affections are set upon things above and our minds stayed on Jehovah.

5. This is seen in grace's dwelling place. In what uncongenial and inimical surroundings is the new nature set — in the depraved soul of a fallen creature. Not only is there nothing in man capable of nourishing the principle of holiness but everything which is directly opposed thereto: "the flesh lusteth against the spirit" (Gal. 5:17). Birds do not fly beneath the waves nor will fish live on dry ground because they are out of their native element: then what a wonder it is for grace to be preserved and grow in a heart which by nature is desperately wicked. Would trees grow if their seeds were planted in salt: why then should communicated grace take root and bring forth the fruit of the Spirit when planted in the midst of corruption? That is truly a miracle of Divine horticulture: a miracle which is far too little attended unto and admired. Well may each believer exclaim "I am a wonder to many" (Ps. 71:7) not failing to add "but Thou art my refuge." The Christian is a mystery to himself, an enigma to the unregenerate, who cannot understand his denying himself the things they delight in and finding pleasure in what they loath: but he is a "wonder," a prodigy of grace, unto his brethren and sisters in Christ.

The miracle of the survival of the principle of grace in a human soul will be the more manifest if we contrast the present case of the believer with that of Adam in the day of this pristine purity. Grace was connatural with our first parents when their Maker pronounced them "very good;" if then they so quickly lost their grace when it was placed in a pure soil, what a wonder it is that it should be preserved in a heart which is essentially evil! When the Son of God became incarnate Herod moved the whole country in a determined attempt to slay Him: and when Christ comes into the heart the whole soul rises up in opposition against Him. The carnal mind, the lusts of the flesh, an intractable will, are all antagonistic to every breathing after holiness. The preservation of grace in the saint is more remarkable than for one to succeed in carrying an unprotected but lighted candle across an open moor in a boisterous wind. Yea, as the Puritans were wont to say, it is as though a fire were kept burning year after year in the midst of the ocean. Grace is not only preserved but maintains its purity amid indwelling sin: as gold cannot be altered in its nature by the dross or transmuted into the rubbish amid which it lies, neither can the new nature be defiled by the mass of corruption wherein it dwells.

6. This is seen in their exposure to Satan's attacks. If there were no Devil at all it would be a miracle that any believer should persevere in the path of obedience while living in such a world as this. Surrounded as he is by the ungodly, ever seeking to allure him into their own sinful ways, carrying within him lusts which are in full accord with the evil around him, it is a wonder of wonders that he should remain steadfast. But over and above that, he is called upon to resist the arch-enemy of God, the mightiest of all His creatures, who is filled with enmity against him and bent upon his destruction. We are plainly warned "your adversary the Devil, as a roaring lion, walketh about seeking whom he may devour" (1 Pet. 5:8): how then shall feeble lambs hope to successfully resist him! We are told that when the woman brought forth the "man-child who was to

rule all nations" that, the red dragon "stood before the woman which was ready to be delivered for to devour her child" (Rev. 12:4). As the dragon acted thus toward the Head Himself so does he still seek to vent his malice upon the members of His mystical body.

Who is capable of estimating the power of Satan and the hosts of evil spirits he commands. And who can adequately describe the weakness and frailty of those called upon to withstand his attacks. If Adam in paradise with no lust within to entice and no world under the curse all around him, fell under the very first assault of Satan upon him, who are we to engage him in conflict. Fallen man could as well move a mountain with his finger as overcome the Prince of this world. Nevertheless of renewed men it is written "For we wrestle not against flesh and blood, but against principalities and powers, against the rulers of the darkness of this world, against wicked spirits in the heavenlies" (Eph. 6:12). Satan with all his wisdom, his power, his myrmidons are marshaled and exerted in tremendous opposition to the interests of the children of God, as the histories of Job, of David (1 Chron. 21:1), of Joshua, (Zech. 3:1), of Peter (Luke 22:31), and of Paul (1 Thess. 2:15) clearly show. We have often marveled at the deliverance of Daniel while spending a night in the lions' den, no less a miracle is the Christian's preservation from the continuous attacks of Satan and all his demons. "They overcame Him by the blood of the Lamb and by the word of their testimony" (Rev. 12:11).

7. This is seen in the renunciations they are required to make. "If any come to Me and hate not his father and mother, and wife and children, and brethren and sisters, yea and his own life also, he cannot be My disciple. And whosoever doth not bear his cross and come after Me, he cannot be My disciple. So likewise whosoever he be of you that forsaketh not all that he hath, he cannot be My disciple" Who can be expected to accept Christian discipleship on such exacting terms as these! No wonder that man of all shades of theological opinion have invented terms which are easier and pleasanter to the flesh, yet such are only blind leaders of the blind. Christ will receive none who refuse His yoke. God will not own as His people those who refuse to give Him their hearts. Sin must be hated, lusts must be mortified, the world must be renounced. A Christian is one who repudiates his own wisdom, strength and righteousness. A Christian is one who holds himself and all that he hath at the disposal of the Lord. As Abram at the call of God turned his back on the old manner of life, so those who are his believing children are made willing to sacrifice all their temporal interests, counting not their lives dear unto themselves. What a marvel is this that grace enables its possessor to pluck out right eyes and cut off right hands, yea which empowers timid women and children to go to the stake rather than apostatize.

8. This is seen in the Way they are required to walk in. It is a "narrow" way, for it is shut in on either side by the Divine commandments, which forbid all that is contrary to the Divine will. It is the way of "holiness," without which no man shall see the Lord. It is the way of obedience, of complete and continuous subjection to the Lord, wherein my own will is set aside. It is a difficult way, hard to find and harder still to traverse, for the whole of it is uphill. It is a lonely way, for there are but few upon it. It is therefore a way which is entirely contrary to flesh and blood, which presents no attraction to fallen human nature. Yet it is the only way which leadeth unto life. That narrow way of

self-abnegation is the one which Christ trod and sufficient for the disciple to be as his Master. He has left us an example that we should follow His steps, so that there is no following of Christ without walking in the way He went, and that way was one of sacrifice, of bearing reproach, of enduring suffering. "Whosoever will save his life (for himself) shall lose it, and whosoever will lose his life for My sake shall find it" (Matt. 16:25). No cross, no crown. What a marvel it is for any sinful creature to voluntarily choose such a path, to accept the cross as the dominant principle of his life.

9. This is seen in the frailty of the Christian. We would naturally think that since God requires His people to overcome such formidable obstacles, perform such difficult tasks and wrestle with such enemies, He would make them strong and powerful. Surely if they are to maintain their piety in a world like this, discharge duties which are contrary to flesh and blood, resist the Devil and all his hosts, the Lord will make each of His saints as mighty spiritually as Samson was physically. If one of them shall chase a thousand and two of them put ten thousand to flight must it not be because of their superior might. How shall they endure opposition, overcome temptations, be fruitful unto every good work unless they be endued with abundant grace. But here again the Lord's thoughts are the very opposite of ours. His people are so frail and helpless in themselves that He declares "without Me ye can do nothing" and sooner or later each of them is made to realize this for himself. Apart from the Lord the believer is as weak as water. Power for the conflict lies not in himself, but in Another: "be strong in the Lord and in the power of His might" (Eph. 6:10). Peter thought he was strong enough in himself to overcome temptation, but he soon discovered that though the spirit was willing the flesh was weak.

But is there not such a thing as growing in grace and in the knowledge of the Lord? Certainly there is, but such progress is of a very different nature from what many imagine. Growth in grace is a deepening realization of where our strength, our wisdom, the supply for every need is to be found. Growing in grace is not an increasing self-sufficiency but an increasing dependency upon God. Those who are spiritually the strongest are they who know most of their own weakness. It is the empty vessel which God fills. "He giveth power to the faint, and to them that have no might (of their own) He increaseth strength" (Isa. 40:29). Surely none of us can hope to attain a higher measure than that of the most favored of the apostles: yet he acknowledged "when lam weak then am I strong" (2 Cor. 12:10). Here then is truly a miracle: that one who is compassed with infirmity, who is not sufficient of himself to think anything as of himself (2 Cor. 3:5)— and therefore still less able to do anything good—who has "no might" of his own, who is utterly helpless in himself, should nevertheless fight a good fight, finish the course and keep the faith. "God hath chosen the weak things of the world to confound the things which are mighty."

10. This is seen in the fruits which the Christian bears. We have already called attention to the survival of the principle of grace despite the uncongenial soil in which it is placed and the foul atmosphere of this world where it grows, and equally wonderful is that which issues from it. This line of thought might be extended considerably, but space requires us to abbreviate. What a marvel that the Christian's faith should be

preserved amid so many trials and buffetings, betrayals by false brethren, and even the hidings of God's face: that notwithstanding the most painful crosses and losses it affirms "yea, though I walk through the valley of the shadow of death, I will fear no evil." Not only have God's saints remained steadfast under persecution, but after being "beaten" they rejoiced that they were counted worthy to suffer shame for the name of Jesus" (Acts 5:40, 41), while others "took joyfully the spoiling of their goods" (Heb. 10:34). What a marvelous fruit is this, to "glory in tribulation" (Rom. 5:3), to "sing praise unto God" (Acts 16:25) while lying in a dungeon with backs bleeding. Such fruits are not the products of nature. To hope against hope (Rom. 4:18), to acknowledge "it is good for me that I have been afflicted" (Ps. 119:71), to cry "Lord, lay not this sin to their charge" (Acts 7:60) while being stoned to death, are the fruits of Divine grace.

11. This is seen in their submission under and triumph of faith over the severest chastisements. It is natural to murmur when everything appears to go wrong and the face of Providence wears a dark frown, but it is supernatural to meekly submit and say "the will of the Lord be done." When "fire from the Lord" went out and devoured Nadab and Abihu because of their presumptuous conduct, so far from their father making an angry outburst at the severity of their punishment we are told that he "held his peace" (Lev. 10:3). When the awful tidings was broken to the aged Eli that both of his wayward sons were to be smitten by Divine judgment on the same day, he quietly acquiesced saying "It is the Lord: let Him do what seemeth Him good" (1 Sam. 3:18). When Job's sons and daughters were suddenly stricken with death and his flocks and herds carried away by thieves, he exclaimed "The Lord gave, and the Lord hath taken away; blessed be the name of the Lord" (1:2 1), and when his own body was smitten with "sore boils from the sole of his foot unto his crown," so far from losing all confidence in God and apostatizing he declared "though He slay me, yet will I trust in Him" (Job 13:15).

12. This is seen in their perseverance in piety when deprived of all public means of grace. When the under-shepherds are taken away what shall the poor sheep do? When corporate testimony breaks down what will become of the individual? When Zion is made desolate and the Lord's people are carried captives into a strange land, will they not pine away? True this is an exceptional state of affairs, yet at various stages of history it has pleased God to deprive numbers of His people of all the external means of grace and preserve them as isolated units. It was thus at a very early stage. Behold Abraham, the father of the faithful, dwelling alone amid the heathen, yet maintaining communion with the Lord. Behold Daniel in Babylon, in the face of deadly peril, preserving his piety. Some of us used to sing as children "Dare to be a Daniel, dare to stand alone, dare to have a purpose true, and dare to make it known." Is not our own lot cast in a day when not a few of the scattered children of God have to lament "I am as a sparrow alone upon the housetop" (Ps. 102:7)! Even so, as God miraculously sustained Elijah in the solitudes of Cherith so He will preserve each of them.

13. This is seen in their deliverance from apostasy. What numbers have been fatally deceived by Romanism. What multitudes of the outer-court worshippers have been stumbled by the multiplication of sects in Protestantism, each claiming to take the Scriptures for their guide yet often differing on the most fundamental truths. What crowds

have been attracted by the false prophets and heretical teachers, especially in America, during the past century. But though the real children of God may have been bewildered yet it drove them to search His Word more closely for themselves, for they know not the voice of strangers (John 10:5). In our own day, because iniquity or lawlessness abounds the love of many has waxed cold and tens of thousands who a little time ago appeared to "run well" have gone right back into the world. Yet there is still a remnant who cleave unto the Lord, and the very fewness of their numbers emphasizes the marvel of their preservation. It is a miracle of grace that any "hold fast the confidence and rejoicing of the hope firm unto the end," never more so than in this dark day.

What an amazing thing it was that Jonah should be cast overboard into the sea, without a lifebelt and with no boat to rescue him, and yet that he was not drowned. Still more remarkable that he should be swallowed by a whale and remain alive in its belly for three days and nights. Most wonderful of all that the whale disgorged the prophet not in the ocean, but vomited him out on the land. So amazing is this that it has been made the favorite subject of jest by infidels. Yet it presents no difficulty to the Christian, who knows that "with God all things are possible." We not only believe the authenticity of this miracle but have long been convinced it is a designed type not only of the resurrection of the Redeemer but of the preservation of the redeemed. The case of Jonah not only adumbrates a backsliding believer, but an extreme case of backsliding at that: showing that when a saint yields to self-will and forsakes the way of obedience, though he will be severely chastened yet the arm of the Lord will reach after and restore him to the paths of righteousness.

14. This is seen in God's manifold workings in and for them. This necessarily follows from all that has been said under the preceding heads. The perseverance of saints must be the consequence of the Divine preservation of them: since believers have no spiritual wisdom and no spiritual strength of their own, God must work in them both to will and to do of His good pleasure. His preventing grace: as the martyr observed a murderer on his way to the gallows he exclaimed "there goes John Bradford but for the grace of God." From how many temptations and sins on which their hearts were set are Christians delivered, as David from slaying Nabal. Protecting grace: "mercy shall compass him about" as a shield (Ps. 32:10). Quickening grace, whereby the principle of holiness is enlivened: "the inward man is renewed day by day" (2 Cor. 4:16). Confirming grace, whereby we are kept from being tossed to and fro: "Now He which establish us with you in Christ, and hath anointed us, is God" (2 Cor. 1:21 and cf. 2 Thess. 2:17). Fructifying grace: "From Me is thy fruit found" (Hos. 14:8). Maturing grace: "make you perfect in every good work to do His will" (Heb. 13:22). These and other operations of Divine grace are all summed up in that acknowledgement "Thou also hast wrought all our works in us" (Isa. 26:12) to which every saint freely ascribes and which alone explains the marvel of his perseverance.

Chapter 5
Its Springs

We now turn to contemplate the most important and blessed aspect of our subject, yea, the very heart and crux thereof. The believer's perseverance in faith and holiness is no detached and isolated thing, but an effect of an all-sufficient cause. It must not be viewed as a separate phenomenon but as the fruit of Divine operations. The believer's continuance in the paths of righteousness is a miracle, and miracle necessarily requires the immediate agency of God. Our present concern then is to trace this stream back to its source and to show the springs from which this marvel issues; to admire the impregnable foundations on which it rests. Only as those springs and foundations are clearly revealed shall we ascribe the glory unto Him to whom alone it is due, only so shall we be able to apprehend the absolute security of the saints, only so shall we perceive the vanity and uselessness of all the Enemy's attacks upon this cardinal truth. The perseverance of the saints is assured by so many infallible guarantees that it is difficult to know which to bring before the reader and which to omit.

The doctrine for which we are here contending follows as a logical consequence from the Divine perfections: whatever is agreeable to them, and they make necessary, must perforce be true; contrariwise whatever is contrary to them and reflects dishonor upon them must be false. Now the doctrine of the saints' final perseverance is agreeable to the Divine perfections, yea is made entirely necessary by them, and therefore must be true; and the contrary doctrine of the falling away of real saints so as to perish everlastingly is repugnant to them and reflects great dishonor upon them, and therefore must be false. That which we have here briefly affirmed will be illustrated in detail and demonstrated at length in all that follows in this and the succeeding section. Summarizing what we propose to set before the reader it will be found that the eternal security of the Christian rests upon the good will of the Father, the mediation of the Son, and the office and operations of the Holy Spirit, and therein we have a "threefold cord" which cannot possibly be broken.

1. The unchanging love of God. This argument however is one which can have little weight with those who have imbibed Arminianism and accepted their false interpretation of John 3:16; but they who perceive the Divine love to be a discriminating and particular and not an indefinite and general one will find here that which is sweeter than the honey or the honeycomb. If it were true that God loves the whole human race then, seeing a large part thereof is already in Hell, I could draw no assurance therefrom that I shall never perish. But when I discover that God's love is restricted to those whom He chose in Christ and that He loves them with an "everlasting love," then I unhesitatingly conclude that "many waters" cannot quench that love (Song of Sol. 8:7). It would lead

too far afield, for us to show wherein so many err concerning the meaning of John 3:16 or to evidence at length the discriminating character of God's love: suffice it here to point out that "For whom the Lord loveth He chasteneth" (Heb. 12:6) would be meaningless did He love everybody—the next clause "and scourgeth every son whom He receiveth" at once defines the objects of His affection. "Jacob have I loved, but Esau have I hated" (Rom. 9:13): therefore Jacob is now in Heaven, but his brother has received the due reward of his iniquities.

"We love Him because He first loved us" (1 John 4:19). God does not love His people because they love Him. No, we read of "His great love wherewith He loved us even when we were dead in sins" (Eph. 2:4, 5): when we had no desire to be loved by Him, yea when we were provoking Him to His face and displaying the fierce enmity of our unrenewed hearts. God loved His people before they had a historical existence, for while they were yet sinners Christ died for them (Rom. 5:8). Why, He declares "I have loved thee with an everlasting love" (Jer. 3 1:3). That love then derives not its strength or its streams from anything in us, but flows spontaneously from the heart of God, finding its deep well-spring within His own bosom. Since God is love He can no more cease to love than He can cease to be, and since God changes not there can be no variation and fluctuation in His love.

The object of God's love is His Church, which is His special delight. From all eternity He loved His elect, and loved them as His elect, as having peculiar propriety in them. He loved them in Christ, chose them in Christ, and blessed them with all spiritual blessings in Christ (Eph. 1:3). He loved them so as to predestinate them unto the adoption of children (Eph. 1:5). He loved their persons in Christ with the same love wherewith He loves Christ their Head (John 17:23). He loved them so as to make them "accepted in the Beloved" (Eph. 1:6). It is a love which can never decay, for it is founded on the good pleasure of His will towards them. God's love to Christ knows no change nor can it to the members of His body: "and hast loved them as Thou hast loved Me" (John 17:23), declares the Savior, and He is speaking there as the Head of His Church. We are loved in Christ and according to the relation we stand in to Him, that is, as members to an Head—loved as freely and immutably.

Though the effects of God's love vary in their manifestations, yet there is no diminution of His affection and none in its perpetuity. Men often love those who prove otherwise than they expected, and come to repent of the affection lavished upon them. But it is not so with God, for He foreknew all that ever we would be and do—our sins, unworthiness, rebellions; yet set His heart upon us notwithstanding—so that He can never say we turned out other than He thought we would. Had God's love been set upon us because of some good or excellency in us, then when that goodness declined, His love would diminish too. "God foresaw all the sins you would ever have: it was all present to His sacred mind, and yet He loved you, and loves you still" (C. H. Spurgeon). The child of God may for a season depart from the paths of righteousness, and then will his Father visit his transgression with the rod and his iniquity with stripes, "nevertheless My lovingkindness will I not make void from him nor suffer My faithfulness to fail" (Ps. 89:32, 33) is His own declaration.

Because God's love is uncreated it is unchanging. God does not love by fits and starts, but forever. Because it is founded upon nothing in its object, no change in that object can forfeit it. In every state and condition into which the elect can come, God's love unto them is invariable and unalterable, constant and permanent. We may repent of the love which we bestowed an some of our fellows because we were unable to make them good: the more we loved them, the more they took advantage of it. Not so with God: whom He loves He makes holy. This is one of the effects of His love: to shed abroad His love in the hearts of its objects, to stamp His own image upon them, to cause them to walk in His fear. His love to the elect is perpetual because it is in Christ; they are joined to Christ by an union which cannot be dissolved. God must cease to love Christ their Head before He can cease to love any member of His Body. Then what madness, what blasphemy, to think of any of them perishing!

Over this blessed attribute of Divine love is written in letters of light "Semper idem," always the same. Those who are once the objects of God's love are so always. If God has ever loved you, my reader, He does so today: loves you with the same love as when He gave His Son to die for you; loves you with the same love as when He sent His Holy Spirit into your heart crying "Abba Father;" loves you with the same love as He will in Heaven throughout the endless ages. And nothing can or shall separate you from that love (see Rom. 8:38, 39). A preacher once called upon a farmer. As he approached his residence he saw over the barn a weathervane and on the top of it in large letters the text "God is love." When the farmer appeared the preacher pointed to that vane and said in tones of rebuke "Do you imagine God's love is as variable as the weather?" No, said the farmer, I put that text there to remind me that no matter what the direction of the wind. God is love!

> "His love no end or measure knows,
> No change can turn its course,
> Immutably the same it flows
> From one eternal source."

2. The immutability of God. The guarantee for the perpetuity of God's love unto His people is found in the immutability of His nature. From everlasting Jehovah is God: underived, independent, self-sufficient, nothing can in anywise affect Him or produce any change in Him. Says the Psalmist "Of old hast Thou laid the foundation of the earth and the heavens are the work of Thy hands. They shall perish, but Thou shalt endure: yea, all of them shall wax old like a garment: as a vesture shalt Thou change them and they shall be changed. But Thou art the same and Thy years shall have no end" (102:25-27). This is one of the excellences of the Creator which distinguishes Him from all creatures. God is perpetually the same: subject to no change in His being, attributes, or determinations. All that He is today He ever has been and ever will be. He cannot change for the better for He is already perfect, and being perfect He cannot change for the worse. He only can say "I am that I am" (Ex. 3:14). Unaffected by anything outside Himself, improvement or deterioration is impossible. His glory is an unfading one.

Now in this immutability of God lies the eternal security of His people. "For I am the

Lord, I change not: therefore ye sons of Jacob are not consumed" (Mal. 3:6). If any of them were lost, "consumed" by His wrath, then He must change in His attitude toward them, so that those whom He once loved He now hates. But that would also involve an alteration in His purpose concerning them, so that whereas He has appointed them "to obtain salvation by our Lord Jesus Christ" (1 Thess. 5:9), He must consign them over to destruction. How entirely different would such a variable and fickle character be from the God of Holy Writ! Of Jehovah it is said "He is of one mind, and who can turn Him?" (Job 23:13). It is because God changes not His people are not consumed: His love wanes not, His will is stable, His word sure. Because He is "The Father of lights, with whom is no variableness neither shadow of turning" (James 1:17) we have an immovable rock on which to stand while everything around us is being swept away.

The foundation of our preservation unto the end is the immutability of God's being, whereunto His love is conformed, so that His everlasting Deity must undergo alteration before any of His children could perish. This is clearly the force of both Malachi 3:6 and James 1:17. In the latter the apostle speaks of "every good and every perfect gift" which the saints receive from their Father, prefacing the same with "Do not err my beloved brethren. "The gifts bestowed upon the elect at their regeneration are not like Jonah's gourd which flourished only for a brief season. No, they are from Him with whom is "no variableness" either in His love or will. "For the gifts and calling of God are without repentance" (Rom. 11:29) or change of mind, and therefore they are never revoked. Let it be noted that those words were added to clinch the certainty of the purpose of God towards the remnant of the Jews according to the election of grace. Thus the immutability of God is the guarantee of the stability of His love and the irrevocableness of His grace unto us.

3. The irreversible purpose of God. Having set His heart upon a chosen people, God formed a purpose of grace toward them: "in love having predestinated them" (Eph. 1:5) and the immutability of His being insures the fulfillment of that purpose. The Most High does not determine to do a thing at one time and decide not to do it at another. "The counsel of the Lord standeth forever, the thoughts of His heart to all generations" (Ps. 33:11): because He has counseled everlasting glory unto His people, nothing can alter it. "For the Lord of hosts hath purposed, and who shall disannul it?" (Isa. 14:27). There are indeed many changes in the external dispensations of His providence toward His elect, but none concerning the thoughts of His heart for them. "I am God, and there is none like unto Me, declaring the end from the beginning and from ancient times the things that are not yet done, saying, My counsel shall stand and I will do all My pleasure. . .1 have spoken, I will also bring it to pass; I have purposed, I will also do it" (Isa. 46:9-11). What a foundation is there here for faith to rest upon: the Divine will is inflexible, His counsels irreversible.

"God is not a man that He should lie, neither the son of man that He should repent" (Num. 23:19). Consider the things which move men to change their minds and alter their purposes, and then mark how utterly inapplicable such things are to the Almighty. Men form a plan and then cancel it through fickleness and inconstancy: but God is immutable. Men make a promise and then revoke it because of their depravity and untruthfulness: but God is infinitely holy and cannot lie. Men devise a project and fail to carry it through because of lack of ability or power: but God is omniscient and omnipotent. Men determine a certain thing for want of foresight and because the unexpected intervenes they are thwarted: but God knows the end from the beginning. Men change their schemes because the influence or threats of superiors deter them: but God has no superior or equal and fears none. No unforeseen occasion can arise which would render it expedient for God to change His mind.

In Romans 8:28 we read of a company who are "the called according to His purpose" and what that signifies the verses which immediately follow tell us. It was a purpose they could neither originate nor frustrate. "For whom He did foreknow" with a knowledge of approbation (contrast "I never knew you": Matt. 7:23) "He also did predestinate," appoint and fore-arrange. That Divine predestination results in their being effectually called out of darkness into God's marvelous light and their being justified or accounted righteous before God because Christ's perfect obedience is reckoned to their account. And then, so infallibly certain is the accomplishment of God's purpose, the apostle added "and whom He justified them He also (not "will glorify," but) glorified." "God, willing more abundantly to show unto the heirs of promise the immutability of His counsel (the immovable fixedness of His design), confirmed it by an oath" (Heb. 6:17). What more can we desire: the Holy One must foreswear Himself before one of His own can perish.

4. The everlasting covenant of God. Having set His heart upon a special people God formed a purpose of grace toward them and that purpose is attested and secured by formal contract. By express stipulation the Eternal Three solemnly undertook for every heir of promise to do all for and in them, so that not one of them shall perish. "I will make an everlasting covenant with them, that I will not turn away from them to do them good, but I will put My fear in their hearts, that they shall not depart from Me" (Jer. 32:40). How comprehensive are those promises! First, Jehovah assures His people that there shall be no alteration in His good will toward them. To that it might be objected, True, God will not turn away from them, but they may turn away from Him, yea utterly apostatize. Therefore He here declares that He will put His fear in their hearts, or grant them such supplies of grace, as to preserve them from falling away. "Were they to return to the service of Satan, He could not continue to do them good consistently with the holiness of His character, but He will preserve them in such a state that He may hold fellowship with them without any impeachment of His holiness" (J. Dick).

This covenant of grace is made with the elect in Christ before the foundation of the world, wherein He became their "Surety" (Heb. 7:22), undertaking to discharge all their liabilities and make full satisfaction for them. Accordingly God has promised the Surety "I will put my laws into their mind and write them upon their hearts: and I will be to them a God, and they shall be to Me a people" (Heb. 8:10). Those promises are of free grace, and there is no contingency or uncertainty about them, for they are "yea," and "Amen" in Christ (2 Cor. 1:20). Mark how God Himself regards His engagement therein: "My covenant will I not break, nor alter the thing that is gone out of My lips" (Ps. 89:34). "He will ever be mindful of His covenant" (Ps. 111:5). 0 what grounds for confidence, for joy, for praise is there here! Therefore may each believer affirm with David "He hath made with me an everlasting covenant, ordered in all things and sure: for this is all my salvation and all my desire" (2 Sam. 23:5). "For the mountains shall depart and the hills be removed, but My kindness shall not depart from thee, neither shall the covenant of my peace be removed, saith the Lord that hath mercy on thee" (Isa. 54:10).

To summarize what has yet been before us. If any saint were eventually lost it could only be because the being and character of God Himself had undergone a change for the worse. His affections must alter, so that one whom He loved must become the object of His hatred. His purpose concerning him must change, so that whereas He appointed him to salvation He must consign him to destruction. He must reverse the promises made and the blessings bestowed upon him. His faithfulness must fail, so that His Word can no longer be relied upon. Thus it is obvious that the alternative to what has been set forth above is unthinkable and impossible. The wisdom of God requires that in appointing the end (the glorification of His people) He has also ordained that the means thereto are sufficient, and His power insures that those means shall prove effectual. Every perfection of God guarantees that all His people shall get safely to Heaven.

5. The irrepealable promises of God. The "exceeding great and precious promises" (2 Pet. 1:4) which God hath made to His people have been likened unto streams along which His covenant engagements run, for they all go back to and have their source in that eternal compact which He made with the elect in Christ. Their Surety undertook to do certain things for them and in return thereof God agreed that certain things should be bestowed upon them on whose behalf He transacted. What those things were that God stipulated to impart unto those Christ represented are revealed in the various promises which He has made unto them. Those promises are God's free and gracious dispensations or discoveries of His good will unto the elect in Christ in a covenant of grace. Therein, upon His veracity and faithfulness, He engages Himself to be their God, to give His Son unto them and for them, and His Spirit to abide with and in them, guaranteeing to supply everything that they need in order to make them acceptable before Him and to bring them all unto the everlasting enjoyment of Himself.

Those promises are free and gracious as to the rise or origin of them, being given to us merely by the good pleasure of God, and not in return for anything demanded of us: that which is of promise is opposed to that which is in any way demanded or procured by us (Rom. 4:13, 14; Gal. 3:18). These promises are made unto us as sinners, and under no other qualification whatever, it being by sovereign mercy alone that any are delivered out of their fallen and depraved state. The promises are given unto them as "shut up under sin" (Gal. 3:22). These discoveries of God's good will are made known in Christ as the sole Medium of their accomplishment and as the alone procuring Cause of the good things contained in them. "For all the promises of God in Him are yea and in Him amen" (2 Cor. 1:20)—in and by Christ's mediation they have all their confirmation and certainty to us. The foundation of our assurance of their accomplishment is the character of their Maker: they are the engagements of Him "who cannot lie" (Titus 1:2; Heb. 6:17, 18)—heaven and earth shall pass away but His word shall endure forever.

The grand fountain-head promise from which all the others flow is that God will be "The God of His people" (Jer. 24:7; 31:33; Ezek. 11:20). In order that He may be "our

God" two chief things are required. First, that all breaches and differences between Him and us shall be removed, perfect peace and agreement made, and we rendered well-pleasing in His sight: sin must be put away and everlasting righteousness brought in. In order to this Christ acted as our Surety, our Priest, our Redeemer, and has become "our Peace" (Eph. 2:14), being of God "made unto us wisdom, righteousness, sanctification and redemption" (1 Cor. 1:30). He "gave Himself for the Church, that He might sanctify and cleanse it with the washing of water by the Word, that He might present it to Himself a glorious Church" (Eph. 5:25, 26). Second, that we might be kept meet for communion with Him as our God and for our eternal enjoyment of Him as our Portion. From this flows the promise of the Holy Spirit (Acts 1:5; 2:33) that He would exercise unto us all the acts of His love and work in us that obedience which He required from and accepts of us in Jesus Christ, so preserving us unto Himself. This promise of the Spirit in the covenant is witnessed in Isaiah 59:21; Ezekiel 36:27, etc.

From the fountain promise that God will be our God in covenant relationship flow the two broad streams that He would give Christ for us and the Holy Spirit to us, and Out from these two main streams issue a thousand rivulets for our refreshment. From those two streams come forth all the blessings Christ hath purchased for us and all the graces that the Holy Spirit produces in the elect, by the first of which they are made acceptable unto God and by the latter of which they have an enjoyment of Him. All the promises of mercy and forgiveness, faith and holiness, obedience and perseverance, joy and consolation, affliction and deliverance issue from them, Thus it follows that whoever hath an interest in one promise hath an interest in them all and in the fountain head from which they flow. Have we a hold on any promise? that is by the Holy Spirit, and from Him to Christ, and thence unto the bosom of the Father. Hence also the most conditional of the promises are ultimately to be resolved into the absolute and unconditional love of God: He who promises to us life upon believing, works faith in us: "according as His Divine power hath given unto us all things that pertain unto life and godliness": 2 Peter 1:3. (Most of the above is condensed from John Owen, the Puritan).

Let us cite a few of the particular promises wherein the Lord has engaged Himself to grant such supplies of His Spirit that we shall be supported against all opposition and preserved from such sins as would separate any of His saints from Him. "For the Lord loveth judgment and forsaketh not His saints: they are preserved forever" (Ps. 37:28). "They that trust in the Lord shall be as mount Zion, which cannot be moved, but abideth forever. As the mountains are round about Jerusalem, so the Lord is round about His people from henceforth even forever" (Ps. 125:1, 2). "Even to your old age lam He, and even to hoar hairs will I carry you: I have made and I will bear, even I will carry and deliver you" (Isa. 46:4). "For the mountains shall depart and the hills be removed, but My kindness shall not depart from them, neither shall the covenant of My peace be removed, saith the Lord that hath mercy on thee" (Isa. 54:10). "He shall confirm you unto the end" (1 Cor. 1:8). "1 will never leave thee nor forsake thee" (Heb. 13:5).

The same Divine protection unto everlasting bliss is confirmed by many assertory passages as well as promissory. "Surely goodness and mercy shall follow me all the days of my life, and I will dwell in the house of the Lord forever" (Psa. 23:4). "I am continually with thee. Thou hast holden me with Thy right hand: thou shalt guide me with Thy counsel and afterward receive me to glory" (Ps. 73:23, 24). "The Lord shall deliver me from every evil work and will preserve me unto His heavenly kingdom" (2 Tim. 4:18). "They went out from us, but they were not of us; for if they had been of us, they would have continued with us" (1 John 2:19). God must forsake His integrity before He would abandon one of His people. But that cannot be: "faithful is He that calleth you, who also will do it" (1 Thess. 5:24). "The Lord is faithful, who shall establish you and keep you from evil" (2 Thess. 3:3). They who affirm that any of God's children will perish are guilty of the fearful sin of charging Him with perjury.

6. The gracious acts of God toward His people. These are of such a nature as insure their everlasting salvation. In addition to His acts of electing them, making a sure covenant with His Son on their behalf and the putting of them into His hands with all grace and glory for them, we may mention the adoption of them into His family. This is an inestimable blessing, little understood today. It is a sonship-in-law, God bestowing upon His elect the legal status of sons. This is "by Jesus Christ" (Eph. 1:5): since Christ is Son of God essentially and the elect are united to Him, they are the sons-in-law of God. Christ as God-man was set up as the Prototype and we are modeled after Him. As a woman becomes a man s daughter-in-law by his son's betrothing himself to her, so we are sons-in-law unto God an inalienable legal title—as the term "adoption" plainly signifies—by marriage union. It is by their relation to the Son of God that the elect are the sons of God. It is not by faith they become sons, rather does faith manifest them to be such.

"Because ye are sons (not to make us such), God hath sent forth the Spirit of His Son into your hearts, crying Abba Father" (Gal. 4:6). "Behold what manner of love the Father hath bestowed upon us that we should be called the children of God" (1 John 3:1). From thence flows all our dignities and honors: "if sons (Greek) then heirs, heirs of God and joint heirs with Christ" (Rom. 8:17). Is Christ King and Priest, so also are we "kings and priests unto God and His Father" (Rev. 1:6). Is Christ Jehovah's "Fellow" (Zech. 13:7)? so are we Christ's "fellows" (Ps. 45:7). Is Christ God's "Firstborn" (Ps. 89:27)? so we read of "The Church of the firstborn" (Heb. 12:22). Even now are we the sons of God, but "it doth not yet appear what we shall be," it is not yet made manifest before the universe, "but we know that when He shall appear we shall be like Him" (1 John 3:2). And why are we so assured? Because "Whom God did foreknow, He also did predestinate to be conformed to the image of His Son that He might be the Firstborn among many brethren" (Rom. 8:30). Because God predestinated us unto the adoption of children by Jesus Christ to Himself "according to the good pleasure of His will" (Eph. 1:5)—by sovereign grace and not because of anything of ours—nothing can possibly sever or annul this wondrous relationship.

The justification of God's people. This is also a legal act. It takes place in the supreme court of Heaven, where God sits as the Judge of all the earth. The believing sinner is measured by the holy Law and pronounced righteous. Of old the question was asked "But how shall man be just before God?" (Job 9:2), for the Law requires nothing less than perfect and perpetual obedience, and pronounces him accursed who continues not in all that it enjoins (Gal. 3:10). Had that question been left for solution to finite intelligence it had remained unsolved forever. How could God show mercy yet not abate one iota of what His justice requires. How could He treat with the guilty as though they were innocent? How could He righteously bestow the reward on those who merited it not? How could He pronounce righteous those who were unrighteous? Such a thing seems utterly impossible, nevertheless Divine omniscience has solved these problems, solved them without tarnishing His honor, yea unto His everlasting glory and to our everlasting admiration. It is the setting forth of this grand display of the Divine wisdom which constitutes the supreme blessedness of the Gospel.

According to the terms of the everlasting covenant Christ became the Sponsor of His people. "When the fullness of the time was come God sent forth His Son, made of a woman, made under the Law" (Gal. 4:4). To the Law the incarnate Son rendered a complete and flawless obedience thereby magnifying and making it honorable (Isa. 42:21): the Divine dignity of His person bestowed more honor on the Law by His obedience thereto than it had been dishonored by all our manifold disobedience. Having perfectly fulfilled the Law, Christ then suffered its curse in His peoples' stead, thereby blotting Out their sins. That perfect obedience of Christ is reckoned to our account the moment we believe on Him, so that believers may say "The Lord our righteousness" (Jer. 23:6). On the ground of Christ's righteousness legally becoming ours, God pronounces us justified (Rom. 3:24; 5:19; 2 Cor. 5:21). And therefore because it is "God that justifieth, who is he that condemneth?" (Rom. 8:33,34). Those justified by God can never be unjustified. The righteousness by which they are justified is an "everlasting" one (Dan. 9:24), the sentence of exoneration passed upon them in the high court of Heaven can never be revoked by man or devil. They have a title to everlasting glory and cannot come into condemnation.

7. The death of Christ. When Adam, the federal head as well as the father of the human race, apostatized, the elect equally with the non-elect fell in him, and thus they are "by nature the children of wrath even as others" (Eph. 2:3). From that dreadful and direful state they are recovered by the mediation of Christ and the operation of the Spirit, the latter being a fruit of the former. We have briefly touched upon the mediation of Christ in the two preceding paragraphs, but as this is of such vital concern to our present theme, it requires to be considered in more detail. A large field is here opened before us, but we can now take only a brief glance at it. Once again we would point out that what we are about to advance can have little weight with Arminians, who erroneously suppose that the mediatory work of Christ was general or universal in its character and design; but to those who have learned from Holy Writ that the redemption of Christ is definite and particular, a specific ransom for a specific people, there will be found here a sufficient answer to every accusation of Satan and an assurance which none of the tribulations of life can shake.

"Who is he that condemneth?" the apostle asks: "it is Christ that died" is his triumphant reply (Rom. 8:34). The force of that reply turns upon the fact that Christ's death is a substitutionary and atoning one. "For the transgression of My people was He stricken" says God (Isa. 53:8). "For Christ also hath once suffered for sins, the Just for the unjust, that He might bring us to God" (1 Pet. 3:18). "He was wounded for our transgressions,

He was bruised for our iniquities: the chastisement of our peace was upon Him, and with His stripes we are healed" (Isa. 53:5). Jehovah laid upon Christ the iniquities of His people (Isa. 53:6) and then cried "Awake 0 sword against My Shepherd and against the Man that is My Fellow, saith the Lord of hosts, smite the Shepherd" (Zech. 13:7). On the cross Christ rendered to God a full satisfaction for the sins of all those whom the Father gave to Him. Being a merciful and faithful High Priest in things pertaining to God "to make propitiation (Gk.) for the sins of the people" (Heb. 2:13). Because Christ was made a curse for sin (Gal. 3:13) nought but blessing is now our portion.

All for whom Christ died shall most certainly be saved, because He paid the full price of their redemption. As a surety stands in the room of the person he represents, the latter reaps the benefit of what the surety has done in his name, so that if his debt has been paid by the surety, the creditor can no more demand payment from him. Since Christ made full reparation to God's Law, making complete atonement for the sins of His people, then it would be a flagrant violation of Divine justice if ever one of them should be punished for the same. Christ has purchased His people by His precious blood, then can we suppose that God will suffer His most avowed enemy to rob His Son of any of them? Were that to happen, the Redeemer's name would be rendered meaningless, for God Himself said "thou shalt call His name Jesus, for He shall save His people from their sins" (Matt. 1:21). Were that to happen, it could not be true that the Redeemer "shall see of the travail of His soul and be satisfied" (Isa. 53:10).

Since all the believer's sins were laid upon Christ and atoned for, what is there that can possibly condemn him? and if there be nothing, how can he be cast into Hell? True, none can reach Heaven without persevering in holiness, but since the atonement of Christ possesses Divine virtue and is of everlasting efficacy, all for whom it was made must and shall persevere in holiness. God's wrath against His people was exhausted upon their Substitute: the black cloud of His vengeance was emptied at Calvary. "When I think of my sin it seems impossible that any atonement should ever be adequate: but when I think of Christ's death it seems impossible that any sin should ever need such an atonement as that. There is in the death of Christ enough and more than enough. There is not only a sea in which to drown our sins, but the very tops of the mountains of our guilt are covered" (C. H. Spurgeon). Therefore is God able to save unto the uttermost them that come unto Him by Christ (Heb. 7:25), yea, even though they have sinned as did Manasseh or Saul of Tarsus.

Christ has removed everything which could cause separation between God and His people. First, He has taken away the guilt of their sins, that it shall never prevail with the Lord to turn from them. Christ hath "obtained eternal redemption" (Heb. 9:12), for them: not a transient and unstable redemption, but an abiding and efficacious one. In consequence thereof God declares, "their sins and iniquities will I remember no more" (Heb. 10:17). How could He do so, seeing that the Redeemer was to "make an end of sins" (Dan. 9:24)—as to the controversy of them between God and those for whom He died. Christ has so satisfied God's justice and fulfilled His Law that no sentence of condemnation can be pronounced against them, and therefore they must infallibly be saved. Second, as Christ removed that which alone might turn God from believers, so

He has annulled that which might cause them to depart from God: neither indwelling sin, Satan or the world, can so prevail as to make them totally fall away. Christ has destroyed Satan's right to rule over them (Col. 2:15; Heb. 2:14), and He has abolished his power by "binding" him. (Matt. 12:29), and therefore are we assured "sin shall not have dominion over you" (Rom. 6:14)—how could it since the Holy Spirit Himself indwells us!

"Since Christ bore our sins, and was condemned in our place; since by His expiatory death the claims of Divine justice are answered, and the holiness of the Divine Law is maintained, who can condemn those for whom He died? Oh, what security is this for the believer in Jesus! Standing beneath the shadow of the cross, the weakest saint can confront his deadliest foe; and every accusation alleged and every sentence of condemnation uttered, he can meet, by pointing to Him who died. In that one fact he sees the great debt cancelled, the entire curse removed, the grand indictment quashed and 'No condemnation to them that are in Christ Jesus' are words written as in letters of living light upon the cross" (O. Winslow).

8. The resurrection of Christ. It seems strange that so many receive more comfort at the cross than they do at the empty grave of Christ, for Scripture itself hesitates not to say, "If Christ be not raised your faith is vain, ye are yet in your sins" (1 Cor. 15:17). A dead Savior could not save: one who was himself vanquished by death would be powerless to deliver sin's slaves. Here is one of the chief defects of Romanism—its deluded subjects are occupied with a lifeless Christ, worshippers of a crucifix. Nor are Protestant preachers above criticism in this matter, for only too often many of them omit the grandest part of the Evangel by going no further than Calvary. The glorious Gospel is not fully preached until we proclaim a risen and victorious Redeemer (1 Cor. 15:1-3; Acts 5:3 1). Christ was "delivered (up to death) for our offences and was raised again for our justification" (Rom. 4:24), and as the apostle goes on to declare, "For if when we were enemies we were reconciled to God by the death of His Son, much more being reconciled, we shall be saved by His life" (Rom. 5:10).

What avail would it have been that Christ died for His people if death had conquered and overwhelmed Him? Had the grave held Him fast, He had been a prisoner still. But in rising from the tomb Christ made demonstration of His victory over sin and death: thereby He was "declared to be the Son of God with power according to the Spirit of holiness, by the resurrection from the dead" (Rom. 1:4); "For to this end Christ both died and rose and revived that He might be Lord both of the dead and living" (Rom. 14:9). Christ's sacrificial work was finished at the cross, but proof was needed of its Divine acceptance. That proof lay with Him who was pleased to "bruise Him and put Him in grief," and by raising the Redeemer God furnished incontestable evidence that all His claims had been met. The death of Christ was the payment of my awful debt: His resurrection God's receipt for the same; it was the public acknowledgement that the bond had been cancelled. Christ's resurrection sealed our justification: it was necessary to give reality to the atonement, and to provide a sure foundation for our faith and hope. Since God is satisfied, the trembling sinner may confide and securely repose upon the work of a triumphant Savior.

"Who is he that condemneth? It is Christ that died, yea rather that is risen again" (Rom.

8:34). Here the resurrection of Christ is presented as the believer's security against condemnation. But how does the former guarantee the latter? There is a causal connection between the two things. First, because Christ rose again not simply as a private person but as the Surety, the Head and Representative of all His people. It has not been sufficiently recognized and emphasized that the Lord Jesus lived, died and rose again as "the Firstborn among many brethren." As all whom the first Adam represented fell when he fell, died when he died, so all whom the last Adam represented died when He died and rose again when He arose. God "quickened us together with Christ, and hath raised us up together" (Eph. 2:5, 6). "Risen with Christ" (Col. 3:1) is judicially true of every believer. The Law can no more condemn him: he has been fully and finally delivered from the wrath to come. Infallibly certain and absolutely secure is he by virtue of his legal union with the risen Savior. "Christ being raised from the dead dieth no more: death hath no more dominion over Him" (Rom. 6:9), nor over me, for His deliverance was mine, the second death cannot touch me.

Second, because there is a vital union between Christ and His people. Said the Lord Jesus, "I am the resurrection and the life: he that believeth on Me, though he were dead, yet shall he live; and whosoever liveth and believeth in Me shall never die" (John 11:25, 26). Nothing could possibly be plainer or more decisive than that. Spiritual resurrection makes the believer one with Him who is "alive for evermore" so that he is forever beyond the reach of death. Well then may we exclaim with the apostle, "Blessed be the God and Father of our Lord Jesus Christ, who according to His abundant mercy hath begotten us again unto a living hope, by the resurrection of Jesus Christ from the dead" (1 Pet. 1:3). Regeneration or being begotten by God is the communication to the soul of the life of the risen Christ. A faint yet striking illustration of this is seen in our awakening each morning out of slumber. While our head sleeps, every member of the body sleeps with it. But the head awakes, and awakes first, and with that awakening each member awakens also — after the head, yet in union with it. Thus it is with the mystical Body of Christ the Head was first quickened, and then in God's good time His life is imparted to each of His members, and before any member could perish the Head must die.

Third, because as Christ was our Surety here so He is our Representative on high, and as He endured our penalty so justice requires that we should enjoy His fullness. Accordingly we read, "Now the God of peace, that brought again from the dead our Lord Jesus, that great Shepherd of the sheep, through the blood of the everlasting covenant, make you perfect in every good work, to do His will, working in you that which is well-pleasing in His sight, through Jesus Christ; to whom be glory forever, Amen" (Heb. 13:20, 21). Note well the coherence of this passage. It is in His character as "the God of peace" He thus acts. Having been pacified or propitiated, God brought again from the dead our Lord Jesus, not as a private person but in His official character, as the "Shepherd," and that, in fulfillment of covenant stipulation and promise. In consequence thereof, God makes perfect (or complete) in every good work the "sheep," preserving and sanctifying them by working in them that which is well pleasing in His sight, and this "through Jesus Christ," or in other words, by communicating to His members the grace, the life, the fullness, which is in their Head.

9. The Exaltation of Christ. There is a little clause, but one of vast purport, which the apostle added to "yea rather that is risen again," namely, "who is even at the right hand of God" (Rom. 8:34). That brief sentence is frequently overlooked, yet is it one which also guarantees the safety and perpetuity of the Church. The ascension of Christ is as vital and cardinal a part of the Truth as is His death and resurrection, and provides the same rich food for faith to feed upon. As it was not possible for death to hold Him, so it was not fitting for the earth to retain Christ. He who humbled Himself and became obedient unto death has been "highly exalted and given a name which is above every name (Phil. 2:9). The head which once was crowned with thorns is crowned with glory now, a royal diadem adorns the mighty Victor's brow. Christ is now in heaven as an everlasting Mediator, as a glorified High Priest over the House of God, as the sceptered King ruling with sovereign sway all things in heaven and earth, angels and principalities and powers being made subject to Him (1 Pet. 3:22). And Christ is entered heaven in our nature, in our name, on our behalf.

The One who descended into the deepest depth has been elevated to the grandest glory. The crowning act of Christ's triumph was not when He issued forth a Victor from the tomb, but when He entered the courts of celestial bliss, when the everlasting doors lifted up their heads and the King of glory went in (Ps. 24:9). The raising of Christ was in order to His glorification. And it was in our nature He is exalted above all: the very hands which were nailed to the cross now wield the scepter of universal dominion. How well fitted then is such an One to succor and "save unto the uttermost!" As faith follows the descent of the Father's Beloved to Bethlehem's manger, to Golgotha, to the sepulcher, so let it follow Him to the loftiest heights of dignity and bliss. This "same Jesus" who was rejected and degraded by Jew and Gentile alike has been "crowned with honor and glory" (Heb. 2:9). The exaltation of Christ was a necessary part of His Mediatorship, for it is from on high He administers His kingdom and makes effectual application of redemption. The ascension of Christ is also an essential part of the gospel.

"Who is even at the right hand of God." First, this is the place of honor and dignity. When Bathsheba appeared before Solomon we are told that the king rose up to meet her and bowed himself unto his mother, and sitting down on this throne he caused a seat to be set for her "on his right hand" (1 Kings 2:19) as a mark of special favor and honor. After the royal proclamation concerning Christ "Thou lovest righteousness and hatest wickedness: therefore God, Thy God, hath anointed Thee with the oil of gladness above Thy fellows; all Thy garments smell of myrrh and aloes and cassia, out of the ivory palaces whereby they have made Thee glad," it is added, "Kings' daughters were among Thy honorable women: upon Thy right hand did stand the Queen in gold of Ophir" (Psa. 45:7-9), indicating the place of privilege and honor which is reserved for the Lamb's wife. "The God of Abraham and of Isaac and of Jacob (God of covenant relationship), the God of our fathers, hath glorified His Son Jesus" (Acts 3:13)—this was His mediatorial glory in answer to His prayer in John 17:5. Christ has "sat down on the right hand of the Majesty on high" (Heb. 1:3).

Second, the "right hand of God" is the place of supreme authority and power. As we read in Ex. 15:6 "Thy right hand, O Lord, is become glorious in power." "And set Him at

His own right hand in the heavenlies: far above all principality and power, and might and dominion, and every name that is named, not only in this world but also in that which is to come: and hath put all things under His feet, and gave Him to be the Head over all things to the Church which is His body, the fullness of Him that filleth all in all" (Eph. 1:20-23). Our Surety, then, was not only delivered from prison but exalted to universal dominion, "all power in heaven and in earth" being conferred upon Him. Then how well suited is He to fight our battles, subdue our iniquities and supply our every need! Christ has been elevated high above all ranks of creatures, however exalted in the scale of being or whatever their titles and dignities, and all have been placed in absolute subjection to Him, as "under His feet" signifies. Thus the entire universe is under His control ("upholding all things by the word of His power": Heb. 1:3) for the well-being of His people, so that no weapon formed against them can prosper. No wonder it is required "that all should honor the Son even as they honor the Father" (John 5:23).

Third, it is the place of all blessedness. Our bounties and benevolences are distributed by our "right hand" (Matt. 6:3). "At Thy right hand there are pleasures for evermore" (Ps. 16:11)—one of the great Messianic Psalms. "It is spoken assuredly of such pleasures as Jesus Christ by way of prerogative enjoyeth beyond all the saints and angels, He being at God's right hand so as none of them are. It was the peculiar encouragement that Jesus Christ had, not to be in Heaven only as a common saint, but to be in Heaven at God's right hand; and to have pleasures answerable, far above all the pleasures of men and angels. . .God doth communicate and impart to Him to the utmost all His felicity, so far forth as that human nature is capable of" (Thos. Goodwin), Thus in the "joy" that was set before Him (Heb. 12:2) Christ has the "preeminence" as in all things else. In accord with this third meaning of the expression, Christ will "set the sheep on His right hand" saying to them "Come, ye blessed of My Father, inherit the kingdom prepared for you from the foundation of the world" (Matt. 25:34).

Fourth, this setting of Christ at the right hand of the Majesty on high denotes the endowing His humanity with capacity and ability accordant with the exalted dignity conferred upon Him. It was not like an earthly king advancing his favorite to high honor, or even elevating his son to share his throne, but that God bestowed upon Christ superlative endowments (anointing Him with the oil of gladness "above His fellows," i.e. giving to Him the Spirit "without measure"), fitting Him to discharge such an office. This is clear from the immediate context of Ephesians 1:21, where prayer is made that we may understand God's "mighty power which He wrought in Christ when He raised Him from the dead and set Him at His own right hand in the heavenlies" (vv. 19, 20). This fitting of Christ for His exalted position appears in Rev. 5. There a mysterious book is held forth, but none either in heaven or earth was found worthy to open it till the Lamb appeared. And wherein lay His fitness? The Lamb as it had been slain, possessed "seven horns and seven eyes" (v. 6)—perfect power and perfect intelligence.

"Who is even at the right hand of God." Here then is a further guarantee of the safety and perpetuity of the Church, and O what consolation and encouragement should it afford the tried and trembling believer. He went up "with a shout" (Ps. 47:5)—of conquest, leading captivity captive. His being seated in heaven is proof that His work is finished and His sacrifice accepted (Heb. 10:11, 12). It was as the Head and Representative of His people Christ entered Heaven to take possession for them: "whither the Forerunner is for us entered, even Jesus" (Heb. 6:20). It is in our nature and name He had gone there, to "prepare a place" for us. (John 14:2). Thus we have a Friend at Court, for "if any one sin we have an Advocate with the Father" (1 John 2:1). His great authority, power, dominion and glory is being exercised on our behalf. The government of the universe is on His shoulder, for the well-being, security and triumph of His Church. Hallelujah, what a Savior! God has laid our help "upon One that is mighty" (Ps. 89:19).

10. Christ's Intercession. "Who is he that condemneth? It is Christ that died, yea rather that is risen again, who is even at the right hand of God, who also maketh intercession for us" (Rom. 8:34). Here is the grand climax. First, Christ made a complete atonement for the sins of His people. Next He rose from the dead in proof that His sacrifice was accepted by God. Then He was advanced to the place of supreme honor and power in reward of His undertaking. And now He sues out or asks for His people the benefits He purchased for them. The inexpressible blessedness of this appears in the above order. How many who have been suddenly elevated from poverty to wealth, from ignominy to honor, from weakness to power, promptly forget their former associates and friends. Not so the Lord Jesus. Though exalted to inconceivable dignity and dominion, though crowned with unrivalled honor and glory, yet this made no difference in the affections of Christ toward His people left here in this world. His love for them is unabated, His care of and concern for His Church undiminished. The good will of the Savior unto His own remains unchanged.

The ascended Christ is not wrapped up in His own enthronement, but is still occupied with the well-being of His people, maintaining their interests, seeking their good: "He ever liveth to make intercession for them" (Heb. 7:25). He knows they are weak and helpless in themselves, and are surrounded by those desiring and seeking their destruction, and therefore does He pray, "I am no more in the world, but these are in the world, and I come to Thee, holy Father, keep through Thine own Name those whom Thou hast given Me" (John 17:11); and He bases that request on the finished work by which He glorified God (v. 4). The plea which our great High Priest urges cannot rest upon our merit, for we have none; it is not in recognition of our worthiness, for we are destitute of such. Nor does our wretchedness furnish the reason which the Intercessor urges on our behalf, for that very wretchedness has been brought upon us by our sins. There are no considerations personal to ourselves which Christ can plead on our behalf. No, His all-sufficient sacrifice is the alone plea, and that must prevail. Christ intercedes in Heaven because He died for us on earth (Heb. 9:24-6).

If left entirely to themselves believers would perish. Temptations and tribulations from without and corruptions from within would prove too strong for them, and therefore does Christ make intercession on their behalf, that God would grant them such supplies of grace and pardoning mercy that they will be preserved from total apostasy. It is not that He prays they may be kept from sin absolutely, but from a fatal and final departure from God. This is evident from the case of the eleven on the night of His betrayal: not one only but all of them "forsook Him and fled" (Matt. 26:56). It was the prevalence of His intercession which brought them back again. That was made more especially evident in the case of Peter. The Lord Jesus foresaw and announced that he would deny Him thrice (and lower than that it would seem a Christian cannot fall), yet He prayed that his faith should fail not: not did it—it wrought by love and produced repentance.

That for which our great High Priest particularly asks is the continuance of our believing. Arminians seek to evade this by saying: Christ prays not for the perseverance of the saints in their faith, or that they who once believed should never cease from believing however wicked they may become, but only for saints while they continue saints; that is, as long as they continue in faith and love God will not reject them. But the very thing Christ does pray for is "that thy faith fail not" (Luke 22:32): for the continuance of a living faith, for where that is, there will be good works. And that for which Christ asks must be performed: not only because He is the Son of God (and therefore could ask for nothing contrary to the Father's will), but because His intercession is based upon His sacrifice: He pleads His own merits and sues only for those things which He has purchased for His people—the things to which they are entitled.

That for which Christ intercedes is clearly revealed in John 17: it is for the preservation, unification, sanctification and glorification of His people. The substance of His petitions is found in verse 11, where (in effect) He says: Holy Father, Thou art concerned for each of these persons and hast been viewing them with unspeakable satisfaction from everlasting: Thou gayest them Me as a special expression of Thy love: My heart is set upon them and My soul delighteth in them because they are Mine by Thy free donation. As I am going to leave them behind Me and they are weak and defenseless in themselves, exposed to many enemies and temptations, I pray Thee keep them. Let them have the person of the Holy Spirit to indwell them: let Him renew their spiritual life and graces day by day: let Him preserve them in Thy sacred Truth. That prayer will be fully answered when Christ will "present the Church to Himself a glorious Church" (Eph. 5:27).

11. The love of Christ. Ah, what pen is capable of expatiating upon such a theme when even the chief of the apostles was obliged to own that it "passeth knowledge" (Eph. 3:19). Such was His wondrous love that in order to save His people the Son of God left Heaven for earth, laid aside the robes of His glory and took upon Him the form of a Servant. Such was His wondrous love that He voluntarily became the homeless Stranger here, having not where to lay His head. Such was His wondrous love that He shrank not from being despised and rejected of men, suffering Himself to be spat upon, buffeted and His hair plucked out. Yea, such was His wondrous love for His Church that He endured the cross, where He was made a curse for her, where the wrath of a sin-hating God was poured upon Him, so that for a season He was actually abandoned by Him. Truly His love is "strong as death. . . .many waters cannot quench it, neither can the floods drown it" (Song of Sol. 8:6, 7).

Mark how that love was tried and proved by the unkind response it met with from the most favored of His disciples. So little did they lay to heart His solemn announcement that He was about to be delivered into the hands of men and be slain by them, they "disputed among themselves who should be the greatest" (Mark 9:31, 34). When the awful cup of woe was presented to Him in Gethsemane and His agony was so intense that He sweat great drops of blood the apostles were unable to watch with Him for a single hour. When His enemies, accompanied by a great rabble armed with swords and staves, came to arrest Him, "all the disciples forsook Him and fled" (Matt. 26:56)—and had writer and reader been in their place we had done no otherwise. Did such base ingratitude freeze the Savior's affection for them and cause Him to abandon their cause? No indeed; "having loved His own which were in the world, He loved them unto the end" (John 13:1)—to the end of their unworthiness and unappreciativeness.

Ah my reader, His people are the objects of Christ's everlasting love. Before ever the earth was His delights were with them (Prov. 8:3 1) and have continued ever since. As the Father hath loved Christ Himself, so Christ loves His people (John 15:9)—with a love that is infinite, immutable, eternal. Nothing can separate us from it (Rom. 8:35). Those whom He loves are the special portion and inheritance given to Him by the Father, and will He lose His portion when it is in His power to keep it? No, He will not: "they shall be Mine, saith the Lord of hosts, in that day when I make up My jewels" (Mal. 3:17). When they were given to Him by the Father it was with the express charge "that of all which He hath given Me I should lose nothing, but should raise it up again at the last day" (John 6:39), and therefore do we find Him saying to the Father, "those that Thou gayest Me I have kept, and none of them is lost but (not 'except') the son of perdition, that the Scripture might be fulfilled" (John 17:12), and he was a devil from the beginning.

Consider well the various relations which believers sustain to Christ. They are the mystical Body of which He is the Head: "members of His body, of His flesh and of His bones" (Eph. 5:30). They are "the fullness of Him that filleth all in all" (Eph. 1:23) and thus He would be incomplete, mutilated, if one of them perished. They are laid upon Him as a "foundation" that is "sure" (Isa. 28:16), built upon Him as a "rock" against which "the gates of hell shall not prevail" (Matt. 16:18). They are His "redeemed," bought with a price, purchased at the cost of His life's blood, then how must He regard them! Consider well the terms of endearment used of them. Christians are "of the travail of His soul" (Isa. 53:11). They are His "brethren" (Rom. 8:29), His 'fellows" (Ps. 45:7), His "wife" (Rev. 19:7). They are set as a seal upon His heart (Song of Sol. 8:6), engraved in the palms of His hands (Isa. 49:16). They are His "crown of glory" and "royal diadem" (Isa. 62:3). Since they are so precious in His sight He will not suffer one to perish.

12. The gift of the Holy Spirit. In contemplating the person and work of the Spirit in the economy of redemption we must needs view Him in connection with the everlasting covenant and the mediation of Christ. The descent of the Spirit is inseparably related to what has been before us in the previous sections. When the Savior ascended on high He "received gifts for men, yea for the rebellious also" (Ps. 68:18), and as His exaltation was in reward for His triumphant undertaking, so also were those "gifts," chiefest of which was the Holy Spirit (Acts 2:33). As Christ is the unspeakable gift of the Father unto us, so the Holy Spirit is the supreme gift of Christ to His people. Since Christ is Man as well as God, it is required of Him that He make request for whatever He receives at the hands of the Father: "Ask of Me, and I shall give Thee the heathen (the Gentiles) for Thine inheritance and the uttermost parts of the earth for Thy possession" (Ps. 2:8). "I will pray the Father and He shall give you another Comforter, that He may abide with

you forever" (John 14:16).

The redemptive work of Christ merited the Spirit for His people. The Spirit was given to Christ in consequence of His having so superlatively glorified God on the earth and in answer to His intercession. It is due to His praying that the Holy Spirit not only renews the regenerate day by day, but that He first brought them from death unto life. This is intimated in the 'for the rebellious also" of Psalm 68:18—even while they were in a state of alienation from God. The dispensing of the Spirit is in the hands of the exalted Christ, therefore is He spoken of as "He that hath the seven Spirits of God" (Rev. 3:1) — the Holy Spirit in the fullness or plenitude of His gifts. To His immediate care is now committed the elect of God. As Christ preserved them during the days of His earthly sojourn (John 17:12), so the Spirit safeguards them while He is on high. This is clearly intimated in John 14:3 where the Lord Jesus declares "I will come again and receive (not "take") you unto Myself, that where lam there ye may be also"—they will be handed back to Him by the blessed Spirit.

13. The indwelling of the Spirit. The Holy Spirit was purchased for His people by the oblation of Christ and is bestowed upon them through His intercession, to abide with them forever. The manner in which He abides with those on whom He is bestowed is by a gracious indwelling. "God sent forth His Son, made of a woman, made under the Law, to redeem them that were under the Law, that we might receive the adoption of sons (that is, that we might have conferred upon us the legal status of sonship). And because ye are sons (by virtue of legal oneness with the Son), God hath sent forth the Spirit of His Son into your hearts" (Gal. 4:4-6). What a marvelous yet mysterious thing this is: that the third Person of the Trinity should take up His abode within fallen creatures! It is not merely that the influences or graces of the Spirit are communicated to us, but that He Himself dwells within us: not in our minds (though they are illumined by Him) but in our hearts—the center of our beings, from which are "the issues of life" (Prov. 4:23).

This was the grand promise of God in the Covenant: "I will put My Spirit within you" (Ezek. .36:27 and cf. 37:14), the fulfillment of which our Surety obtained for us—"being by the right hand of God exalted and having received of the Father the promise of the Holy Spirit, He hath shed forth this" (Acts 2:33), for the dispensing of Him is now in the hands of Christ as we have pointed Out above. Thus it is that the inhabitation of the Spirit is the distinguishing mark of the regenerate: "But ye are not in the flesh (as to your legal standing before God) but in the spirit, if so be that the Spirit of God dwell in you. Now if any man have not the Spirit of Christ, he is none of His" (Rom. 8:9). It is the indwelling of the Spirit of God which identifies the Christian, and thus He is called "the Spirit of Christ" because He occupies the believer with Christ and conforms him to His image. The apprehension of this wondrous fact exerts a sobering influence upon the believer, causing him to "possess his vessel in sanctification and honour," "What! know ye not that your body is the temple of the Holy Spirit?" (1 Cor. 6:19).

Now the Spirit takes up His residence in the saints not for a season only but never to leave them. "This is My covenant with them, saith the Lord (unto the Redeemer, see v. 20), My Spirit that is upon Thee and My word which I have put in Thy mouth shall not depart out of Thy mouth, nor out of the mouth of Thy seed, nor out of the mouth of Thy seed's seed, saith the Lord, from henceforth and forever" (Isa. 59:21): that was a solemn promise of the Father unto the Mediator that the Spirit should continue forever with the Redeemer and the redeemed. The blessed Spirit comes not as a transient Visitor but as a permanent Guest of the soul: "And I will pray the Father and He shall give you another Comforter, that He may abide with you forever" (John 14:16). Since then the Spirit takes up His abode in the renewed soul forever, how certain it is that he will be preserved from apostasy. This will be the more evident from our next division, when it will appear that the Spirit is a powerful, active and sanctifying Agent with the Christian.

14. The operations of the Spirit. These are summed up in "He which hath begun a good work in you will finish it" (Phil. 1:6). The reference is to our regeneration, completed in our sanctification, preservation and glorification. First He imparts spiritual life to one who is dead in trespasses and sins and then He sustains and maintains that life by nourishing it and calling it forth into exercise and act, so that it becomes fruitful and abounds in good works. Every growth of spirituality is the work of the Holy Spirit: as the green blade was His so is the ripening corn. The increase of life, as much as the beginning thereof, must still come by the gracious power of the Spirit of God. We never have more life or even know we need more or groan after it, except as He works in us to desire and agonize after it. Were the Spirit totally withdrawn from the Christian he would soon lapse back into spiritual death. But thank God there is no possibility of any such dire calamity: every born-again soul has the infallible guarantee "the Lord will perfect that which concerneth me" (Ps. 138:8).

Let us now consider more particularly some eminent acts of the Spirit in the believer and effects of His grace exercised in them. He empowers and moves them unto obedience: "I will put My Spirit within you and cause you to walk in My statutes and ye shall keep My judgments and do them" (Ezek. 36:27). The two things are inseparable: an indwelling Spirit and holy conduct from those indwelt. "As many as are led by the Spirit of God they are the sons of God" (Rom. 8:14). The Spirit guides into the paths of righteousness by a blessed combination of invincible power and gentle suasion: not forcing us against our wills, but sweetly constraining us. He directs the activities of the Christian by enlightening his understanding, warming his affections, stimulating his holy inclinations and moving his will to do that which is pleasing unto God. In this way is that divine promise fulfilled, "Iam the Lord thy God which teacheth thee to profit, which leadeth thee by the way that thou shouldest go" (Isa. 48:17), and thus is his prayer answered "Order my steps in Thy Word" (Ps. 119:133). By His gracious indwelling the Spirit affords the saints supportment: "likewise the Spirit also helpeth our infirmities" (Rom. 8:26). If the believer were left to himself he would never see (by faith) the all-wise hand of God in his afflictions, still less would his heart ever honestly say concerning them, "Thy will be done." If left to himself the believer would never seek grace to patiently endure chastisement, still less cherish the hope that afterward it would "yield the peaceable fruit of righteousness" (Heb. 12:11). No, rather would he chafe and kick like "a bullock unaccustomed to the yoke" (Jer. 31:18) and yield to the vile temptation to "curse God and die" (Job 2:9). If the believer were left to himself he would never have the assurance that his acutest sufferings were among the all things which work together for his ultimate good, still less would he glory in his infirmity that the power of Christ might rest upon him (2 Cor. 12:9). No, such holy exercises of heart are not the products of fallen human nature: instead they are the immediate, gracious, lovely fruits of the Spirit, brought forth in such uncongenial soil.

By His gracious indwelling the Spirit energies the believer: "strengthened with might by His Spirit in the inner man" (Eph. 3:16). This is manifested in many directions. How often He exerts upon the believer a restraining influence, subduing the lusts of the flesh and holding him back from a course of folly by causing a solemn awe to fall upon him: "the fear of the Lord is to depart from evil," and the Spirit is the Author of that holy fear. "That good thing which was committed unto thee keep by the Holy Spirit which dwelleth in us" (2 Tim. 1:14)—He is the one who oils the wheels of the saint's obedience. "For we through the Spirit wait for the hope of righteousness by faith" (Gal. 5:5) otherwise the deferring of our hope would cause the soul to utterly pine away. Hence we find the Spouse praying to the Spirit for invigoration and fructification, "Awake 0 north wind, and come thou south; blow upon my garden that the spices thereof may flow out" (Song of Sol. 4:16).

The graces which the indwelling Spirit produces are durable and lasting, particularly the three cardinal ones: "now abideth faith, hope, love" (1 Cor. 13:13). Faith is that grace which is "much more precious than of gold that perisheth" (1 Pet. 1:7)— it is its imperishability which constitutes its superior excellency. It is "of the operation of God" (Col. 2:12) and we know that whatsoever is of Him "it shall be forever" (Eccl. 3:14), Christ praying that it "fail not," and therefore no matter how severely it shall be tested its possessor can declare "though He slay me, yet will I trust in Him" (Job 13:15). The hope of the Christian is "as an anchor of the soul both sure and steadfast," for it is cast on Christ the foundation, from whence it can never be removed (Heb. 6:18, 19). As to the believer's love, though its initial ardor may be cooled yet it cannot be quenched, though first love any be "left" it cannot be lost. Under the darkest times Christ is still the object of his love, as the cases of the Church in Song of Solomon 3:1-3 and of Peter (John 21:17) evidence.

15. The relations which the Holy Spirit sustains to the Christian. In Ephesians 1:14 He is designated "the earnest of our inheritance until the redemption of the purchased possession" (cf. 2 Cor. 1:22). Now an "earnest" is part payment assuring the full reward in due season: it is more than a pledge, being an actual portion and token of that which is promised. If the inheritance were precarious, suspended on conditions of uncertain performance, the Spirit could not in truth or propriety be termed the earnest thereof. If an "earnest" is a guaranty among men, much more so between God and His people. He is also "the first fruits" of glorification unto the believer (Rom. 8:23), an antepast of Heaven, the initial beams of the rising sun of eternal bliss in the Christian's soul. He is also the "anointing" which we have received from Christ (cf. 2 Cor. 1:21) and this "abideth" in us (1 John 2:17). Again, He is the believer's seal: "grieve not the Holy Spirit of God whereby ye are sealed unto the day of redemption" (Eph. 4:30), that is, until their bodies are delivered from the grave. Among other purposes a "seal" is to secure: can then the treasure which the Spirit guards be lost? No: as Christ was "sealed" (John 6:27) and in consequence "upheld" by the Spirit so that He failed not (Isa. 42:1, 4), so is the believer. It is impossible for any saint to perish.

Chapter 6
Its Blessedness

In an earlier section we dwelt upon the deep importance of this doctrine, here we wish to show something of its great preciousness. Let us begin by pointing Out the opposite. Suppose that the Gospel proclaimed only a forgiveness of all sins up to the moment of conversion and announced that believers must henceforth keep themselves from everything unworthy of this signal mercy: that means are provided, motives supplied, and warnings given of the fatal consequences which will surely befall those who fail to make a good use of those means and diligently respond to those motives; that whether or not he shall ultimately reach Heaven is thus left entirely in the believer's own hands. Then what? We may well ask what would be the consequences of such a dismal outlook: what would be the thoughts begotten and the spirit engendered by such a gospel? what effect would it produce upon those who really believed it? Answers to these questions should prepare us to the more deeply appreciate the converse.

It hardly requires a profound theologian to reply to the above queries; they have only to be carefully pondered and the simplest Christian should be able to perceive for himself what would be the inevitable result. If the Christian's entrance into Heaven turns entirely upon his own fidelity and his treading the path of righteousness unto the end of his course, then he is far worse off than was Adam in Eden, for when God placed him under the covenant of works he was not heavily handicapped from the beginning by indwelling sin, but each of his fallen descendants is born into this world with a carnal nature which remains unchanged to the moment of death. Thus the believer would enter into the fight not only without any assurance of victory but face almost certain defeat. If such a gospel were true then those who really believed it would be entire strangers to peace and joy, for they must inevitably spend their days in a perpetual dread of Hell. Or, the first time they were overcome by temptation and worsted by the Enemy, they would at once abandon the fight and give way to hopeless despair. "I will not turn away from them to do them good" (Jer. 32:40). "I will never leave thee nor forsake thee" (Heb. 13:5). Nothing whatever can or "shall be able to separate us from the love of God which is in Christ Jesus our Lord" (Rom. 8:39). "He will keep the feet of His saints" (1 Sam. 2:9). How immeasurable the difference between the vain imaginations of men and the sure declarations of God: it is the contrast of the darkness of a moonless and starless midnight from the radiance of the midday sun. "Of them which Thou gavest Me have I lost none" (John 18:9) affirmed the Redeemer. Is not that inexpressibly blessed! That every one of the redeemed shall be brought safely to Heaven. The final apostasy of a believer is an utter impossibility, not in the nature of things but by the Divine constitution: not one who has once been received into the Divine favor can ever be cast out thereof. God has bestowed on each of His children a life than cannot die, He has brought him into a relationship which nothing can change or effect, He has wrought a work in him which lasts "forever" (Eccl. 3:14).

It is sadly true that multitudes of empty professors have "wrested" this truth to their destruction, just as many of our fellows have put to an ill use some of the most valuable of God's temporal gifts; but because foolish gluttons destroy their health through intemperance that is no reason why sane people should refuse to be nourished by wholesome food; and because the carnal pervert the doctrine of Divine preservation that is no valid argument for Christians being afraid to draw comfort from the same. Most certainly it is the design of God that His people should be strengthened and established by this grand article of the faith. Note how in John 17 Christ mentions again and again the words "keep" and "kept" (vv. 6, 11, 12, 13, 15). And His reason for so doing is clearly stated: "these things I speak in the world that they may have My joy fulfilled in them" (v. 13). He would not have them spend their days in the wretchedness of doubts about their ultimate bliss, uncertain as to the issue of their fight. It is His revealed will that they should go forward with a song in their hearts, praising Him for the certainty of ultimate victory.

But the joy which issues from a knowledge of our security is not obtained by a casual acquaintance with this truth. Christ's very repetition "I kept them those that Thou gayest Me I have kept" (John 17:12) intimates to us that we must meditate frequently upon this Divine preservation unto eternal life. It is to be laid hold of in no transient manner but should daily engage the Christian's heart till he is warmed and influenced by it. A few sprinklings of water do not go to the roots of a tree, but frequent and plentiful showers are needed: so it is not an occasional thought about Christ's power to keep His people safe for Heaven which will deeply affect them, but only a constant spiritual and believing pondering thereon. As Jacob said to the Angel "I will not let thee go except thou bless me" (Gen. 32:26), so the believer should say to this truth, I will not turn from it until it has blessed me.

When our great High Priest prayed "Holy Father, keep through Thine own name those whom Thou hast given Me" (John 17:11) it was not (as the Arminians say) that He asked merely that they might be provided with adequate means, by the use of which they must preserve themselves. No, my reader, it was for something more valuable and essential. The Savior made request that faith should be continually wrought in them by the exceeding greatness of God's power (Eph. 1:19), and where that is there will be works of sincere (though imperfect) obedience and it will operate by responding to the holiness of the Law so that sins are mortified. The Father answers that prayer of the Redeemer's by working in the redeemed "both to will and to do of His good pleasure" (Phil. 2:13), fulfilling in them "all the good pleasure of His goodness and the work of faith with power" (2 Thess. 1:11) preserving them "through faith unto salvation" (1 Pet. 1:5). He leaves them not to their feeble and fickle wills, but renews them in the inner man "day by day" (2 Cor. 4:16).

That Christ would have His redeemed draw comfort from their security is clear again from His words "Rejoice because your names are written in heaven" (Luke 10:20). To what purpose did the Lord Jesus thus address His disciples, but to denote that infallible certainty of their final salvation by a contrast from those who perish: that is, whose names were written only "in the earth" (Jer. 17:13) or on the sands which may be defaced. Surely He had never spoken thus if there was the slightest possibility of their names being blotted Out. Rejoice because your names are written in heaven;" is not the implication both necessary and clear as a sunbeam; such rejoicing would be premature if there was any likelihood of final apostasy. This call to rejoice is not given at the moment of the believer's death, as he sees the angels about to convoy him to the realm of ineffable bliss, but while he is still here on the battlefield. Those names are written by none other than the finger of God, indelibly inscribed in the Book of Life, and not one of them will ever be erased.

Take again His words in the parable of the lost sheep: "I say unto you, that likewise joy shall be in heaven over one sinner that repenteth" (Luke 15:7). "Such exalted hosannas would not resound on these occasions among the inhabitants of the skies if the doctrine of final perseverance was untrue. Tell me, ye seraphs of light; tell me, ye spirits of elect men made perfect in glory, why this exuberance of holy rapture on the real recovery of a sinner to God? Because ye know assuredly that every true conversion is (1) a certain proof that the person converted is one of the elect number, and (2) that he shall be infallibly preserved and brought to that very region of blessedness into which ye yourselves are come. The contrary belief would silence your harps and chill your praises. If it be uncertain whether the person who is regenerated today may ultimately reign with you in heaven or take up his eternal abode among apostate spirits in hell, your rejoicings are too sanguine and your praises too presumptuous. You should suspend your songs until he actually arrives among you and not give thanks for his conversion until he has persevered unto glorification" (A. Toplady).

1. What encouragement is there here for the babe in Christ! Conscious of his weakness, he is fearful that the flesh and the world and the Devil may prove too powerful for him. Aware of his ignorance, bewildered by the confusion of tongues in the religious realm, he dreads lest he be led astray by false prophets. Beholding many of his companions, who made a similar profession of faith, so quickly losing their fervor and going back again into the world, he trembles lest he make shipwreck of the faith. Stumbled by the inconsistencies of those called "the pillars of the church," chilled by older Christians who tell him he must not be too extreme, he is alarmed and wonders how it can be expected that he shall hold on his way almost alone. But if these fears empty him of self-confidence and make him cling the closer to Christ, then are they blessings in disguise, for he will then prove for himself that "underneath are the everlasting arms," and that those arms are all-mighty and all-sufficient.

The babe in Christ is as much a member of God's family as is the mature "father" (1 John 2:13) and the former is as truly the object of Divine love and faithfulness as is the latter. Yea, the younger ones in His flock are more the subjects of the Shepherd's care than are the full-grown sheep: "He shall gather the lambs with His arm and carry them in His bosom" (Isa. 40:11). The Lord does not break the bruised reed nor quench the smoking flax (Matt. 12:20). He gave proof of this in the days of His flesh. He found some "smoking flax" in the nobleman who came to Him on behalf of his sick son: his faith was so weak that he supposed the Savior must come down to his house and heal him ere he died—as though the Lord Jesus could not recover him while at a distance or after he had expired (John 4:49): nevertheless He cured him. So too after His ascension, He took note of a "little strength" (Rev. 3:8) and opened a door which none can shut. The highest oak was once an acorn and God was the maintainer of its life. When we affirm the final perseverance of every born-again soul we do not mean that saints are not in themselves prone to fall away, nor that at regeneration such a work is wrought in them once for all that they now have sufficient strength of their own to overcome sin and Satan and that there is no likelihood of their spiritual life decaying. So far from it, we hesitate not to declare that the very principle of grace (or "new nature") in the believer considered abstractedly in itself — apart from the renewing and sustaining power of God — would assuredly perish under the corruptions of the flesh and the assaults of the Devil. No, the preservation of the Christian's faith and his continuance in the path of obedience lies in something entirely external to himself or his state. Wherein lay the impossibility of any bone of Christ being broken? Not because they were in themselves incapable of being broken, for they were as liable to be broken as His flesh to be pierced, but solely because of the unbreakable decree of God. So it is with the mystical Body of Christ: no member of His can perish because of the purpose, power and promise of God Himself.

How important it is then that the babe in Christ should be instructed in the ground of Christian perseverance, that the foundation on which his eternal security rests is nothing whatever in himself but wholly outside. The preservation of the believer depends not upon his continuing to love God, believe in Christ, tread the highway of holiness, or make diligent use of the means of grace, but on the Covenant-engagements entered into between the Father and the Son. That is the basic and grand Cause which produces as a necessary and infallible effect our continuing to love God, believe in Christ and perform sincere obedience. O what a sure foundation is that! What a firm ground for the soul to rest upon! What unspeakable peace and joy issues from faith's apprehension of the same! Though fickle in ourselves, the Covenant is immutable. Though weak and unstable as water we are, yet that is "ordered in all things and sure." Though full of sin and unworthiness, yet the sacrifice of Christ is of infinite merit. Though often the spirit of prayer be quenched in us, yet our great High Priest ever liveth to make intercession for us. Here then is the "anchor of the soul," and it is "both sure and steadfast" (Heb. 6:19).

Ere concluding this subdivision it is necessary to point out in such days as these that it must not be inferred from the above that because the grace, the power and the faithfulness of God insures the preservation of the feeblest babe in Christ that henceforth he is relieved of all responsibility in the matter. Not so: such a blessed truth has not been revealed for the purpose of encouraging slothfulness, but rather to provide an impetus to use the means of preservation which God has appointed. Though we must not anticipate too much what we purpose to bring before the reader under a later division of our subject, when we shall consider at more length the safeguards which Divine wisdom has placed around this truth, yet a few words of warning, or rather explanation, should be given here to prevent a wrong conclusion being drawn from the preceding paragraphs.

The babe in Christ is weak in himself, he is left in a hostile world, he is confronted with powerful temptations, both from within and from without, to apostatize. But strength is available unto faith, armor is provided against all enemies, deliverance from temptations is given in answer to prevailing prayer. But he must seek that strength, put on that armor, and resist those temptations. He must fight for his very life, and refuse to acknowledge defeat. Nor shall he fight in vain, for Another shall gird his arm and enable him to overcome. The blessedness of this doctrine is that he shall not be left to himself nor suffered to perish. The Holy spirit shall renew him day by day, quicken his graces, move him to perseverance and make him "more than conqueror through Him that loved him."

2. What comfort is there here for fearing saints! All Christians have a reverential and filial fear of God and an evangelical horror of sin. Some are beset with legal fears, and most of them with anxieties which are the product of a mingling of legal and evangelical principles. These latter are occasioned more immediately by anxious doubts, painful misgivings, evil surmisings of unbelief. More remotely, they are the result of the permissive appointment of God, who has decreed that perfect happiness must be waited till His people get home to Heaven. Were our graces complete, our bliss would be complete too. In the meantime it is needful for the Christian traveler to be exercised with a thorn in the flesh, and that "thorn" assumes a variety of forms with different believers; but whatever its form it is effectual in convincing them that this earth is not their rest or a mount whereon to pitch tabernacles of continuance. In many instances that "thorn" consists of anxious misgivings, as the frequent "fear not" of Scripture intimates: the fear of being completely overcome by temptation, or making shipwreck of the faith, of failing to endure unto the end.

Once again we would quote those words of Christ, "Of them whom Thou hast given Me have I lost none" (John 18:9). Is not that inexpressibly blessed! That every one of the dear children whom the Father has entrusted to the care and custody of the Mediator shall be brought safely to glory; the feeblest as much as the strongest, those with the least degree of grace as those of the highest, the babes as truly as the full grown. Where true grace is imparted, though it be as a grain of mustard seed, yet it shall be quickened and nourished so that it shall not perish. This should be of great consolation to those timid and doubting ones who are apt to think it will be well with Christians of great faith and eminent gifts, but that such frail creatures as they know themselves to be will never hold out, who dread that Satan's next attack will utterly vanquish them. Let them know that the self-same Divine protection is given to all the redeemed. It is not because one is more godly than another, but because both are held fast in the hand of God. The tiny mouse was as safe in the ark as the ponderous elephant.

What encouragement is there here for the godly, who when they view the numerous Anakims in the way and hear of the giants and walled cities before them are prone to dread their meeting with them. How many a one has trembled as he has pondered that word of Christ's "Verily I say unto you, That a rich man shall hardly enter into the kingdom of heaven. And again I say unto you, It is easier for a camel to go through the eye of a needle than for a rich man to enter into the kingdom of God" (Matt. 19:23, 24) and said with the apostles, "Who then can be saved?" If it be such a difficult matter to get to

Heaven, if the gate be so strait and the way so narrow, and so many of those professing to tread it turn out to be hypocrites and apostates, what will become of me? When thus exercised, remember Christ's answer to the astonished disciples, "with God all things are possible." He who kept Israel on the march for forty years without their shoes wearing out, can quite easily preserve thee, O thou of little faith.

"Thou has a mighty arm: strong is Thy hand, high is Thy right hand" (Ps. 89:13). Grandly is that fact displayed in creation. Who has stretched out the heavens with a span? Who upholds the pillars of the earth? Who has set limits to the raging ocean, so that it cannot overflow its bounds? Whose finger kindled the sun, the moon, and the stars, and kept those mysterious Lamps of the sky alight all these thousands of years? Whose hand has filled the sea with fishes, the fields with herds, and made the earth fertile and fruitful? So too the mightiness of the Lord's arm is manifest in providence. Who directs the destinies of nations and shapes the affairs of kingdoms? Who sets the monarch upon his throne and casts him from thence when it so pleases Him? Who supplies the daily needs of a countless myriad of creatures so that even the sparrow is provided for when the earth is blanketed with snow? Who makes all things work together for good —even in a world which lieth in the Wicked one — to them that love Him, who are the called according to His purpose?

When a soul is truly reconciled to God and brought to delight in Him, it rejoices in all His attributes. At first it is apt to dwell much upon His move and mercy, but as it grows in grace and experience it delights in His holiness and power. It is a mark of spiritual understanding when we have learned to distinguish the manifold perfections of God, to take pleasure in each of them. It is a proof of more intimate communion with the Lord when we perceive how adorable is the Divine character, so that we meditate upon its excellences separately and in detail, and praise and bless Him for each of them. The more we are given to behold all the varied rays of His pure light, the more we are occupied with the many glories of His crown, the more shall we bow in wonderment before Him. Not only shall we perceive how infinitely He is above us, but how there is everything in Him suited to our need; grace to meet our unworthiness, mercy to pardon our sins, wisdom to supply our ignorance, strength to minister to our weakness. "Who is like unto Thee, 0 Lord among the gods? who is like Thee, glorious in holiness, fearful in praises, doing wonders!" (Ex. 15:11).

How this glorious attribute of God's power ensures the final perseverance of the saints! Some of our readers have passed through sore trials and severe tribulations, yet they prevailed not against them: they shook them to their foundations, but they did not overthrow their faith. "Many are the afflictions of the righteous, but the Lord delivereth him out of them all" (Ps. 34:19). Fierce were the foes which many a time gathered against thee, and had not the Lord been on thy side thou hadst quickly been devoured, but in Him thou didst find a sure refuge. The Divine strength has been manifested in your weakness. Is it not so, my brother, my sister: that such a frail worm as yourself has never been crushed by the weight of opposition that has come upon you—Ah, "underneath were the everlasting arms." Though you trembled at your feebleness, yet, "out of weakness were made strong" (Heb. 11:34) has been your case too. Kept alive with death all around you, preserved when Satan and his hosts encompassed you. Must you not say "strong is Thy right hand!"

3. What comfort is there here for souls who are tempted to entertain hard thoughts of God! The awful corruptions of the flesh which still remain in the believer and which are ever ready to complain at the difficulties of the way and murmur against the dispensations of Divine providence, and the questionings of unbelief which constantly ask, Has God ceased to be gracious? how can He love me if He deals with me thus? are sufficient in themselves to destroy his peace and quench his joy. But when to these are added the infidelities of Arminianism which declares that God takes no more care of His children than to suffer the Devil to enter in among and devour them, that the Lord Jesus, that great Shepherd of the sheep, affords no more security to His flock than to allow wolves and lions to come among and devour them at their pleasure, how shall the poor Christian maintain his confidence in the love and faithfulness of the Lord? Such blasphemies are like buckets of cold water poured upon the flames of his affection for God and are calculated only to destroy that delight which he has taken in the riches of Divine grace.

The uninstructed and unestablished believer is apt to think within himself I may for the present be in a good state and condition, but what assurance is there that I shall continue thus? Were not the apostate angels once in a far better state and more excellent condition than mine: they dwelt in Heaven itself, but now they are cast down into Hell, being "reserved in everlasting chains under darkness unto the judgment of the great day" (Jude 6)! Adam in paradise had no lusts within to tempt and seduce him, no world without to oppose and entangle, yet "being in honor" he continued not, but apostatized and perished. If it was not in their power to persevere much less so in mine, who am "sold under sin" and encompassed with a world of temptations. What hope is there left to me? Let a man be exercised with such thoughts as these, let him be cast back solely upon himself, and what is there that can give him any relief or bring his soul to any degree of composure? Nothing whatever, for the so-called "power of free will" availed not either the angels which fell or our first parents.

And what is it which will deliver the distressed soul from these breathings of despair? Nothing but a believing laying hold of this grand comfort: that the child of God has an infallible promise from his Father that he shall be preserved unto His heavenly kingdom, that he shall be kept from apostasy, that the intercession of his great High Priest prevents the total failing of his faith. So far from God being indifferent to the welfare of His children and failing in His care for them, He has sworn that "I will not turn away from them to do them good." So far from the good Shepherd proving unfaithful to His trust, He has given express assurance that not one of His sheep shall perish. Rest on those assurances my reader, and thy hard thoughts about God will be effectually silenced. As to the stability and excellency of the Divine love, is it not written, "The Lord thy God in the midst of thee is mighty, He will rejoice over thee with joy; He will rest in His love, He will joy over thee with singing" (Zeph. 3:17). What can more endear God to His people than that! How it should fix their souls in their love to Him. Well might Stephen Charnock say of Arminians, "Can these men fancy Infinite Tenderness so unconcerned as to let the apple of His eye be plucked out, as to be a careless Spectator of the pillage of His jewels by the powers of Hell, to have the delight of His soul (if I may so speak) tossed like a tennis ball between himself and the Devil." He that does the greater thing for His people shall He not also do the less: to regenerate them is more wonderful than to preserve them, as the bestowal of life exceeds the maintaining of it. The reconciliation of enemies is far harder than dealing with the failings of friends: "while we were yet sinners, Christ died for us. Much more then being now justified by His blood we shall be saved from wrath through Him. For if, when we were enemies, we were reconciled to God by the death of His Son much more, being reconciled, we shall be saved by His life" (Rom. 5:8-10). If there was such efficacy in the death of Christ, who can estimate the virtue of His resurrection! "He ever liveth to make intercession for us."

4. What comfort is there here for aged pilgrims! Some perhaps may be surprised at this heading, supposing that those who have been longest in the way and have experienced most of God's faithfulness have the least need of consolation from the truth. But such a view is sadly superficial to say the least of it. No matter how matured in the faith one may be, nor how well acquainted with the Divine goodness, so long as he is left down here he has no might of his own and is completely dependent upon Divine grace to preserve him. Methuselah stood in as much need of God's supporting hand during the closing days of his pilgrimage as does the veriest babe in Christ. Look at it from the human side of things: the aged believer, filled with infirmities, the spiritual companions of his youth all gone, perhaps bereft of the partner of his bosom, cut off from the public means of grace, he looks forward to the final conflict with trepidation.

"And even to your old age I am He, and even to hoar hairs will I carry you" (Isa. 46:4). Why has such a tender and appropriate promise been given by God if His aged saints have no need of the same? They, any more than the young, are not immune from Satan's attacks. He is not slow to tell the tottering believer that as many a ship has foundered when in sight of port so the closing storm of life will prove too much for him: that though God has borne long with his unbelief and waywardness, even His patience is now exhausted. How then is he to meet such assaults of the Fiend? In the same way as he has done all through his course. By taking the shield of faith, wherewith he shall be able to quench all the fiery darts of the Wicked one (Eph. 6:16), by having recourse to the sure promise of Him who has said "Lo, I am with you always, even unto the end."

Ah, my aged friend, how often have you proved in your experience the truth of those words "thine enemies shall be found liars unto thee" (Deut. 33:29). What a shameless liar the Devil is! Did he not tell thee in some severe trial, The hand of the Lord is gone out against thee: He has forsaken thee and will no more be gracious to thee: He has deserted thee as He did Saul the king and now thou art wholly given up unto the powers of evil: the Lord will no more answer thee from His holy oracle; He has utterly cast thee off. Yet you found that God had not deserted you after all, and this very day you are able to join the writer in thanking Him for His lovingkindness and to testify of His unfailing faithfulness. How often has thine own unbelief whispered to thee, I shall one day perish at the hand of this foe who seeks my life: my strength is gone, the Spirit withholds His assistance, I am left alone and must perish. Yet year after year has passed, and though faint you are still pursuing, though feeble you will hold on your way.

Has not Satan often told you in the past, Your profession is a sham, iniquities prevail over you, the root of the matter is not in thee. Thou was a fool to make a profession and cast in thy lot with God's people: there is no stability in thee, thou art certain to apostatize and bring reproach upon the cause of Christ. And did not your own doubts second his motion, telling you that your experience was but a flash in the pan, some evanescent emotion, which like a firebrand would die out into black ashes. Unbelief has whispered a thousand falsehoods into your ear, saying this duty is too difficult, this toil will prove too great, this adversity will drown you. What madness it was to lend an ear to such lies. Can God ever cast away one on whom He has fixed His everlasting love? Can He renounce one who was purchased by the blood of Christ? Thus will it prove of thy last fears: "Thine enemies shall be found liars unto thee."

5. What comfort is there here for preachers! Many a rural minister views with uneasiness the departure into cities of some of his young converts. And may well he be exercised at the prospect of them leaving their sheltered homes to be brought into close contact with temptations to which they were formerly strangers. It is both his duty and privilege to give them godly counsel and warning, to follow them with his prayers, to write them: but if they he soundly converted he need not fear about their ultimate well-being. Servants of God called to move into other parts are fearful about the babes in Christ which they will leave behind, yet if they really be such they may find consolation in the blessed fact that the great Shepherd of the sheep will never leave nor forsake them.

Chapter 7
Its Perversion

Nowhere is the depravity of man and the enmity of their minds against God more terribly displayed than in the treatment which His Holy Word receives at their hands. By many it is criminally neglected, by others it is wickedly wrested and made to teach the most horrible heresies. To slight such a revelation, to despise such an inestimable treasure, is an insult which the Most High will certainly avenge. To corrupt the sacred Scriptures, to force from them a meaning the opposite of what they bear, to handle them deceitfully by picking and choosing from their contents, is a crime of fearful magnitude. Yet this, in varying measure, is what all the false cults of Christendom are guilty of. Unitarians, Universalists, those who teach the unconsciousness of the soul between death and resurrection and the annihilation of the wicked, single out certain snippets of Scripture but ignore or explain away anything which makes against them. A very high percentage of the errors propagated by the pulpit are nothing more or less than Truth itself, but the Truth distorted and perverted.

Broadly speaking the doctrine which we have been expounding in this series has been perverted by two main classes. First, by open Arminians, who expressly repudiate most of what has been advanced in the preceding sections. With them we are not here directly concerned. Second, by what we can only designate "mongrel Calvinists." This class deny the sovereign and unconditional election of God and also the limited or particular redemption of Christ. They are one with Arminians in believing that election is based on God's foreknowledge of those who would believe the Gospel, and they affirm Christ atoned for the sins of all of Adam's race, and yet they term themselves "Calvinists" because they hold the eternal security of the saints, or "once in grace, always in grace." In their crude and ill-balanced presentation of this doctrine they woefully pervert the Truth and do incalculable damage unto those who give ear to them. As they do not all proceed along exactly the same line or distort the Truth at the same particular point we will divide this branch of our subject so as to cover as many errors as possible.

1. It is perverted by those who predicate of mere professors what pertains only to the regenerate. Here is a young man who attends a service at a church where a "special evangelistic campaign" is being held. He is not seriously inclined, in fact rarely enters a place of worship, but is visiting one now to please a friend. The evangelist makes a fervent emotional appeal and many are induced to "go forward" and be prayed for, our young man among them—again to please his friend. He is persuaded to "become a Christian" by signing a "decision card" and then he is congratulated on the "manly step" he has taken. He is duly "received into the church" and at once given a class of boys in the "Sunday School." He is conscious there has been no change within and though

somewhat puzzled supposes the preacher and church-members know more about the matter than he does. They regard him as a Christian and assure him he is now safe for eternity. Here is another young man who is passing a "Gospel Hall" on a Lord's day evening; attracted by the hearty singing, he enters. The speaker expatiates at length on John 3:16 and similar passages. He declares with such vigor that God loves everybody and points out in proof thereof that He gave His Son to die for the sins of all mankind. The unsaved are urged to believe this and are told that the only thing which can now send them to Hell is their unbelief. As soon as the service is over the speaker makes for our young man and asks him if he is saved. Upon receiving a negative reply, he says, "Would you not like to be, here and now?" Acts 16:3 1 is read to him and he is asked "Will you believe?" If he says yes, John 5:24 is quoted to him and he is told that he is now eternally secure. He is welcomed into the homes of these new friends, frequents their meetings and is addressed as "Brother."

The above are far more than imaginary cases: we have come into personal contact with many from both classes. And what was the sequel? In the great majority of instances the tide of emotion and enthusiasm soon subsided, the novelty quickly wore off, attending "Bible readings" soon palled, and the dog returned to its vomit and the sow to her wallowing in the mire. They were then regarded as "backsliders" and perhaps told "The Lord will bring you back again into the fold," and some of these man-made converts are foolish enough to believe their deceivers and assured that "once saved, saved forever" they go on their worldly way with no trepidation as to the ultimate outcome. They have been fatally deceived. And what of their deceivers? They are guilty of perverting the Truth, they have cast pearls before swine, they have taken the children's bread and thrown it to the dogs; they gave to empty professors what pertained only to the regenerate.

2. It is perverted by those who fail to insist upon credible evidences of regeneration, as is the case with the above examples. The burden of proof always rests upon the one who affirms. When a person avers that he is a Christian that averment does not make him one, and if he be mistaken it certainly is not kindness on my part to confirm him in a delusion. A church is weakened spiritually in proportion to the number of its unregenerate members. Regeneration is a supernatural work of grace and therefore it is a great insult to the Holy Spirit to imagine that there is not a radical difference between one who has been miraculously quickened by Him and one who is dead in trespasses and sins, between one who is indwelt by Him and one in whom Satan is working (Eph. 2:2). Not until we see clear evidence that a supernatural work of grace has been wrought in a soul are we justified in regarding him as a brother in Christ. The tree is known by the fruits it bears: good fruit must be manifested on its branches ere we can identify it as a good tree.

We will not enter into a labored attempt to describe at length the principal birth-marks of a Christian; instead we will mention some things which if they be absent indicate that "the root of the matter" (Job 19:28) is not in the person. One who regards sin lightly, who thinks nothing of breaking a promise, who is careless in the performance of temporal duties, who gives no sign of a tender conscience which is exercised over what are commonly called "trifles," lacks the one thing needful. A person who is vain and self-important, who pushes to the fore seeking the notice of others, who parades his fancied knowledge and attainments, has not learned of Him who is "meek and lowly in heart." One who is hyper-sensitive, who is deeply hurt if someone slights her, who resents a word of reproof no matter how kindly spoken, betrays the lack of a humble and teachable spirit. One who frets over disappointments, murmurs each time his will is crossed and rebels against the dispensations of Providence, exhibits a will which has not been Divinely subdued.

That a person belongs to some "evangelical church" or "assembly" and is regular in his attendance there, is no proof that he is a member of the Church which is Christ's (mystical) body. That a person goes about with a Bible in his hand is no guaranty that the Divine Law is within his heart. Though he may talk freely and fluently about spiritual things, of what worth is it if they do not regulate his daily walk? One who is dishonest in business, undutiful in the home, thoughtless of others, censorious and unmerciful, has no title to be regarded as a new creature in Christ Jesus, no matter how saintly his pose be on the Sabbath Day. When the Pharisees and Sadducees came to Christ's forerunner to be baptized of him, he said, "Bring forth therefore fruits meet for repentance" (Matt. 3:8): I must first see some signs of godly sorrow for sin, some manifestations of a change of heart, some tokens of a transformed life. So we must demand the evidences of regeneration before we are justified in crediting a Christian profession, otherwise we endorse what is false and bolster up one in his self-deceit.

3. It is perverted by those who sever the cause from its necessary effect. The cause of the believer's perseverance is one and indivisible, for it is Divine and nothing whatever of the creature is mingled with it; yet to our apprehension at least it appears as a compound one and we may view its component parts separately. The unchanging love, the immutable purpose, the everlasting covenant and the invincible power of God are conjoint elements in making the saint infallibly secure. But each of those elements is active and brings forth fruit after its own kind. God's love is not confined to the Divine bosom but is "shed abroad" in the hearts of His people by the Holy Spirit (Rom. 5:5), from whence it flows forth again unto its Giver: "we love Him because He first loved us" (1 John 4:19). Our love is indeed feeble and fluctuating, yet it exists, and cannot be quenched, so that we can say with Peter "Thou knowest that I love Thee." "I know My sheep and (though imperfectly) am known of Mine." (John 10:14) shows the response made.

The preacher who has much to say upon the love of God and little or nothing about the believer's love to Him is partial and fails in his duty. How can I ascertain that I am an object of God's love but by discovering the manifest effects of His love being shed abroad in my heart? "If any man love God, the same in known of God" (1 Cor. 8:3). "All things work together for good to them that love God, to them who are the called according to His purpose" (Rom. 8:28). It is by their love for Him they give proof they are the subjects of His effectual call. And how is genuine love for God to be identified? First, by its eminency: God is loved above all others so as He has no rival in the soul: "whom have I in heaven but Thee, and there in none upon earth that I desire beside Thee" (Ps. 73:25). All things give way to His love; "Because Thy lovingkindness is better than life, my lips shall praise Thee" (Ps. 63:3). The real Christian is content to do and suffer anything rather than lose God's favor, for that is his all. Second, true love for God may be recognized by its component parts. Repentance is a mourning love, because of the wrongs done its Beloved and the loss accruing to ourselves. Faith is a receptive love, thankfully accepting Christ and all His benefits. Obedience is a pleasing love, seeking to honor and glorify the One who has set His heart upon me. Filial fear is a restraining love which prevents me offending Him whom I esteem above all others. Hope is love expecting, anticipating the time when there shall be. nothing to come between my soul and Him. Communion is love finding satisfaction in its Object. All true piety is the expression and outflow of love to God and those who bear His image. Hungering and thirsting after righteousness is love desiring more of God and His holiness. Joy is the exuberance of love, delighting itself in its all-sufficient portion. Patience is love waiting for God to make good His promise, moving us to endure the trials of the way until He comes to our relief. Love "beareth all things, believeth all things, hopeth all things, endureth all things" (1 Cor. 13:7).

Third, real love for God expresses itself in obedience. Where there is genuine love for God it will be our chief concern to please Him and fulfill His will. "He that hath My commandments and keepeth them, he it is that loveth Me" (John 14:21). "This is the love of God, that we keep His commandments" (1 John 5:3). Inasmuch as it is the love of an inferior to a superior it must show itself in a respectful subjection, in the performance of duty. God returneth love with love: "I love them that love Me" (Prov. 8:17 and cf. John 14:21). "A Christian is rewarded as a lover rather than as a servant: not as doing work, but as doing work out of love" (Manton). If we love God we shall do his bidding, promote His interests, seek His glory. And this not sporadically but uniformly and constantly; not in being devout at certain set times and the observance of the Lord's supper, but respecting His authority in all the details of our daily lives. Only thus does love perform its function and fulfill its design: "whoso keepeth His Word, in him verily is the love of God perfected (attains its proper goal): hereby know we that we are in Him"(1 John 2:5).

From what has been pointed out in the last three paragraphs it is clear that those who dwell upon the love of God for His people to the virtual exclusion of their love for Him do pervert the truth of the security of the saints, as the individual who persuades himself that he is the object of God's love without producing the fruit of his love for Him is treading on very dangerous ground. This divorcing of the necessary effect from its cause might be demonstrated just as conclusively of the other elements or parts, but because we entered into so much detail with the first we will barely state the other three. The immutability of God's purpose to conduct His elect to Heaven must not be considered as a thing apart; the means have been predestinated as much as the end, and they who despise the means perish. The very term "covenant" signifies a compact entered into by two or more persons, wherein terms are prescribed and rewards promised: nowhere has God promised covenant blessings to those who comply not with covenant stipulations. Nor have I any warrant to believe the saving power of God is working in me unless I am expressly proving the sufficiency of His grace.

4. It is perverted by those who lose the balance of Truth between Divine preservation and Christian perseverance. We may think it vastly more honoring unto God to write or

say ten times as much about His sovereignty as we do upon man's responsibility, but that is only a vain attempt to be wise above what is written, and therefore is to display our own presumption and folly. We may attempt to excuse our failure by declaring it is a difficult matter to present the Divine supremacy and human accountability in their due proportions, but with the Word of God in our hands it will avail us nothing. The business of God's servant is not only to contend earnestly for the Faith but to set forth the Truth in its Scriptural proportions. Far more error consists in misrepresenting and distorting the Truth than in expressly repudiating it. Professing Christians are not deceived by an avowed infidel or atheist, but are taken in by men who quote and re-quote certain portions of Holy Writ, but are silent upon all the passages which clash with their lop-sided views.

Just as we may dwell so much upon the Deity of Christ as to lose sight of the reality of His humanity so we may become so occupied with God's keeping of His people as to overlook those verses where the Christian is bidden to keep himself. The incarnation in nowise changed or modified the fact that Christ was none other than Immanuel tabernacling among men, that "God was manifest in flesh," nevertheless we read "Wherefore in all things it behoved Him to be made like unto His brethren" (Heb. 2:17), and again "Jesus increased in wisdom and stature and in favor with God and man" (Luke 2:51). The theanthropic person or the Mediator is grossly caricatured if either His Godhead or manhood be omitted from consideration. Whatever difficulty it may involve to our finite minds, whatever mystery which transcends our grasp, yet we must hold fast to the fact that the Child born, the Son given, was "the mighty God" (Isa. 9:6); nor must we suffer the truth of God's garrisoning of His people to crowd out the necessity of their discharging their responsibility.

It is perfectly true there is a danger in the other side and that we need to be on our guard against erring in the opposite direction. Some have done so. There are those who consider the humanity of Christ could not be true humanity in the real sense of that word unless it were peccable, arguing that His temptation was nothing more than a meaningless show unless He was capable of yielding to Satan's attacks. One error leads to another. If the last Adam met the Devil on the same plane as did the first Adam, simply as a sinless man, and if His victory (as well as all His wondrous works) is to be attributed solely to the power of the Holy Spirit, then it follows that the exercise of His divine prerogatives and attributes were entirely suspended during the years of His humiliation. Hence we find that those who hold this fantastic view endorse the "kenosis" theory, interpreting the "made Himself of no reputation" or "who emptied Himself" of Phil. 2:7 as the temporary setting aside of His omniscience and omnipotence.

Contending for Christian perseverance no more warrants the repudiation of Divine preservation than insisting on the true manhood of Christ justifies the impugning of His Godhood. Both must be held fast: on the one hand reasoning must be bridled by refusing to go one step further than Scripture goes; on the other hand faith must be freely exercised, receiving all that God has revealed thereon. That which is central in Philippians 2:5-7 is the position Christ entered and the character in which He appeared. He who was "in the form of God" and deemed it not robbery "to be equal with God" took upon Him "the form of a servant" and was "made in the likeness of men." He laid aside the robes of His incomprehensible glory, divested Himself of His incommunicable honors, and assumed the mediatorial office instead of continuing to act as the universal Sovereign. He descended into the sphere of servitude, yet without the slightest injury to His Godhead. There was a voluntary abnegation of the exercise of full dominion and sovereignty, though He still remained "The Lord of glory" (1 Cor. 2:8). He "became obedient unto death" but He did not become either feeble or fallible. He was and is both perfect and "the mighty God."

As the person of the God-man Mediator is falsified if either His Godhead or manhood be denied, or perverted if either be practically ignored, so it is with the security of the saints when either their Divine preservation or their own perseverance is repudiated, or perverted if either be emphasized to the virtual exclusion of the other. Both must be maintained in their due proportions. Scripture designates our Savior "the true God" (1 John 5:20), yet it also speaks of Him as "the man Christ Jesus" (1 Tim. 2:5); again and again He is denominated "the Son of man," yet Thomas owned Him as "my Lord and my God." So too the Psalmist affirmed "He will not suffer thy foot to be moved: He that keepeth thee, will not slumber. . . The Lord shall preserve thee from all evil: He shall preserve thy soul. The Lord shall preserve thy going out and thy coming in from this time forth and for evermore" (121:3, 7, 8); nevertheless, He also declared "By the Word of Thy lips I have kept me from the paths of the destroyer" (17:4), and again "I have kept the ways of the Lord. . .1 have kept myself from mine iniquity" (18:21, 23).Jude exhorts believers "keep yourselves in the love of God" and then speaks of Him "that is able to keep you from falling" (21:24). The one complements, and not contradicts, the other.

5. It is perverted by those who divorce the purpose of God from the means through which it is accomplished. God has purposed the eternal felicity of His people and that purpose is certain of full fruition, nevertheless it is not effected without the use of means on their part, any more than a harvest is obtained and secured apart from human industry and persevering diligence. God has made promise to His saints that "bread shall be given" them and their "water shall be sure" (Isa. 33:16), but that does not exempt them from the discharge of their duty or provide them with an indulgence to take their ease. The Lord gave a plentiful supply of manna from heaven, but the Israelites had to get up early and gather it each morning, for it melted when the sun shone on it. So His people are now required to "labor for the meat which endureth unto everlasting life "(John 6:2 7). Promises of Divine preservation are not made to sluggards and idlers but those called unto the use of means for the establishing of their souls in the practice of obedience; those promises are not given to promote idleness but are so many encouragements to the diligent, assurances that sincere endeavors shall have a successful issue.

God has purposed to preserve believers in holiness and not in wickedness. His promises are made to those who strive against sin and mourn over it, not to those who take their full thereof and delight therein. If I presume upon God's goodness and count upon His shielding me when I deliberately run into the place of temptation, then I shall be justly left to reap as I have sown. It is Satan who tempts souls to recklessness and to the perverting of the Divine promises. This is clear from the attack which he made upon the

Savior. When he bade Him cast Himself from the pinnacle of the temple and to rely upon the angels to preserve Him from harm, it was an urging Him to presume upon the end by disdaining the means; Our Lord stopped his mouth by pointing out that, notwithstanding His assurance from God and of His faithfulness concerning the end, yet Scripture requires that the means tending to that end be employed, the neglect of which is a sinful tempting of God. If I deliberately drink deadly poison I have no ground for concluding that prayer will deliver me from its fatal effects.

The Divine preservation of the saints no more renders their own activities, constant care and exertions superfluous, than does God's gift of breath make it unnecessary for us to breathe. It is their own preservation in faith and holiness which is the very thing made certain: they themselves, therefore, must live by faith and in the practice of holiness, for they cannot persevere in any other way than by watching and praying, carefully avoiding the snares of Satan and the seductions of the world, resisting and mortifying the lusts of the flesh, working out their own salvation with fear and trembling. To neglect those duties, to follow a contrary course, is to "draw back unto perdition" and not to "believe to the saving of the soul" (Heb. 10:39). He who argues that since his perseverance in faith and holiness is assured he needs exercise no concern about it or trouble to do anything toward it, is not only guilty of a palpable contradiction but gives proof that he is a stranger to regeneration and has neither part nor lot in the matter. "Make me to go in the path of Thy commandments, for therein do I delight" (Ps. 119:35) is the cry of the renewed.

6. It is perverted by those who deny the truth of Christian responsibility. In this section we shall turn away from the "mongrel Calvinists" to consider a serious defect on the part of "hyper-Calvinists," or as some prefer to call them, "fatalists." These people not only repudiate the general offer of the Gospel, arguing that it is a virtual denial of man's spiritual impotency to call upon the unregenerate to savingly repent and believe, but they are also woefully remiss in exhorting believers unto the performance of Christian duties. Their favorite text is "without Me ye can do nothing. "but they are silent upon "I can do all things through Christ which strengtheneth me" (Phil. 4:13). They delight to quote the promises wherein God declares "I will" and "I shall" but they ignore those verses which contain the qualifying "if ye" (John 8:31) and "if we" (Heb. 3:6).

They are sound and strong in the truth of God's preservation of His people, but they are weak and unsound on the correlative truth of the saints' perseverance. They say much about the power and operations of the Holy Spirit, but very little on the method He employs or the means and motives He makes use of.

"As many as are led by the Spirit of God they are the sons of God" (Rom. 8:14). He does not compel but inclines: it is not by the use of physical power but by the employment of moral suasion and sweet inducements that He leads for He deals with the saints not as stocks and stones but as rational entities. "I will instruct thee and teach thee in the way which thou shalt go: I will guide thee with Mine eye" (Ps. 32:8), The meaning of that is more apparent from the contrast presented in the next verse: "Be ye not as the horse (rushing where it should not) or as the mule (stubbornly refusing to go where it should) which have no understanding: whose mouth must be held in with bit and bridle. " God does not drive His children like unintelligent animals, but guides by enlightening their minds, directing their inclinations, moving their wills. God led Israel across the wilderness by a pillar of cloud by day and a pillar of fire by night: but they had to respond thereto, to follow it. So the good Shepherd goes before His sheep, and they follow Him.

It is true, blessedly true, that God "draws," yet that drawing is not a mechanical one as though we were machines, but a moral one in keeping with our nature and constitution. Beautifully is this expressed in Hosea 11:4, "1 drew them with cords as a man, with bands of love." Every moral virtue, every spiritual grace, is appealed to and called into action. There is perfect love and gracious care on God's part toward us; there is the intelligence of faith and response of love on our part toward Him; and thereby He keeps us in the way. Blessed and wondrous indeed is the inter-working of Divine grace and the believer's responsibility. All the affections of the new creature are wrought upon by the Holy Spirit. He draws out our love by setting before us God's love: "we love Him, because He first loved us," but we do love Him, we are not passive, nor is love inactive. He quickens our desires and revives our assurance, and we "rejoice in hope of the glory of God." He brings into view "the prize of the high calling" and we "press toward the mark, forgetting those things which are behind and reaching forth unto those things which are before" (Phil. 3:13, 14). It is very much like a skilled musician and a harp: as his fingers touch its strings they produce melodious sounds. God works in us and produces the beauty of Holiness. But how? By setting before our minds weighty considerations and powerful motives, and causing us to respond thereto. By giving us a tender conscience which is sensitive to His still small voice. By appealing to every motive-power in us: fear, desire, love, hatred, hope, ambition. God preserves His saints not as He does the mountain pine which is enabled to withstand the storm without its own concurrence, but by calling into exercise and act the principle that was imparted to them at the new birth. There is the working of Divine grace first, and then the outflow of Christian energy. God works in His people both to will and to do of His good pleasure, and they work out their own salvation with fear and trembling (Phil. 2:12,13). And it is the office of God's servants to be used as instruments in the hands of the Spirit. It is their task to enforce the responsibility of the saints, to admonish slothfulness, to warn against apostasy, to call unto the use of means and the performance of duty.

If the hyper-Calvinist preacher compares the method he follows with the policy pursued by the apostles, he should quickly perceive the vast difference there is between them. True, the apostles gave attention to doctrinal instruction, but they also devoted themselves to exhortation and expostulation. True, they magnified the free and sovereign grace of God and were careful to set the crown of glory upon the One to whom alone it belonged, yet they were far from addressing their hearers as so many paralytics or creatures who must lie impotent till the waters be moved. "No," they said, "Let us not sleep, as do others" (1 Thess. 5:6), but "awake to righteousness and sin not" (1 Cor. 15:34). They bade them "run with patience the race that is set before us" (Heb. 12:2) and not sit down and mope and hug their miseries. They called upon them to "resist the Devil" (James 4:7), not take the attitude they were helpless in the matter. They gave direction "keep yourselves from idols" (1 John 5:21) and did not at once negative it by adding, "but you are unable to do so." When the apostle said "I think it meet, as long as I am in this tabernacle, to stir you up by putting you in remembrance" (2 Pet. 1:13), he was not usurping the prerogative of the Spirit but was enforcing the responsibility of the saints.

7. It is perverted by those who use the doctrine of justification to crowd out the companion doctrine of sanctification. Though they are inseparably connected yet they may be and should be considered singly and distinctly. Under the Law the ablutions and oblations, the washings and sacrifices went together, and justification and sanctification are blessings which must not be disjointed. God never bestows the one without the other, yet we have no means of knowing we have received the former apart from the evidences of the latter. Justification refers to the relative or legal change which takes place in the status of God's people. Sanctification to the real and experimental change which takes place in their state, a change which is begun at the new birth, developed during the course of their earthly pilgrimage and is made perfect in Heaven. The one gives the believer a title to Heaven, the other a meetness for the inheritance of the saints in light; the former clears him from the guilt of sin, the latter cleanses from sin's defilement. In sanctification something is actually imparted to the believer, whereas in justification it is only imputed. Justification is based entirely on the work which Christ wrought for His people, but sanctification is principally a work wrought in them.

By our fall in Adam we not only lost the favor of God but also the purity of our nature, and therefore we need to be both reconciled to God and renewed in our inner man, for without personal holiness "no man shall see the Lord" (Heb. 12:14). "As He which hath called you is holy, so be ye holy in all manner of conversation (behavior); because it is written, Be ye holy for I am holy" (1 Pet. 1:15, 16). God's nature is such that unless we be sanctified there can be no intercourse between Him and us. But can persons be sinful and holy at one and the same time? Genuine Christians discover so much carnality, filth and vileness in themselves that they find it almost impossible to be assured they are holy. Nor is this difficulty solved, as in justification, by recognizing that though completely unholy in ourselves we are holy in Christ, for Scripture teaches that those who are sanctified by God are holy in themselves, though the evil nature has not been removed from them.

None but "the pure in heart" will ever "see God" (Matt. 5:8). There must be that renovation of soul whereby our minds, affections and wills are brought into harmony with God. There must be that impartial compliance with the revealed will of God and abstinence from evil which issues from faith and love. There must be that directing of all our actions to the glory of God, by Jesus Christ, according to the Gospel. There must be a spirit of holiness working within the believer's heart so as to sanctify his outward actions if they are to be acceptable unto Him in whom "there is no darkness." True, there is perfect holiness in Christ for the believer, but there must also be a holy nature received from Him. There are some who appear to delight in the imputed obedience of Christ who make little or no concern about personal holiness. They have much to say about being arrayed in "the garments of salvation and covered with the robe of righteousness" (Isa. 61:10), who give no evidence that they "are clothed with humility" (1 Pet. 5:4) or that they have "put on. . .bowels of mercies, kindness, humbleness of mind, meekness, long-suffering, forbearing one another and forgiving one another" (Col. 3:12).

How many there are today who suppose that if they have trusted in Christ all is sure to be well with them at the last, even though they are not personally holy. Under the pretense of honoring faith, Satan, as an angel of light, has deceived and is now deceiving multitudes of souls. When their "faith" is examined and tested, what is it worth? Nothing at all so far as insuring an entrance into Heaven is concerned: it is a powerless, lifeless, fruitless thing. The faith of God's elect is unto "the acknowledging of the truth which is after godliness" (Titus 1:1). It is a faith which purifieth the heart (Acts 15:9), and it grieves over all impurity. It is a faith which produces an unquestioning obedience (Heb. 11:8). They therefore do but delude themselves who suppose they are daily drawing nearer to Heaven while they are following those courses which lead only to Hell. He who thinks to come to the enjoyment of God without being personally holy, makes Him Out to be an unholy God, and puts the highest indignity upon Him. The genuineness of saving faith is only proved as it bears the blossoms of experimental godliness and the fruits of true piety.

Sanctification consists of receiving a holy nature from Christ and being indwelt by the Spirit so that the body becomes His temple, set apart unto God. By the Spirit's giving me vital union with "the Holy One" I am "sanctified in Christ Jesus" (1 Cor. 1:2). Where there is life there is growth, and even when growth ceases there is a development and maturing of what has grown. There is a living principle, a moral quality communicated at the new birth, and under sanctification it is drawn out into action and exercised in living unto God. In regeneration the Spirit imparts saving grace, in sanctification He strengthens and develops it: the one is a birth, the other a growth.. Therein it differs from justification: justification is a single act of grace, sanctification is a continued work of grace; the one is complete the other progressive. Some do not like the term "progressive sanctification" hut the thing itself is clearly taught in Scripture. "Every branch that beareth fruit, He purgeth it that it may bring forth more fruit" (John 15:2). "I pray that your love may abound yet more and more in knowledge and all judgment" (Phil. 1:9). That you "may grow up in Him in all things" (Eph. 4:15) is an exhortation thereto.

8. It is perverted by those who fail to accord the example of Christ its proper place. Few indeed have maintained an even keel on this important matter. If the Socinians have made the exemplary life of Christ to be the whole end of the incarnation, others have so stressed His atoning death as to reduce His model walk to comparative insignificance. While the pulpit must make it clear that the main and chief reason why the Son of God became flesh, was in order that He might honor God in rendering to the Law a perfect satisfaction on behalf of His people, yet it should also make equally plain that a prominent design and important end of Christ's incarnation was to set before His people a pattern of holiness for their emulation. Thus declares The Scriptures: "He hath left us an example that we should follow His steps" (1 Pet. 2:21) and that example imperatively obligates believers unto its imitation. If some have unduly pressed the example of Christ upon unbelievers, others have woefully failed to press it on believers. Because it has no place in the justification of a sinner, it is a serious mistake to suppose it exerts no influence upon the sanctification of a saint.

The very name "Christian" intimates that there is an intimate relation between Christ and the believer. It signifies "an anointed one," that he has been endued with a measure of that Divine unction which his Master received "without measure" (John 3:34). And as Flavel, the Puritan, pointed out "Believers are called 'fellows' or co-partners (Ps. 45:7) of Christ from their participation with Him of the same Spirit. God giveth the same spirit unto us which He most plentifully poured out upon Christ. Now where the same spirit and principle is, there the same fruits and operations must he produced, according to the proportions and measures of the Spirit of grace communicated. Its nature also is assimilating, and changeth those in whom it is into the same image with Christ, their heavenly Head (2 Cor. 3:18)." Again; believers are denominated "Christians" because they are disciples of Christ (Matt. 28:19 margin, Acts 11:26), that is, learners and followers of His, and therefore it is a misuse of terms to designate a man a "Christian" who is not sincerely endeavoring to mortify and forsake whatever is contrary to His character: to justify his name he must be Christlike.

Though the perfect life of Christ must not be exalted to the exclusion of His atoning death, neither must it be omitted as the believer's model. If it be true that no attempt to imitate Christ can obtain a sinner's acceptance with God, it is equally true that the emulating of Him is imperatively necessary and absolutely essential in order to the saints' preservation and final salvation. "Every man is bound to the imitation of Christ under penalty of forfeiting his claim to Christ. The necessity of this imitation convincingly appears from the established order of salvation, which is fixed and unalterable. Now conformity to Christ is the established method in which God will bring many souls to glory. 'For whom He did foreknow, He also did predestinate to be conformed to the image of His Son, that He might be the Firstborn among many brethren' (Rom. 8:29). The same God who hath predestinated men to salvation, hath in order thereto, predestinated them unto conformity to Christ, and this order of heaven is never to be reversed. We may as well think to be saved without Christ, as to be saved without conformity to Christ" (John Flavel).

In Christ God has set before His people that standard of moral excellence which He requires them to aim and strive after. In His life we behold a glorious representation in our own nature of the walk of obedience which He demands of us. Christ conformed Himself to us by His abasing incarnation, how reasonable therefore is it that we should conform ourselves to Him in the way of obedience and sanctification. "Let this mind be in you which was also in Christ Jesus" (Phil. 2:5). He came as near to us as was possible for Him to do, how reasonable then is it that we should endeavor to come as near as it is possible for us to do. "Take My yoke upon you, and learn of Me." If "even Christ pleased not Himself" (Rom. 15:3), how reasonable is it that we should be required to deny ourselves and take up our cross and follow Him (Matt. 16:24), for without so doing we cannot be His disciples (Luke 15:27). If we are to he conformed to Christ in glory how necessary that we first be conformed to Him in holiness: "he that saith he abideth in Him ought himself so to walk even as He walked" (1 John 2:6). "Let everyone that nameth the name of Christ depart from iniquity" (2 Tim. 2:19): let him either put on the life of Christ or drop the name of Christ.

Chapter 8
Its Safeguards

There may be some who will at once take exception to the employment of this term in such a connection, affirming that the Truth of God requires no safeguarding at the hands of those called by Him to expound it: that their business is to faithfully preach the same and leave results entirely to its Author. We fully agree that God's eternal Truth stands in no need of any carnal assistance from us, either in the way of dressing it up to render it more attractive or toning down to make it less offensive; yea, we heartily subscribe to the apostle's dictum that "we can do nothing against the Truth, but for the Truth" (2 Cor. 13:8)—God overrules the opposition of those who hate it and makes the wrath of His enemies to praise Him. Nevertheless in view of such passages as Mark 4:33; John 16:12; 1 Cor. 3:2; Heb. 5:12 it is clear that our presentation of the Truth needs to be regulated by the condition of those to whom it is ministered. Moreover, this raises the question, What is faithfully presenting the Truth? Are there not other modifying adverbs which are not to be omitted?

The Truth should not only be preached "faithfully" but wisely, proportionately, seasonably as well. There is a zeal which is not according to knowledge nor tempered by wisdom. There is an unbalanced presentation of the Truth which accomplishes more harm than good. We read of "the present Truth" (2 Pet. 1:12) and of "a word in due season" (Prov. 15:23 and cf. Isa. 50:4), which implies there is such a thing as speaking unseasonably, even though it be the Truth itself which is spoken and that "faithfully." What is a "word in season?" Is it not a timely and pertinent one, a message suited to the condition, circumstances and needs of the persons addressed? In His wisdom and goodness God has provided cordials for the faint and comfort for those who mourn, as He has also given exhortations to the slothful, admonitions to the careless, solemn warnings to the reckless, and fearful threatenings to those who are defiant. Discrimination needs to be used in our appropriation and application of the Scriptures. As it would be cruel to quote terrifying passages to one who is already mourning over his sins, so it would be wrong to press the promises of Divine preservation upon a professing Christian who is living a carnal and worldly life.

"Watch and pray that ye enter not into temptation: the spirit indeed is willing, but the flesh is weak" (Matt. 26:41). Those words furnish an illustration of a "word in due season." The disciples (not Peter only) had boasted "though I should die with Thee, yet will I not deny Thee." They were self-confident and temporarily blind to their own instability. Their Lord therefore bade them guard against self-reliance and seek grace from above, for though they were quite sincere in their avowal, yet were they much too feeble to resist Satan's attacks in their own strength. They thought themselves immune from such a horrible sin as denying their Master, but instead of bolstering them up in their sense of security He warned them of their danger. Another example of a seasonable word is the apostle's exhortation to the one who claims that he "standeth by faith," namely, "Be not high-minded, but fear. For if God spared not the natural branches take heed lest He also spare not thee. Behold therefore the goodness and severity of God: on those that fell, severity; but toward thee goodness, if thou continue in His goodness; otherwise thou also shalt be cut off" (Rom. 11:20,22).

But it is rather those safeguards by which God Himself has hedged about the subject of the everlasting security of His people that we would now particularly consider, those defenses which are designed to shut out unholy trespassers from this garden of delights; or to change the figure, those descriptions of character and conduct which serve to make known the particular persons to whom alone His promises belong. In the preceding section we dwelt at some length on how this blessed doctrine is misrepresented by Arminians and perverted by Antinomians. To use a term employed by an apostle, it has been grievously "wrested," torn from its setting, disproportionately contorted, divorced from its qualifying terms, detached from the necessary means by which it is attained, applied unto those to whom it does not belong. Hence our present object is to direct attention unto some of the principal bulwarks by which this precious truth is protected and which must be duly emphasized and continually pressed by the servants of God if it is to be portrayed in its true perspective and if souls are not to be fatally misled. Only thus shall we "faithfully" present this truth.

1. By insisting that it is the preservation of saints and not everyone who deems himself a Christian. It is of deep importance to define clearly and sharply the character of those who are Divinely assured of being preserved unto the heavenly kingdom—that God be not dishonored, His Truth falsified, and souls deceived. "He preserveth the souls of His saints" (Ps. 87:10), but of none others. It is so easy to appropriate (or misappropriate) such a promise as "Thou shalt guide me with Thy counsel and afterward receive me to glory" (Ps. 73:24), but before so doing honesty requires that I ascertain whether the experiences of the one described in the context are those of mine. Asaph confesses to being envious at the prosperity of the wicked (vv. 3, 12) until he felt he had cleansed his own heart and hands "in vain" (v. 13). But he checks himself, tender lest by such murmuring he should stumble God's children (v. 15), recording how his "heart was grieved" and his conscience pricked at giving way to such foolish repinings, until he owned unto God "I was as a beast before Thee" (v. 22). The recollection of God's gracious forbearance (v. 23) moved him to say "it is good for me to draw near to God" (v. 28).

When I can find such marks in myself as the Psalmist had, such graces operating in my heart as did in, his, then—but not before — am I warranted in comforting myself as he did. If I challenge the utterances of my mouth as to whether or no they are likely to offend God's little ones, if I make conscience of envying the prosperity of the wicked and mourn over it, if I am deeply humbled thereby, if I realize "my steps had well-nigh slipped" (v. 2) and that it was a longsuffering God who had "holden me by my right hand," alone preserving me from apostasy; if this sense of His sovereign goodness enables me to affirm "Whom have I in heaven but Thee? and there is none upon earth that

I desire besides Thee" (v. 25); if all of this produces in me such a sense of my utter insufficiency as to own "My flesh and my heart faileth, but God is the strength of my heart" (v. 26), then am I justified in saying "Thou shalt guide me with Thy counsel and afterward receive me to glory." Yes, God "preserveth the souls of His saints," but what avails that for me unless I be one of them!

Again; how many there are who eagerly grasp at those words of Christ concerning His sheep, who have only the vaguest idea of the ones whom He thus designates: "And I give unto them eternal life, and they shall never perish; neither shall any pluck them out of My hand" (John 10:27). The very fact that the verse opens with "and" requires us to ponder what immediately precedes, and because His flock is but a "little" one (Luke 12:32) it behooves each one who values his soul to spare no pains in seeking to ascertain whether he belongs to it. In the context the Savior says "My sheep hear My voice, and I know them, and they follow Me." Observe diligently the three things which are here predicated of them. First, they hear Christ's voice. Now to hear His voice means far more than to be acquainted with His words as they are recorded in Scripture—more than believing they are His words. When it was said unto Israel "the Lord will not hear you in that day" (1 Sam. 8:18) it signified that He would not heed their requests or grant their petitions. When God complained "When I spoke, ye did not hear," it was not that they were physically deaf but their hearts were steeled against Him, as the remainder of the verse indicates: "But did evil before Mine eyes, and did choose that wherein I delighted not" (Isa. 65:12).

When God says "This is My beloved Son in whom I am well pleased: hear ye Him" (Matt. 17:5) He is requiring something more of us than that we simply listen respectfully and believingly to what He says: He is demanding that we submit ourselves unreservedly to His authority, that we respond promptly to His orders, that we obey Him. In Prov. 8:33 "hearing" is contrasted from refusing, and in Heb. 3:15 we read "If ye will hear His voice harden not your hearts." When Christ declares of His flock "My sheep hear My voice" He signifies they heed it — they are not intractable but responsive, doing what He bids. Second, He declares "and I know them," that is, with a knowledge of approbation. Third, "and they follow Me ": not the bent of the flesh, not the solicitations of Satan, not the ways of the world, but the example which Christ hast left them (1 Pet. 2:21). Of this it said "they follow the Lamb whithersoever He goeth" (Rev. 14:4) But in order to follow Christ, self has to be denied and the cross taken up (Matt. 16:24). Only those who thus "hear," are "known" of Christ, and who "follow" Him, shall "never perish."

2. By insisting that no person has any warrant to derive comfort from the doctrine of Divine Security until he is sure that he possesses the character and conduct of a saint. This naturally grows out of the first point, though we have somewhat anticipated what should be said here. Not everyone who bears the name of Christ will enter Heaven, but only His sheep. It therefore follows that only those bearing the marks of such have any claim upon the promises made to that favored company. And the burden of proof always rests upon the one who affirms. If one answers some advertisement from an employer of labor for a skilled workman, he is required to give evidence of his qualifications by well-accredited testimonials. If a person puts in a claim to an estate he must produce proof

that he is a legitimate heir and satisfy the court of his bona fides. If a captain requires an additional hand for his ship he demands that the applicant show his papers or give demonstration that he is a fully qualified seaman. Before I can procure a passport I must produce my birth certificate. And one who avers himself a saint must authenticate his profession and evidence his new birth before he is entitled to be regarded as such.

God's saints are distinguished from all other people, not only by what He has done for them but also by what He has wrought in them. He set His heart upon them from all eternity, having loved them "with an everlasting love" (Jer. 31:3) and therefore were they "blessed with all spiritual blessings in the heavenlies in Christ," chosen in Him before the foundation of the world, predestinated "unto the adoption of children by Jesus Christ to Himself," and "accepted in the Beloved" (Eph. 1:3-6). It is true that they fell in Adam and became guilty before God, but an all-sufficient Redeemer was provided for them, appointed to assume and discharge all their liabilities and make full reparation to the broken Law on their behalf. It is also true that they are "by nature the children of wrath even as others," being born into this world "dead in trespasses and sins" (Eph. 2:1-3); but at the ordained hour a miracle of grace is performed within them so that they become "new creatures in Christ Jesus" (2 Cor. 5:17) and their bodies are made "the temple of the Holy Spirit" (1 Cor. 6:19). Faith and holiness have been communicated to them, so that though they are still in the world they are not of it (John 17:14).

The saints are endowed with a new life, with a spiritual and supernatural principle or "nature" which affects their whole souls. So radical and transforming is the change wrought in them by this miracle of grace that it is described as a passing from death unto life (John 5:24), from the power of darkness into the kingdom of God's dear Son (Col. 1:13), from "having no hope and without God in the world" to being "made nigh by the blood of Christ" (Eph. 2:12, 13), from a state of alienation to one of reconciliation (Col. 1:21), out of darkness into God's marvelous light (1 Pet. 2:9). Of them God says "This people have I formed for Myself: they shall show forth My praise" (Isa. 43:21). Obviously such a tremendous change in their state and standing must effect a real and marked change in their character and conduct. From rebellion against God they are brought unto subjection to Him, so that they throw down their weapons of opposition and yield to His scepter. From love of sin they are turned to hate it, and from dread of God they now delight in Him. Formerly they thought only of gratifying self, now their deepest longing is to please Him who has shown them such amazing grace.

The saints are those who enter into a solemn covenant with the Lord, unreservedly dedicating themselves unto Him, making His glory their paramount concern. "Formerly soldiers used to take an oath not to flinch from their colors, but faithfully to cleave to their leaders; this they called sacramentum militare, a military oath; such an oath lies upon every Christian. It is so essential to the being of a saint, that they are described by this: "gather My saints together unto Me; those that have made a covenant with Me" (Ps. 50:5). We are not Christians till we have subscribed this covenant, and that without any reservation. When we take upon us the profession of Christ's name, we enlist ourselves in His muster-roll, and by it do promise that we will live and die with Him in opposition to all His enemies. . .He will not entertain us till we resign up ourselves freely to His disposal, that there may be no disputing with His commands afterwards, but, as one under His authority, go and come at His word" (W. Gurnall, 1660).

3. By insisting that perseverance is an imperative necessity. Adherence to the Truth no matter what opposition is encountered, living a life of faith in and upon God despite all the antagonism of the flesh, steadfastly treading the path of obedience in face of the scoffs of the world, continuing to go forward along the highway of holiness notwithstanding the hindrances of Satan and his emissaries, is not optional but obligatory. It is according to the unalterable decree of God: no one can reach Heaven except by going along the only way that reaches there—Christ "endured the cross" before He received the crown. It is according to the irreversible appointment of God: "For we are His workmanship, created in Christ Jesus unto good works, which God hath before ordained that we should walk in them" (Eph. 2:10). It is according to the established order of God: "that ye be not slothful but followers of them who through faith and patience (the Greek word may be rendered, perseverance with equal propriety) inherit the promises" (Heb. 6:12). It is according to the design of the Atonement, for Christ lived and died that He might "purify unto Himself a peculiar people zealous of good works" (Titus 2:14)

Assurance of Divine preservation no more renders less imperative the saints own perseverance than God's informing Hezekiah he should live a further fifteen years abolished the necessity of his eating and drinking, resting and sleeping, as hitherto. "The elect are as much chosen to intermediate sanctification on their way as they are to that ultimate glorification which crowns their journey's end, and there is no coming to the one but through the other. So that neither the value, nor the necessity, nor the practical value of good works is superseded by this glorious truth. . .It is impossible that either the Son of God, who came down from heaven to propose and make known His Father's will; or that the Spirit of God, speaking in the Scriptures and acting on the heart, should administer the least encouragement to negligence and unholiness of life. Therefore that opinion that personal holiness is unnecessary to final glorification is in direct opposition to every dictate of reason, to every declaration of Scripture" (A. Toplady). Alas, the attitude of multitudes of professing Christians is, "Soul, thou hast much good laid up. . .take thine ease" (Luke 12:19), and the doom of the fool will be theirs.

Concerning the imperativeness of perseverance C. H. Spurgeon said in the introductory portion of his sermon on "The righteous shall hold on his way" (Job 17:9), "The man who is righteous before God has a way of his own. It is not the way of the flesh, nor the way of the world; it is a way marked Out for him by the Divine command, in which he walks by faith. It is the king's highway of holiness, the unclean shall not pass over it: only the ransomed of the Lord shall walk there, and these shall find it a path of separation from the world. Once entered upon the way of life, the pilgrim must persevere in it or perish, for thus saith the Lord 'If any man draw back, My soul shall have no pleasure in him.' Perseverance in the path of faith and holiness is a necessity of the Christian, for only 'he that endureth to the end shall be saved.' It is in vain to spring up quickly like the seed that was sown on the rock, and then by-and-by to wither when the sun is up; that would but prove that such a plant has no root in itself, but 'the trees of the Lord are full of sap' and they abide and continue and bring forth fruit, even in old age, to show that the Lord is upright.

"There is a great difference between nominal Christianity and real Christianity, and this is generally seen in the failure of the one and the continuance of the other. Now, the declaration of the text is, that the truly righteous man shall hold on his way: he shall not go back, he shall not leap the hedges and wander to the right hand or the left, he shall not lie down in idleness, neither shall he faint and cease to go upon his journey; but he 'shall hold on his way.' It will frequently be very difficult for him to do so, but he will have such resolution, such power of inward grace given him, that he will hold on his way' with stern determination, as though he held on by his teeth, resolving never to let go. Perhaps he may not always travel with equal speed; it is not said that he shall hold on his pace, but he shall hold on his way. There are times when we run and are not weary, and anon when we walk and are thankful that we do not faint; ay, and there are periods when we are glad to go on all fours and creep upwards with pain; but still we prove that 'the righteous shall hold on his way.' Under all difficulties the face of the man whom God has justified is steadfastly set towards Jerusalem, nor will he turn aside till his eyes shall see the King in his beauty."

4. By insisting on continuance in well doing. It is not how a person commences but how he ends which is the all-important matter. We certainly do not believe that one who has been born of God can perish, but one of the marks of regeneration is its permanent effects, and therefore I must produce those permanent fruits if my profession is to be credited. Both Scripture and observation testify to the fact that there are those who appear to run well for a season and then drop out of the race. Not only are there numbers induced to "come forward" and "join the church" under the high-pressure methods used by the professional evangelists, who quickly return to their former manner of life: but there are not a few who enter upon a religious profession more soberly and wear longer. Some seem to be genuinely converted: they separate from ungodly companions, seek fellowship with God's people, manifest an earnest desire to know more of the Word, become quite intelligent in the Scriptures, and for a number of years give every outward sign of being Christians. But gradually their zeal abates, or they are offended at some wrong done them, and ultimately they go right back again into the world.

We read of a certain class "who for a while believed, and in time of temptation fall away" (Luke 8:13). There were those who followed Christ for a season, yet of them we read "From that time many of His disciples went back and walked no more with Him" (John 6:66). There have been many such in every age. All is not gold that glitters, and not every one who makes a promising start in the race reaches the goal. It is therefore incumbent upon us to take note of those passages which press upon us the necessity of continuance, for they constitute another of those safeguards which God has placed around the doctrine of the security of His saints. On a certain occasion "many believed on Him" (John 8:30), but so far from Christ assuring them that Heaven was now their settled portion, we are told "Then said Jesus to those Jews which believed on Him, IF ye continue in MY word then are ye My disciples indeed" (v. 31). Unless we abide in subjection to Christ, unless we walk in obedience to Him unto the end of our earthly course, we are but disciples in name and semblance.

We read of certain men who "came to Antioch and spoke unto the Grecians there, preaching the Lord Jesus." The power of God accompanied them and richly blessed their efforts, for "The hand of the Lord was with them and a great multitude believed and turned unto the Lord" (Acts 11:20,21). Tidings of this reached the church at Jerusalem, and mark well their response: they sent Barnabas to them, "who, when he came and had seen the grace of God, was glad, and exhorted them all that with purpose of heart they would cleave unto the Lord" (v. 22). Barnabas was not one of those fatalistic hyper-Calvinists who argued that since God has begun a good work in them all would be well, that the Holy Spirit will care for, instruct, and guard them, whether or no they be furnished with ministerial nurses and teachers. Instead, he recognized and discharged his own Christian responsibility, dealt with them as accountable agents, addressed to them suitable exhortations, pressed upon them the indispensable duty of their cleaving to the Lord. Alas that there are so few like Barnabas today.

At a later date we find that Barnabas returned to Antioch accompanied by Paul, and while there they were engaged in "confirming the souls of the disciples, exhorting them to continue in the faith" and warning them that "we must through much tribulation enter into the kingdom of God" (Acts 14:22). How far were they from believing in a mechanical salvation, reasoning that if these people had been genuinely converted they would necessarily "continue in the faith!" Writing to the Corinthians, the apostle reminded them of the Gospel he had preached unto them and which they had received, yet failing not to add "By which also ye are saved IF ye hold fast that which I preached unto you, unless ye have believed in vain" (1 Cor. 15:2). In like manner he reminded the Colossians that they were reconciled to God and would be preserved unblameable and unreproveable "IF ye continue in the faith, grounded and settled, and be not moved away from the hope of the Gospel" (1:23). There are those who dare to say there is no "if" about it, but such people are taking direct issue with Holy Writ.

Even when writing to a minister of the Gospel, his own "son in the faith," Paul hesitated not to exhort him, "Take heed unto thyself and unto the doctrine; continue in them," adding "for in doing this thou shalt both save thyself (from apostasy) and them that hear thee" (1 Tim. 4:6). To the Hebrews he said "But Christ as a Son over His own house, whose house are we IF we hold fast the confidence and the rejoicing of the hope firm unto the end" (3:6). And again, "For we are made partakers of Christ IF we hold the beginning of our confidence steadfast unto the end" (3:15). How dishonestly has the Word of God been handled by many! Such passages as these are never heard from many pulpits from one year's end to another. It is much to be feared that many pastors of "Calvinistic" churches are afraid to quote such verses lest their people should charge them with Arminianism. Such will yet have to face the Divine indictment "Ye have not kept My ways, but have been partial in the Law" or Word (Mal. 2:9).

We find precisely the same thing in the writings of another apostle. James though addressing those whom he terms "my beloved brethren," calls upon his readers "But be ye doers of the Word, and not hearers only, deceiving your own selves. For if anyone be a hearer of the Word and not a doer, he is like unto a man beholding his natural face in a glass: for he beholdeth himself, and goeth his way, and straightway forgetteth what manner of man he was (that is, nothing but a superficial and fleeting effect is produced upon him). But whoso looketh into the perfect Law of liberty, and continueth therein, he being not a forgetful hearer, but a doer of the work, this man shall be blessed in his deed" (1:22-25). The word for 'beholdeth" is a metaphor taken from those who not only glance at a thing but bend their bodies towards it that they may carefully scrutinize it —used in Luke 24:12, and 1 Peter 1:12; denoting earnestness of desire, and diligent enquiry. To "continue therein" signifies a persevering study of the Truth, and abiding in the belief of and obedience to the same, thereby evidencing our love for it. Many have a brief taste for it, but their appetite is quickly quenched again by the things of this world.

It is perfectly true, blessedly true, that there is no "if," no uncertainty, from the Divine side in connection with the Christian's reaching Heaven: everyone who has been justified by God shall without fail be glorified. Those who have been Divinely quickened will most assuredly continue in the faith and persevere in holiness unto the end of their earthly course. This is clear from 1 John 2:19, where the apostle alludes to some in his day who had apostatized: "They went out from us, but they were not of us"—they belonged not to the family of God, though for a while they had fraternized with some of its members. "For" adds the apostle, "if they had been of us (had they really been one in a personal experience of the regenerating power of the Spirit) they would have continued with us" —nothing could have induced them to heed the siren voice of their seducers. "But they went Out from us that they might be made manifest that they were not all of us"—but merely temporary professors, stony-ground hearers, nominal Christians, members of a totally different family. Previously they had every appearance of being the genuine article, but by their defection they were exposed as counterfeits. No, there is no "if" from the Divine side.

Nevertheless, there is an "if" from the human side of things, from the standpoint of our responsibility, in connection with my making sure that I am one of those whom God has promised to preserve unto His heavenly kingdom. Continuance in the faith in the path of obedience, in denying self and following Christ, is not simply desirable but indispensable. No matter how excellent a beginning I have made, if I do not continue to press forward I shall be lost. Yes, lost, and not merely miss some particular crown or millennial honors as the deluded dispensationalists teach. It is persevere or perish: it is final perseverance or perish eternally—there is no other alternative. Romans 11:22 makes that unmistakably clear; "Behold therefore the goodness and severity of God: on them that fell (the unbelieving Jews) severity: but toward thee (saved Gentiles, v. 11) goodness, IF thou continue in His goodness; otherwise thou also shalt be cut off" To continue in God's goodness is the opposite of returning to our badness. The evidence that we are the recipients of God's goodness is that we continue in the faith and obedience of the Gospel. The end cannot be reached apart from the appointed means.

But I cannot see the consistency between what has been set forth in the last two paragraphs, some will exclaim. What of it: who are you? who am I? Merely short-sighted creatures of yesterday, upon whom God has written "folly and vanity." Shall human ignorance set itself against Divine wisdom! Does any reader dare call into question the practice of Christ and His apostles: they pressed the "if" and insisted upon the needs-be for this "continuing"; and those ministers who fail to do so—no matter what their standing or reputation—are no servants of God. Can you see the consistency between the apostle affirming so positively of those who have received the Holy Spirit from Christ "ye shall abide ("continue" - the same Greek word as in all the above passages) in Him," and then in the very next breath exhorting them "And now, little children, abide ("continue") in Him" (1 John 2:27,28)—if you cannot it must be because of theological blinders. Can you see the consistency of David asserting so confidently "The Lord will perfect that which concerneth me: Thy mercy 0 Lord, endureth forever" and then immediately after praying, "forsake not the works of Thine own hands" (Ps. 138:8)—if you cannot then this writer places a big question-mark against your religious profession.

5. By insisting that there are dangers to guard against. Here again there will be those who object against the use of this term is such a connection. What sort of dangers, they will ask: dangers of the Christian's severing his fellowship with God, losing his peace, spoiling his usefulness, rendering himself unfruitful?—granted, but not of missing Heaven itself. They will point Out that safety and danger are opposites and that one who is secure in Christ cannot be in any peril of perishing. However plausible, logical, and apparently Christ-honoring that may sound, we would ask, Is that how Scripture represents the case? Do the Epistles picture the saints as being in no danger of apostasy? Or, to state it less baldly: are there no sins warned against, no evils denounced, no paths of unrighteousness described, which if persisted in do not certainly terminate in destruction? And is there no responsibility resting on me in connection therewith? Apostasy is not reached at a single bound, but is the final culmination of an evil process, and it is against those things which have a tendency unto apostasy against which the saints are repeatedly and most solemnly warned.

One who is now experiencing good health is in no immediate danger of dying from tuberculosis, nevertheless if he recklessly exposes himself to the wet and cold, if he refrains from taking sufficient nourishing food which supplies strength to resist disease, or if he incurs a heavy cough on his chest and makes no effort to break it up, he is most likely to fall a victim to consumption. So, while the Christian remains spiritually healthy he is in no danger of apostatizing, but if he starts to keep company with the wicked and recklessly exposes himself to temptation, if he fails to use the means of grace, if he experiences a sad fall, and repents not of it and returns to his first works, he is deliberately heading for disaster. The seed of eternal death is still in the Christian: that seed is sin, and it is only as Divine grace is diligently and constantly sought, for the thwarting of its inclinations and suppressing of its activities, that it is hindered from developing to a fatal end. A small leak which is neglected will sink a ship just as effectually as the most boisterous sea. And as Spurgeon said on Psalm 19:13, "Secret sin is a steppingstone to presumptuous sin, and that is the vestibule of 'the sin which is unto death' " (Treasury of David).

Did no dangers menace Israel after Jehovah brought them Out of Egypt with a high hand and by His mighty arm conducted them safely through the Red Sea? Did all who entered upon the journey to Canaan actually arrive at the promised land? Perhaps someone replies, They were under the old covenant and therefore supply no analogy to the case of Christians today. What says the Word? This, they "were all baptized unto Moses in the cloud and in the sea, and did all eat the same spiritual meat, and did all drink the same spiritual drink, for they drank of that spiritual Rock that followed them, and that Rock was Christ." What analogy could be closer than that? Yet the passage goes on to say, "But with many of them God was not well pleased: for they were overthrown in the wilderness" (1 Cor. 10:2-5). And what is the use which the apostle makes of this solemn history? Does he say that it has no application unto us? The very reverse: "Now these things were our examples, to the intent that we should not lust after evil things as they also lusted. . .neither let us tempt Christ, as some of them also tempted and were destroyed of serpents" (vv. 6-9). Here is a most deadly danger for us to guard against.

Nor did the apostle leave it at that. He was still more definite, saying "Neither murmur ye as some of them also murmured, and were destroyed of the destroyer. Now all these things happened unto them for examples, and they are written for our admonition upon whom the ends of the world are come," making this specific application unto Christians, "Wherefore let him that thinketh he standeth take heed lest he fall" (vv. 10-12). Paul was no fatalist but one who ever enforced moral responsibility. He inculcated no mechanical salvation, but one which must be worked Out "with fear and trembling." Chas. Hodge of Princeton was a very strong Calvinist, yet on 1 Corinthians 10:12 he failed not to say: "There is perpetual danger of falling. No degree of progress we have already made, no amount of privileges which we may have enjoyed, can justify the want of caution. 'Let him that thinketh he standeth,' that is, who thinketh himself secure. . .neither the members of the church nor the elect can be saved unless they persevere in holiness, and they cannot persevere in holiness without continual watchfulness and effort," i.e., against the dangers menacing them.

The above is not the only instance when the apostle made use of the case of those Israelites who perished on their way to Canaan to warn N.T. saints of their danger. After affirming that God was grieved with that generation, saying "They do alway err in their heart and they have not known (loved) My ways, so I sware in My wrath, They shall not enter into My rest," Paul added, "Take heed, brethren, lest there be in any of you an evil heart of unbelief in departing from the living God. But exhort one another daily, while it is called Today, lest any of you be hardened through the deceitfulness of sin" (Heb. 3:12, 13). We are not here warned against an imaginary peril but a real one. "Take heed" signifies watch against carelessness and sloth, be on the alert as a soldier who knows the enemy is near, lest you fall an easy prey. Those here exhorted are specifically addressed as "brethren" to intimate there are times when the best of saints need to be cautioned against the worst of evils. An "evil heart of unbelief" is a heart which dislikes the strictness of obedience and universality of holiness which God requires of us.

After referring again to those "whose carcasses fell in the wilderness" to whom God swore "they shall not enter into My rest, because of their unbelief" or "disobedience" (3:18, 19), the apostle said "Let us therefore fear lest a promise being left us of entering into His rest, any of you should seem to come short of it" (Heb. 4:1). "Fear" is as truly a Christian grace as is faith, peace or joy. The Christian is to fear temptations, the dangers which menace him, the sin which indwells him, the warnings pointed by others who have made shipwreck of the faith and the severity of God in His dealings with such. He is to fear the threatenings of God against sin and those who indulge themselves in it. It was because Noah was "moved with fear" at the warning he had received from God that he took precautions against the impending flood (Heb. 11:7). God has plainly announced the awful doom of all who continue in allowed sin, and fear of that doom will inspire caution and circumspection, and will preserve from carnal security and presumption. And therefore are we counseled "passing the time of your sojourn here in fear" (1 Pet. 1:17)—not only in exceptional seasons, but the whole of our time here.

We can barely glance at a few more of the solemn cautions addressed not merely to formal professors but to those who are recognized as genuine saints. "Be sober, be vigilant, because your adversary the Devil, as a roaring lion, walketh about seeking whom he may devour. Whom resist steadfast in the faith" (1 Pet. 5:8, 9). Obviously such a warning would be meaningless if the Christian were not threatened with a most deadly danger. "Ye therefore, beloved, seeing ye know these things before, beware lest ye also, being led away with the error of the wicked, fall from your own steadfastness" (2 Pet. 3:17). This warning looks back to the false prophets of (2:1, 2) and what is said of them in vv. 18-22. The "error of the wicked" here cautioned against includes both doctrinal and practical, especially the latter—forsaking of the "narrow way," the highway of holiness which alone leads to Heaven. "Hold that fast which thou hast, that no man take thy crown" (Rev. 3:11)—cling tenaciously to the Truth you have received, the faith which has been planted in your heart, to the measure of grace given you.

But how do you reconcile the Christian's danger with his safety? There is nothing to reconcile, for there is no antagonism. It is enemies and not friends who need reconciling, and warnings are the Christian's friend, one of the safeguards which God has placed around the truth of the security of His people, preventing them from wresting it to their destruction. By revealing the certain consequences of total apostasy Christians are thereby cautioned and kept from the same: a holy fear moves their hearts and so becomes the means of preventing the very evil they denounce. A lighthouse is to warn against recklessness as mariners near the coast, so that they will steer away from the fatal rocks. A fence before a precipice is not superfluous, but is designed to call to a halt those journeying in that direction. When the driver of a train sees the signals change to red he shuts off steam, thereby preserving the passengers under his care. The danger signals of Scripture to which we have called attention are heeded by the regenerate and therefore are among the very means appointed by God for the preservation of His people, for it is only by attending to the same they are kept from destroying themselves.

In the foregoing volume we devoted four sections to a setting forth of the principal springs from which the final perseverance of the saints (in their cleaving unto the Lord, their love of the Truth, and their treading the path of obedience) does issue, or the grounds on which their eternal security rests.

In this book we devoted a chapter to a setting forth of the principal springs from which the final perseverance of the saints (in their cleaving unto the Lord, their love of the Truth, and their treading the path of obedience) does issue, or the grounds on which their eternal security rests. It is therefore fitting, if the balance of truth is to be duly observed, that we should give space unto a presentation of the safeguards by which God has hedged about this doctrine, thereby forbidding empty professors and presumptuous Antinomians from trespassing upon this sacred ground. In this chapter we have already dwelt upon five of these safeguards and we now proceed to point out others. In such a day as this it is the more necessary to enter into detail upon the present branch of our subject that the mouths of certain enemies of the Truth may be closed, that formalists may be shown they have no part or lot in the matter, that hyper-Calvinists may be instructed in the way of the Lord more perfectly, and His own people stirred out of their lethargy.

6. By insisting on the necessity for using the means of grace. There are some who assert that if God has regenerated a soul he is infallibly certain of reaching Heaven whether or not he uses the means appointed, yea that no matter to what extent he fails in the performance of duty or how carnally he lives, he cannot perish. Now we have no hesitation in saying that such an assertion is a grievous perversion of the Truth, and in view of Satan's words to Christ "If Thou be the Son of God cast Thyself down (from a pinnacle of the temple),for it is written, He shall give His angels charge over Thee, and in their hands they shall bear Thee up" (Matt. 4:6), there is no room for doubt as to who is the author of such a lie. It is a grievous perversion because a tearing asunder of what God Himself has joined together. The same One who has decreed the end has also ordained the means necessary unto that end. He has promised certain things unto His people, but He requires to be inquired of concerning them; and if they have not, it is because they ask not.

Even among those who would turn away with abhorrence from the extreme form of Antinomianism mentioned above, there are those who regard the use of means quite indifferently in this connection, arguing that whatever be required in order to preserve from apostasy the Lord Himself will attend unto, that He will so work in His people both to will and to do of His good pleasure that it is quite unnecessary for ministers of the Gospel to be constantly addressing exhortations unto them and urging to the performance of duty. But such a conclusion is thoroughly defective and erroneous, for it quite loses sight of the fact that God deals with His people throughout as moral agents, enforcing their responsibility. Whether or not we can see the consistency between the Divine fore-ordination and the discharge of human accountability, between the Divine decree and the imperativeness of our making use of the means of grace, is entirely beside the point. Christ exhorted and admonished His apostles, and they in turn the churches; and that is sufficient. It is vain to pit our puny objections against their regular practice.

Just as God has ordained material means for the accomplishment of His pleasure in the material realm, so He has appointed that rational agents shall use spiritual means for the fulfilling of His will in connection with spiritual things. He could make the fields fertile and the trees fruitful without the instrumentality of rain and sunshine, but it has pleased Him to employ secondary causes and subordinate agents in the production of our food. In like manner He could cause His people to grow in grace, make them fruitful unto every good work, and preserve them from everything injurious to their welfare, without requiring any industry and diligence on their part; but it has not so pleased Him to dispense with their concurrence. Accordingly we find Him bidding them "Work out your own salvation with fear and trembling" (Phil. 2:12), "Labor therefore to enter into that rest, lest any man fall after the same example of unbelief" (Heb. 4:11). Promises and precepts, exhortations and threatenings, suitable to moral agents are given to them, calling for the employment of those faculties and the exercise of those graces which He has bestowed upon them.

It is a serious mistake to suppose that there is any conflict between one class of passages which contain God's promises of sufficient grace unto His people, and another class in which He requires of them the performance of their duty. In his exposition of Hebrews 3:14 John Owen pointed out that the force of the Greek rendered "if we hold the beginning of our confidence firm unto the end" denotes "our utmost endeavor to hold it fast and to keep it firm and steadfast"; adding "Shaken it will be, opposed it will be, kept it will not be, without our utmost diligence and endeavor. It is true our persistency in Christ does not, as to the issue and event, depend absolutely on our own diligence. The unalterableness of our union with Christ, on the account of the faithfulness of the covenant, is that which does and shall eventually secure it. But yet our own diligent endeavor is such an indispensable means for that end that without it, it will not be brought about." Our diligent endeavor is necessitated by the precept, which God commands us to make use of, and by the order He has established in the relations of one spiritual thing to another.

The older writers were wont to illustrate the consistency between God's purpose and our performance of duty by an appeal to Acts 27. The ship which carried the apostle and other prisoners encountered a fearful gale and it continued so long and with such severity that the inspired narrative declares "all hope that we should be saved was then taken away" (v. 20). A Divine messenger then assured the apostle, "Fear not Paul, thou must be brought before Caesar; and lo God hath given thee all (the lives of) them that sail with thee," and so sure was the apostle that this promise would be fulfilled, he said unto the ship's company "Be of good cheer, for there shall be no loss of life among you, but of the ship, for I believe that it shall be even as it was told me" (vv. 21-25). Yet next day, when the sailors feared they would be smashed upon the rocks and started to flee out of the ship, Paul said to the centurion "except these abide in the ship, ye cannot be saved" (v. 31)!

Now there is a nice problem which we would submit to the more extreme Calvinists: how can the positive promise "there shall be no loss of life" (v. 22) and the contingent "except these abide in the ship ye cannot be saved" (v. 31) stand together? How are you going to reconcile them according to your principles? But in reality there is no difficulty: God made no absolute promise that He would preserve those in the ship regardless of their use of appropriate means. They were not irrational creatures He would safeguard, but moral agents who must discharge their own responsibility, and neither be inert nor act presumptuously. Accordingly we find Paul bidding his companions "take meat," saying "This is for your health" (v. 34), and later the ship was lightened of its cargo (v. 38) and its main-sail hoisted (v. 40), which further conduced to their safety. The certainty of God's promise was not suspended upon their remaining in the ship, but it was a making known of the means whereby God would affect their security.

Reverting to Owen's exposition of Hebrews 3:14, he said: "Our persistency in our sub-sistence in Christ is the emergence and effect of our acting grace unto that purpose. Diligence and endeavors in this matter are like Paul's mariners when he was ship-wrecked at Melita. The preservation of their lives depended absolutely on the faithful-ness and power of God, yet when the mariners began to fly out of the ship Paul tells the centurion that unless his men stayed therein they could not be saved. But why need he think of the shipmen when God took upon Himself the preservation of them all? He knew full well that He would preserve them; but yet that He would do so in and by the use of means. If we are in Christ God has given us the lives of our souls, and hath taken upon Himself, in His covenant, the preservation of them. But yet we may say, with ref-erence unto the means that He hath appointed, when storms and trials arise, unless we use our own diligent endeavors we cannot be saved." Alas that some who profess to so greatly admire this Puritan and endorse his teaching have wandered so far from the course which he followed.

If it be asked, Did the purpose of God that Paul and his companions should all reach land safely depend upon the uncertain will and actions of men? The answer is, No, as a cause from which the purpose of God received its strength and support. But yes, as a means, appointed by Him, to secure the end He had ordained, for God has decreed the subordinate agencies by which the end shall be accomplished as truly as He has de-creed the end itself. In His Word God has revealed a conjunction of means and ends, and there is a necessity lying upon men to use the means and not to expect the end without them. It is at our peril that we tear asunder what God has joined together and disrupt the order He has appointed. The same God who bids us believe His promises, forbids us to tempt His providences (Matt. 4:7). Even though the means may appear to us to have no adequate connection with the end, seeing God has enjoined them, we must use the same. Naaman must wash in the Jordan if he would be cleansed of his leprosy (2 Kings 4:10) and Hezekiah must take a lump of figs and lay it on his boil if he is to be recovered (2 Kings 20:4-7).

They are greatly mistaken who suppose that since the preservation of believers is guar-anteed in the covenant of grace that this renders all means and motives, exhortations and threatenings, useless and senseless. Not so. The doctrine of the everlasting security of the saint does not mean that God will preserve him whether or not he perseveres, but rather that He has promised to give him all needed grace for him to continue in the path of holiness. This supposes that believers will be under such advantages and have suit-able aids used with them in order to this, and that they shall have motives constantly set before them which induce and persuade unto obedience and personal piety and to guard them against the contrary. Hence the propriety and usefulness of the ordinances of the Gospel, the instructions and precepts, the promises and incentives which are fur-nished us to perseverance, without which the purpose of God that we should persevere could not be effected in a way suited to our moral nature.

Christians are indeed "kept by the power of God" (1 Pet. 1:5), yet it needs to be pointed out that they are not preserved mechanically, as a child is kept in the nursery from falling into the fire by a tall metal fender or guard, or as the unwilling horse is held in by bit and bridle; but spiritually so by the workings of Divine grace in them and by means of motives and inducements from without which call forth that grace into exercise and action. We quite miss the force of that declaration unless we complete the verse: "Who are kept by the power of God through faith, unto salvation ready to be revealed in the last time." It is not "for" or "because of faith" but "through faith" yet not without it, for faith is the hand which, from a sense of utter insufficiency and helplessness, clings to God and grasps His strength—not always firmly, but often feebly; not always consciously, but instinctively. Though the saint be "kept by the power of God" yet he himself has to fight every step of the way. If we read of "this grace wherein ye stand" (Rom. 5:2), we are also told "for by faith ye stand" (2 Cor. 1:24).

Viewing the event from the standpoint of the Divine decree it was not possible that Herod should slay Christ in His infancy, nevertheless God commanded Joseph to use means to prevent it, by fleeing into Egypt. In like manner, from the standpoint of God's eternal purpose it is not possible that any saint should perish, yet He has placed upon him the necessity of using means to prevent apostasy and everything which has a tendency thereto. True, he must not trust in the means to the exclusion of God, for those means are only efficacious by His appointment and blessing; on the other hand, it is presumption and not faith which talks of trusting God while the means are despised or ignored. Nor have we said anything in this section which warrants the inference that Heaven is a wage that we earn by our own industry and fidelity, rather do the means appointed by God mark out the course we must take if we would reach the desired Goal. It is "through faith and patience" we "inherit the promises" (Heb. 6:12): our glorification will not be bestowed in return for them, yet there can be no glorification to those devoid of these graces.

The sun shines into our rooms through their windows: those windows contribute nothing whatever to our comfort and enjoyment of the sun, yet are they necessary as means for its beams to enter. The means and mediums which God has designed for the accomplishment of His ends concerning us are not such as to be "conditions" on which those ends are suspended in uncertainty as to their issue, but are the sure links by which He has connected the one with the other. Exhortations and warnings are not so much the means whereby God's promises are accomplished, as the means by which the things promised are wrought. God has promised His people sufficient grace to enable and cause them to make such a use of the means that they will be preserved from fatal sins or apostasy, and the exhortations, consolations, admonitions of Scripture are designed for the stirring up into exercise of that grace. The certainty of the end is assured not by the nature or sufficiency of the means in themselves considered, but because of God's ordination in connection therewith.

God has assured His people that His grace shall be all-sufficient and that His strength shall be made perfect in their weakness, but nowhere has He promised a continuance of His love and favor unto dogs returning to their vomit or to sows which are content to wallow in the mire. If our thoughts on this subject be formed entirely by the teaching of God's Word (and not partly by carnal reason), then we shall expect perseverance only in that way wherein God has promised it, and that is by availing ourselves of the helps and advantages He has provided, especially the study of and meditation upon His Word and the hearing or reading the messages of His servants. Though God has promised grace unto His people, yet He requires them to—sincerely, believingly, earnestly—seek it: "Let us therefore come boldly unto the Throne of Grace, that we may obtain mercy and find grace to help in time of need" (Heb. 4:16). And that grace we are constantly in need of as long as we are left here:—"Day by day the manna fell, O to learn that lesson well."

Much confusion has resulted on this and other points through failure to distinguish between impetration and application, or what Christ purchased for His people and God's actually making over the same unto them according to the order of things He has established. As faith is indispensable before justification so is perseverance before glorification, and that necessarily involves the use of means. True, our faith adds nothing whatever to the merits of Christ in order to our justification, yet until we believe, we are under the curse of the Law; nor does our perseverance entitle us to glorification, yet only those who do persevere unto the end will be glorified. Now as God requires obedience from all the parts and faculties of our souls, so in His Word He has provided motives to the obedience required, motives suited unto "all that is within us" — that love, fear, hope, etc. may be called into action. Of ourselves we are not sufficient to make a good use of the means, and therefore we beg God to work in us that which He requireth: Colossians 1:29.

God has promised to repair the spiritual decays of His people and to heal their backslidings freely, yet He will do so in such a way as wherein He may communicate His grace righteously to the praise of His glory. Therefore are duties, especially that of confession of sins to God, prescribed to us in order thereto. "He that covereth his sins shall not prosper, but whoso confesseth and forsaketh them shall have mercy" (Prov. 28:13). "I will heal their backsliding" (Hos. 14:4): there is the promise and the end. But first "Take with you words and turn to the Lord: say unto Him, Take away all iniquity, and receive us graciously" (v. 2): there is the duty and the means unto that end. Although repentance and confession be not the procuring cause of God's grace and love, from whence alone our healing or recovery proceeds, yet are they required in the appointed method of God's dispensing His grace.

It must be insisted upon that the Christian's concurrence with the Divine will by no means warrants the horrible conclusion that he is entitled to divide the honors with God. How could this possibly be, seeing that if he does what he is bidden he remains but an "unprofitable servant?" How could it be, when to whatever extent he does improve the means it is only the power of Divine grace which so enabled him? How could it be, when he is most sensible in himself that far more of failure than success attends his efforts? No, when the redeemed have safely crossed the Jordan and are safely landed on the shores of the heavenly Canaan they will exclaim with one accord "Not unto us, O Lord, not unto us, but unto Thy name give glory, for Thy mercy, for Thy Truth's sake" (Ps. 115:1).

To sum up. The doctrine of the perseverance of the saints, in the pursuit and practice of holiness as it is set forth in God's Word, provides no shelter for either laziness or licentiousness: it supplies no encouragement for us to take our regeneration and glorification for granted, but bids us "give diligence to make your calling and election sure" (2 Pet. 1:10). Exhortations and threatenings are not made unto us as those already assured of final perseverance, but as those who are called to the use of means for the establishment of our souls in the ways of obedience, being annexed to those ways of grace and peace which God calls His saints unto. Perseverance consists in a continual exercise of spiritual graces in the saints, and exhortations are the Divinely appointed means for stirring those graces into action and for a further increase of them. Therefore those preachers who do not press upon the Lord's people the discharge of their duties and are remiss in warning and admonishing them, fail grievously at one of the most vital points in the charge committed to them.

7. By enforcing the threatenings of Scripture. The One with whom we have to do is ineffably holy and therefore does He hate sin wherever it is found. He will not ignore sin in His own children when it is unjudged and unconfessed any more than He will in those who are the children of the Devil. The pope and his underlings may traffic in their vile "indulgences" and "special dispensations," but the Lord God never lowers His standard, and even those in Christ are not exempted from bitter consequences if they pursue a course of folly. But God is also merciful and faithful, and therefore He threatens before He punishes and warns before He smites. In His Word He has described those ways which lead to disaster and destruction, that we may shun them; yet those who deliberately follow them may know for certain that they shall receive the due reward of their defiance. It is therefore incumbent upon the minister of the Gospel to press the Divine threatenings, as it is the part of wisdom for his hearers or readers to take the same to heart.

"If ye forgive not men their trespasses, neither will your Father forgive your trespasses" (Matt. 6:15). "And that servant which knew his Lord's will and prepared not himself, neither did according to His will, shall be beaten with many stripes" (Luke 12:47—spoken to Peter: 5:41). "Behold, thou art made whole: sin no more, lest a worse thing come unto thee" (John 5:14). "If a man abide not in Me, he is cast forth as a branch and is withered, and men gather them and cast into the fire and they are burned" (John 15:6—spoken to the eleven apostles). "For if ye live after the flesh, ye shall die; but if ye through the Spirit do mortify the deeds of the body, ye shall live" (Rom. 8:13). "Be not deceived, God is not mocked: for whatsoever a man soweth, that shall he also reap. For he that soweth to his flesh, shall of the flesh reap corruption; but he that soweth to the spirit, shall of the spirit reap life everlasting" (Gal. 6:7, 8). Have such passages as these been given due place in the preachings and writings of the orthodox during the past fifty years? No indeed: why?

There are three particular passages which claim a fuller notice from us in this connection, passages which are among the most solemn and frightful to be found in all the Word of God, yet which are nevertheless addressed immediately unto the people of God. Before citing the same we would preface our remarks upon them with this general observation: they have not received the attention they ought in the practical ministrations of God's servants. The minister of the Gospel has only discharged half his duty when he clears these verses of the false glosses which his opponents have placed upon them. It is quite true that Arminians have made an altogether unwarrantable and wrong use of them, but probably God suffered His enemies to thereby bring them into prominent notice because His friends ignored them. The Christian teacher must not only show there is no conflict between these passages and such verses as John 10:28 and Phil. 1:6, but he must also bring out their positive meaning and the solemn bearing which they have upon Christians themselves.

"For it is impossible for those who were once enlightened, and have tasted of the heavenly gift, and were made partakers of the Holy Spirit, and have tasted the good Word of God, and the powers of the world to come, if they shall fall away—to renew them again unto repentance; seeing they crucify to themselves the Son of God afresh, and put Him to an open shame. For the earth which drinketh in the rain that cometh oft upon it, and bringeth forth herbs, meet for them by whom it is dressed, receiveth blessing from God. But that which beareth thorns and briers is rejected, and is nigh unto cursing; whose end is to be burned" (Heb. 6:4-8). Those words are addressed to "holy brethren, partakers of the heavenly calling" (3:1), and their connection is as follows. In 5:11-14 the apostle had reproved the Hebrews for being slow in their apprehension of the Truth and in walking suitably thereto, and after the exhortation of 6:1-3 he warns them of the awful danger of continuing in a slothful state—"For it is impossible."

But, it may be objected. Surely it is not the intention of our Heavenly Father to terrorize His own dear children. No, certainly not; yet He would have them suitably affected thereby. Though such threatenings are not designed to work in Christians a fear of damnation, yet they should beget in them a holy care and diligence of avoiding the evils denounced. There is no more incongruity between a Christian's being comforted by the Divine promises and alarmed by the Divine threatenings, than there is between his living a life of joyful confidence in God and also one of humble dependence upon Him. We must distinguish between things that differ: there is a fear of caution as well as of distrust, a fear that produces carefulness and watchfulness as well as one which fills with anxiety. There is a vast difference between a thing that is meant to weaken the security of the flesh, and the confidence that faith has in Christ. Assurance of perseverance is quite consistent with and ought ever to be accompanied by "fear and trembling" (Phil. 2:12, 13).

In his opening remarks on Hebrews 6:4-6 John Owen said, It "is a needful and wholesome commination (denunciation) duly to be considered by all professors of the Gospel." And in the course of his masterly exposition pointed out, "For not to proceed in the way of the Gospel and obedience thereto is an untoward entrance into a total relinquishment of the one and the other. That they therefore may be acquainted with the danger hereof, and be stirred up to avoid that danger, the apostle gives them an account of those who, after a profession of the Gospel, beginning at a non-proficiency under it, do end in apostasy from it. And we may see that the severest comminations are not only useful in the preaching of the Gospel, but exceeding necessary towards persons that are observed to be slothful in their profession." Scripture nowhere teaches that the saint is so secure that he needs not to be wary of himself, nor unmindful of the defection of those who for a time seemed to run well.

Another of the Puritans said on this passage, "Certainly all of us should stand in fear of this heavy judgment of being given up to perish by our apostasy, to an obstinate heart, never to reconcile ourselves by repentance, even the children of God; for he proposeth it to them. . .The apostle saith, It is impossible they should be saved, because it is impossible they should repent. This is a fearful state, and yet, as fearful as it is, it is not unusual: it is a thing we see often in some that have made a savory profession of the name of God, and afterwards have been blasted. 0, then, you that have begun and have had a taste of the ways of God, and to walk closely with Him, you should lay this to heart! Therefore this is propounded to believers, that they should keep at a very great distance from such a judgment, lest we grow to such an impenitent state as to be given up to a reprobate mind and vile affections" (Thos. Manton). The best preventative is a conscience kept tender of sin, which mourns over and confesses to God our transgressions, and seeks grace to mortify our lusts.

"For if we sin willfully after that we have received the knowledge of the Truth, there remaineth no more sacrifice for sins; but a certain fearful looking for of judgment and fiery indignation, which shall devour the adversaries. He that despised Moses' law died without mercy under two or three witnesses; of how much sorer punishment, suppose ye, shall he be thought worthy who bath trodden underfoot the Son of God, and bath counted the blood of the covenant wherewith He was sanctified an unholy thing, and bath done despite unto the Spirit of grace? For we know Him that bath said, Vengeance belongeth unto Me, I will recompense, saith the Lord. And again, The Lord shall judge His people. It is a fearful thing to fall in to the hands of the living God" (Heb. 10:26-31). It is outside our present design to give an exposition of these verses (which we did when going through that Epistle), as we shall not now expose the Arminian errors thereon (which we hope to very shortly); rather do we now direct attention unto them as another example of the fearful threatenings which are directly addressed to Christians, and which it is madness and not wisdom to scoff at.

The scope of the above passage is easily grasped: Hebrews 10:23 gives an exhortation, verses 24, 25 announce the means of continuing in that profession, while verses 26-31 declare what will befall those who relinquish the Truth. In his comments John Owen points out, "The apostle puts himself among them ("if we sin" etc.), as is his manner in comminations: both to show that there is no respect of persons in this matter, but that those who had equally sinned shall be equally punished; and to take off all appearances of severity towards them, seeing he speaks nothing of this nature but on such suppositions as wherein if he were himself concerned he pronounceth it against himself also. The word 'willingly' signifies, of choice—without surprise, compulsion or fear . . . If a voluntary relinquishment of the profession of the Gospel and the duties of it be the highest sin, and be attended with the height of wrath and punishment, we ought earnestly to watch against everything that inclineth or disposeth us thereto."

John Owen concluded his remarks on these verses by saying, "This therefore is a passage of Holy Writ which is much to be considered, especially in these days wherein we live, wherein men are apt to grow cold and careless in this profession, and to decline gradually from what they had attained unto. To be useful in such a season it was first written, and it belongs unto us no less than unto them to whom it was first originally sent. And we live in days wherein the security and contempt of God, the despite of the Lord Christ and His Spirit, are come to the full, so as to justify the truth that we have insisted on." If the pressing of this passage on the attention of all professing Christians was deemed so necessary in the palmy days of the Puritans, how much more so in the dark times in which our lot is cast! How woefully remiss, then, are those preachers who not only fail to devote a whole sermon to these verses, but who never so much as quote them from one years' end to another, except it be to refute the Arminians in such a manner that empty professors are made to believe there is nothing for them to fear.

"For if after they have escaped the pollutions of the world through the knowledge of the Lord and Savior Jesus Christ, they are again entangled therein, and overcome, the latter end is worse with them than the beginning. For it had been better for them not to have known the way of righteousness, than after they have known it, to turn from the holy commandment delivered unto them. But it is happened unto them according to the true proverb, The dog is turned to his own vomit again, and the sow that was washed to her wallowing in the mire" (2 Pet. 2:20-22). At the close of his remarks on this passage Matthew Henry says, "If the Scriptures give such an account of Christianity on the one hand and of sin on the other as we have in these verses, we certainly ought highly to approve of the former and persevere therein, because it is a 'way of righteousness' and a 'holy commandment,' and to loathe and keep at the greatest distance from the latter because it is set forth as offensive and abominable." Far better never to make a profession, than make a fair one and then sully and repudiate it.

"He that being often reproved hardeneth his neck, shall suddenly be cut off, and that without remedy" (Prov. 29:1). The solemn threatenings of Scripture are so many discoveries to the Church in particular and to the world in general of the severity of God against sin and that He adjudges them worthy of eternal destruction who persist therein. If professing Christians turn a deaf ear to exhortations, admonitions and warnings, if they steel their hearts against entreaties and threatenings, and determine to follow a course of self-will and self-pleasing, they place themselves beyond the hope of mercy. It is therefore the imperative duty of the servant of Christ to faithfully warn God's people of the fearful danger of backsliding and of what awaits them if they remain in that state: to definitely point out the connection which God has established between sin and punishment, between apostasy and damnation, so that a holy fear may be instilled to preserve them from making shipwreck of the faith, and to prevent carnal professors from indulging the vain hope of once in grace always in grace.

8. By holding up the rewards. Many preachers have failed to do so, allowing the fear of man to withhold from God's children a portion of their necessary bread. Because certain enemies of the Truth have wrested this subject, they deemed it wisest to be silent thereon. Because Papists have grievously perverted the teaching of Scripture upon "rewards," insidiously bringing in their lie of creature-merits at this point, not a few Protestants have been chary of preaching thereon, lest they be charged with leaning toward Romanism. Rather should this very abuse move them to be the more diligent and

zealous in presenting their right and true meaning and use. Threatenings and rewards: does not the one naturally suggest the other? The former to act as deterrents, the latter as stimulants: deterrents against evil doing, stimulants or incentives unto the discharge of duty. But if the one has been shelved in the pulpit, the other has received scant attention even in orthodox quarters. We can but briefly touch upon the subject here, but hope to devote a separate article to it in the next section.

In Scripture "eternal life" is presented both as a "gift" and as a "reward"—the reward of perseverance. To some it may appear that such terms and concepts are mutually opposed. Yet is not prayer both a privilege and a duty? Is not the natural man startled when he finds that God bids His people to "rejoice with trembling"—what a seeming paradox! The apparent difficulty is removed when it is seen that the "rewards" which God has promised His people are not those of justice but of bounty; that they are not a proportioned remuneration or return for the duties which we perform or the services we have rendered, but the end to which our obedience is suited. Thus the rewards proposed unto us by God are not calculated to work in His people a legal spirit but are designed to support our hearts under the self-denials to which we are called, to cheer us amid the sufferings we encounter for Christ's sake, and to stir us to acts of obedience meet for what is promised. Certainly Moses was inspired by no mercenary spirit when "he had respect unto the recompense of the reward" (Heb. 11:26).

That eternal life and glory is set forth in God's Word as the reward and end of perseverance which await all faithful Christians is clear from Hebrews 10:35, to cite no other passages now: "Cast not away therefore your confidence which hath great recompense of reward." On those words Matt. Henry said, "He exhorts them not to cast away their confidence, that is, their holy courage and boldness, but to hold fast the profession for which they had suffered so much before, and borne those sufferings so well. Second, he encourages them to this by assuring them that the reward of their holy confidence is very great: it carries a present reward in it, in holy peace and joy and much of God's presence and power visited upon them; and it shall have a great recompense of reward hereafter." While the Christian sincerely endeavors to walk obediently and mix faith with God's promises the Spirit comforts and witnesses with his spirit that he is a child of God; but when he becomes careless of duty, and neglects the means of grace, He not only withholds His witness but suffers the threatenings of Scripture to so lay hold of him that Psalm 38:2, 3 becomes his experiences.

9. By insisting on steadfastness. "Let us hold fast the profession of our faith without wavering" (Heb. 10:23). Press forward along the path of holiness, no matter what obstacles and opposition you meet with. Your very safety depends upon it, for if you deny the faith either by words or actions, you are "worse than an infidel" who never professed it. The very fact that we are here bidden to "hold fast" our Christian profession implies that it is no easy task assigned us, that there are difficulties to be overcome which call for the putting forth of our utmost strength and endeavors in the defense and furtherance of it. "Without wavering" means, with unvarying and unflinching constancy. Sin is ever seeking to vanquish the Christian; the world is ever endeavoring to draw him back into its seductive embraces; the Devil, like a roaring lion, is ever waiting to devour him.

Therefore the call to him is "be ye steadfast, immovable, always abounding in the work of the Lord"— the duties He has assigned (1 Cor. 15:58).

The need for pressing such exhortations as the above appears from the solemn warning addressed to those whom the apostle calls "beloved" in 2 Pet. 3:17: "Beware lest ye also being led away with the error of the wicked, fall from your own steadfastness." Upon this Matt. Henry says, "We are in great danger of being seduced and turned away from the Truth. Many who have the Scriptures and read them do not understand what they read, and too many of those who have a right understanding of the sense and meaning of the Word are not established in the belief of the Truth, and all these are liable to fall into error. Few attain to the knowledge and acknowledgement of doctrinal Christianity; and fewer find so as to keep in the way of practical godliness, which is the narrow way which only leadeth unto life. There must be a great deal of self-denial and suspicion of ourselves, and submitting to the authority of Christ Jesus our great Prophet, before we can heartily receive all the truths of the Gospel, and therefore we are in great danger of rejecting the Truth." Ministers of Christ, then, need to insist much upon the imperativeness of steadfastness and constancy.

10. By withholding from backsliders the comfort of the truth of eternal security. After all that has been said under the previous heads there is little need for us to enlarge upon this point. Any preacher who encourages the slothful and the undutiful is doing great harm to souls. To tell those who have deserted the paths of righteousness that because they once believed in Christ all will come out well with them in the end, is to put a premium on their carnality. To assure those who have forsaken the means of grace and gone back again into the world that because they formerly made a credible profession God will recover and restore them, is to say what Scripture nowhere warrants. A griping purgative and not rich and savory viands is what is needed by one whose system is out of order. The Divine threatenings and not the promises need to be pressed upon those who are following the desires and devices of their own hearts. Only by heeding the ten things mentioned in these sections is the precious truth of the eternal security of the saints safeguarded from profanation.

Chapter 9
Its Opposition

It has been shown at length in earlier sections that the concept of a total and final apostasy of a regenerated soul is not according to Truth. To postulate the eternal destruction of one to whom Divine grace has been savingly communicated to the soul is contrary to the whole tenor of the Covenant of redemption, to the attributes of God engaged in it, to the design and work of the Redeemer in it, to the Spirit's mission and His abiding with God's children "forever" (John 14:16). One who is indwelt by the Triune God shall not and cannot so fall from holiness and serve sin as to give himself wholly to its behests (authoritative commands). One who has been delivered from the power of darkness and translated into the kingdom of God's dear Son shall never again become the willing subject of Satan. One who has been made the recipient of a supernatural experience of the Truth shall never be fatally deceived by the Devil's lies. True, his will is mutable, but God's promise is unchangeable; his own strength is feeble, but God's power is invincible, his prayers are weak, but Christ's intercession is prevalent.

Yet in all ages this doctrine of the final perseverance of the saints has been opposed and denied. Satan himself believed in the apostasy of Job and had the effrontery to avow it unto Jehovah (Job 1:8-11). We need not be surprised then to find that the supreme imposture of the religious realm repudiates most vehemently this precious truth and pronounces accursed all who hold it. The merit-mongers of Rome are inveterately opposed to everything which exalts free grace. Moreover, they who so hotly deny unconditional election, particular redemption, and effectual calling, must, in order to be consistent, deny the eternal security of the Christian. Since Papists are such rabid sticklers for the "free will" of fallen man, logically, they must deny the indefectibility of all who are in Christ. If I have by an act of my own volition brought myself into a state of grace, then it clearly follows that I am capable of forsaking the same. If the "free will" of the sinner first inclines him to exercise repentance and faith, then obviously he may relapse into a state of confirmed impenitence and unbelief.

But Rome has by no means stood alone in antagonizing this blessed article of the Father. Others who differ widely from her in many other respects have made common cause with her in this. Considerable sections of "Protestantism," whole denominations which claim to take the Word of God for their sole Rule of faith and practice, have also strenuously and bitterly fought against those who maintained this truth. These are what are known as Arminians, for James Arminius or Van Harmin, a Dutchman of the sixteenth century, was the first man of any prominence in orthodox circles who opposed the theology taught by John Calvin—opposed it covertly and slyly and contrary to the most solemn and particular promise and pledge which he gave to the Classis (church governing bodies) before he was installed as professor of divinity at Leyden in 1602. Since then, for the purpose of theological classification, non-Calvinists and anti-Calvinists have been termed "Arminians." The one man who did more than any other to popularize and spread Arminianism in the English-speaking world was John Wesley.

We shall now make it our business to examine the attacks which Arminians have made upon this truth of the final perseverance of the saints and the leading arguments they employ to prejudice and overturn it. But let us say at the outset, it is not because we entertain any hope of delivering such people from their errors that we are now writing, still less that we are prepared to enter the lists against them. No, it is useless to argue with those whose hearts are set against the Truth: convince a man against his will and he is of the same opinion still. Moreover God's eternal Truth is infinitely too sacred to be made the matter of carnal debate and wrangling. Rather is it our design to help those of God's people who have been harassed by the dogs who yapped at their heels and show that their bark is worse than their bite. We write now with the object of delivering the "babes" from being "corrupted from the simplicity that is in Christ" (2 Cor. 11:3).

1. By misrepresenting and misstating the truth for which we contend. It is a favorite device of Arminians to set up a "man of straw" and because he is incapable of withstanding their assaults, pretend they have overthrown the Calvinistic tenet itself. To caricature a doctrine and then hold up that caricature to ridicule, to falsify a doctrine and then denounce that falsification as a thing of evil, is tantamount to acknowledging that they are unable to overthrow the doctrine as it is held and presented by its friends. Yet this is the very practice of which Arminian dialecticians are guilty. They select a single part of our doctrine and then take it up as though it were the whole. They sever the means from the end and claim we teach that the end will be reached irrespective of the means. They ignore the safeguards by which God has hedged around this part of His Truth, and which His true servants have ever maintained, and then affirm that such a doctrine is injurious, dangerous, inimical to the promotion of practical godliness. In plain language, they seek to terrify the simple by a bogey of their own manufacture.

That we have not brought an unjust and unfair charge against Arminians will appear from the following citation. "The common doctrine that perseverance requireth and commandeth all saints or believers to be fully persuaded, and this with the greatest and most indubitable certainty of faith, that there is an absolute and utter impossibility either of a total or a final defection of their faith: that though they shall fall into ten thousand enormities and most abominable sins and lie wallowing in them like a swine in the mire, yet they should remain all the while in an estate of grace, and that God will by a strong hand of irresistible grace bring them off from their sins by repentance before they die." Those were the words of one of the most influential of English Arminians in the palmy days of the Puritans, issuing from the pen of one, John Goodwin, a nephew of the pious and eminent expositor, Thos. Goodwin. In the light of what we have written in previous sections of this series few of our readers should have much difficulty in perceiving the sophistry of this miserable shift.

No well-instructed scribe of Christ ever set forth the doctrine of the saints perseverance in any such distorted manner and extravagant terms as the above, yet such is a fair sample of the devices employed by Arminians when engaged in assailing this truth: they detach a single element of it and then render repugnant their one-sided misrepresentation of the whole. The perseverance which we contend for, and which the operations of Divine grace effectually provide for and secure, is a perseverance of faith and holiness,—a continuing steadfast in believing and in bringing forth all the fruits of righteousness. Whereas as anyone can see at a glance, the travesty presented in the above quotation is a preservation in spite of and in the midst of perseverance in abominable sins and lie wallowing in them like a swine in the mire (i.e. quite at home in such filth and content therewith), and yet they shall remain all the while in an estate of grace" is a palpable contradiction of terms, for an "estate of grace" is one of subjection and obedience to God.

Again, Goodwin makes out the Calvinist to say in God's name, "You that truly believe in My Son, and have been made partakers of the Holy Spirit, and therefore are fully persuaded and assured from My will and command given unto you in that behalf, yea, according to the infallible Word of Truth you have from Me, that you cannot possibly, no, not by the most horrid sins and abominable practices, that you shall or can commit, fall away either totally or finally from your faith; for in the midst of your foulest actings and courses, there remains a seed in you which is sufficient to make you true believers, and to preserve you from falling away finally, that it is impossible you should die in your sins; you that know and are assured that I will by an irresistible hand work perseverance in you, and consequently that you are out of all danger of condemnation, and that heaven and salvation belong unto you, and are as good as yours already, so that nothing but giving of thanks appertains to you."

The incongruity of such a fiction should at once be apparent. First, all true saints do not have a firm and comfortable assurance of their perseverance: many of them are frequently beset by doubts and fears. Second, it is by means of God's promises and precepts, exhortations and threatenings, that they are stirred up to the use of those things by which perseverance is wrought and assurance is obtained. Third, no rightly-taught saint ever expected his perseverance or the least assurance of it under such a foul supposition as falling into and continuing in horrid sins and abominable practices." Fourth, the promises of eternal security are made to those in whose mind God writes His laws and in whose hearts He places His holy fear, so that they shall not depart from Him: they are made to those who "hear" the voice of the good Shepherd and who "follow" the example He has left them. Fifth, so far from "nothing but giving of thanks" appertaining to them, they are bidden to work out their own salvation with fear and trembling, to run with patience the race set before them, to make their calling and election sure by adding to their graces and bringing forth the fruits of righteousness.

Let us say once more, and it cannot be insisted upon too frequently and emphatically in this degenerate age, that the perseverance of saints which is depicted in Holy Writ is not a simple continuance of Christians on this earth for a number of years after regeneration and faith have been wrought in them, and then their being admitted as a matter of course to Heaven, without any regard to their moral history in the intervening period. No, though that may be how incompetent novices have portrayed it, and how Antinomians have perverted it, yet such a concept is as far removed from the reality as darkness is from light. The perseverance of the saints is a steady pressing forward in the course on which they entered at conversion—an enduring unto the end in the exercise of faith and in the practice of holiness. The perseverance of the saints consists in a continuing to deny self, to mortify the lusts of the flesh, to resist the Devil, to fight the good fight of faith; and though they suffer many falls by the way, and receive numerous wounds from their foes, yet, if "faint," they "hold on their way."

2. By insisting that this doctrine encourages loose living. We have heard numbers of Arminians declare "If I were absolutely sure that Heaven would be my everlasting portion; then I would drop all religion and take my fill of the world," to which we replied, Perhaps you would, but the regenerate feel quite different: they find their delight in One who is infinitely preferable to all that can be found in this perishing world. Yet Arminians never tire of saying that this article of the non-apostasy of the saints is a vicious and dangerous one, affording great encouragement unto those who believe themselves to be Christians to indulge themselves in iniquities, such as Lot, David, Solomon and Peter committed. It is granted that those who commit such sins and die without repentance for them and faith in the blood of the Lamb have no inheritance in the kingdom of God and Christ. It is also a fact that God visited the transgressions of those men with His rod and recovered them from their falls. Nor are such instances recorded in the Word to encourage us in sin, but rather to caution us against and make us distrustful of ourselves.

Such a gross view as is propounded in the above objection loses sight entirely of the nature of regeneration, tacitly denying that the new birth is a miracle of grace, effecting a radical change within, renewing the faculties of the soul, giving an entirely different bent to a person's inclinations. To talk of a child of God falling in love again with sin is tantamount to suggesting that there is no real difference between one who has passed from death unto life, who has had the principle of holiness communicated to him, who is indwelt by the Spirit of God, and those who are unregenerate. That one who has been merely intellectually impressed and emotionally stirred to temporarily reform his outward conduct may indeed return to his former manner of life, is readily conceded; but that one who has experienced a supernatural work of grace within, who has been made "a new creature in Christ Jesus," can or will lose all relish for spiritual things and become satisfied with the husks which the swine feed on, we emphatically deny.

3. By asserting our doctrine deprives God's people of the sharpest bit which He has given for curtailing the flesh in them. It is affirmed by many Arminians that the most effectual means for restraining their evil inclinations, alike in the regenerate and the unregenerate, is the fear of the everlasting burnings, and from this premise they draw the conclusion that when a person is definitely assured he has been once and for all delivered from the wrath to come, the strongest deterrent against carnality and lasciviousness has been taken from him. There would be considerable force in this objection if God had not communicated to His children that which operates in them more mightily and effectually than the dread of punishment, and since He has, then the argument has little point or weight to it. Whatever influence the fear of Hell exerts in curtailing

the lusts of the flesh, certain it is that the righteous are withheld from a life of sin by far more potent considerations. Faith purifieth the heart (Acts 15:9), faith overcometh the world (1 John 5:4), but Scripture nowhere ascribes such virtues to a dread of the Lake of fire. An unruly horse needs to be held in by a bridle, but one that is well broken in is better managed by a gentler hand than a biting bit.

The case of the saint would certainly be a perilous one if there was no stronger restraint upon his lusts than the fear of Hell: how far does such fear restrain the ungodly! As the nature of a cause determines the nature of its effects, and as a man's conduct will be determined by the most powerful principle governing him, so a slavish fear can produce only slavish observance, and surely God requires something better than that from His people. Such service as the fear of Hell produces will be weak and wavering, for nothing more unsettles the mind and enervates the soul than alarms and horrors. Nabal's heart "died within" him for fear (1 Sam. 25:37), and the soldiers that kept the sepulcher "became as dead men" for fear (Matt. 28:4): thus any obedience from thence can only be a dead obedience. Moreover, it will be fickle and fleeting at the best: Pharaoh relaxed his persecution of the Hebrews when no longer tormented by God's plagues, and even gave them permission to leave Egypt; but soon after he repented of his leniency, chiding himself for it, and pursued them with murder in his heart (Ex. 14:5). Those hypocrites whom "fearfulness" surprised, remained hypocrites still (Isa. 33:14).

It is true that believers are bidden to "fear Him which is able to destroy both body and soul in Hell" (Matt. 10:28), yet it should be pointed out that there is a vast difference between fearing God and dreading eternal punishment: in the parallel and fuller passage Christ added, "yea, I say unto you, fear Him" (Luke 12:5)—not fear Hell! One of the covenant promises which God has made concerning His elect is, "I will put My fear in their hearts, that they shall not depart from Me" (Jer. 32:40), and that is a filial fear, a respect for His authority, an awesome veneration of His majesty; whereas the fear of the unregenerate is a servile, anxious and tormenting one. The holy fear of the righteous causes them to be vigilant and watchful against those ways which lead to destruction, but the fear of the wicked is occupied only with the destruction itself: the one is concerned about the evils which occasion God's wrath, the other is confined to the effects of His wrath. But the exercise of faith and the operations of filial fear are not the only principles which regulate the saint: the love of Christ constrains him, gratitude unto God for His wondrous grace has a powerful effect upon his conduct.

4. By declaring it neutralizes the force of exhortations. The argument used by Arminians on this point may be fairly stated thus: if it be absolutely certain that all regenerated souls will reach Heaven then there can be no real need to bid them tread the path that leads thither, that in such case it is meaningless to urge them to run with patience the race set before them; but since God has uttered such calls to His people, then it follows that their final perseverance is by no means sure, the less so seeing that failure to heed those calls is threatened with eternal death. It is insisted upon that exhortations to effort, watchfulness, diligence etc., clearly imply the contingency of the believer's salvation, that all such calls to the discharge of these duties signify that security is conditional upon his own fidelity, upon the response which he makes unto these demands

of God upon him. It should be a sufficient reply to point out that if this objection were really valid then no Christian could have any firm persuasion of his everlasting bliss so long as he was left upon earth: hence the inference drawn by Arminians from the exhortations must be an erroneous one.

What strange logic is this: because I am persuaded that God loves me with an unchanging and unquenchable love therefore I feel free to trample upon His revealed will, and have no concern whether my conduct pleases or displeases Him. Because I am assured that Christ, at the cost of unparalleled shame and suffering, purchased for me eternal redemption, an inalienable inheritance, therefore I am encouraged to forsake instead of to follow Him, vilify rather than glorify Him. That might be the theology of devils, and those they possess, but it would be repudiated and abhorred by any one renewed by the Holy Spirit. How preposterous to argue that because a person believes he shall persevere to the end, that he will therefore despise and neglect everything that promotes such perseverance. Such an argument as the above is tantamount to saying that because God has regenerated a soul He now requires no obedience from him, whereas one of the chief ends for which he is renewed is to capacitate him for obedience, that he may be conformed to the image of His son.

So far from the absolute promises of God concerning the everlasting safety of His people weakening the force of motives to righteousness, they are the very means made use of by the Spirit to stir up the saints, and to encourage them in the practice of righteousness and engage them in the continuance thereof. Most certainly the apostles perceived no inconsistency or incongruity between the Divine promises and the precepts. They did not judge it meaningless to argue from such blessed assurances to the performance of the duties of holiness. One of them said "Having therefore these promises, dearly beloved, let us cleanse ourselves from all filthiness of the flesh and spirit, perfecting holiness in the fear of God" (2 Cor. 7:1). Those promises were, "I will dwell in them and walk in them, and I will be their God and they shall be My people: I will be a Father unto you and ye shall be My sons and daughters"(6:16, 18), and on them he based his exhortation. After saying, ye "are kept by the power of God through faith unto salvation" another apostle proceeded to urge, "Wherefore gird up the loins of your mind, be sober and hope to the end. . . And if ye call on the Father ... pass the time of your sojourning here in fear" (1 Pet. 1:5, 13, 17)—apparently it never occurred to him that such exhortations had been neutralized or even weakened by the doctrine before advanced.

5. By appealing to cases and examples which, though plausible, are quite inconclusive. In order to prove their contention that a real child of God may so backslide as to lose all relish for spiritual things, renounce his profession and die an infidel, Arminians are fond of referring to alleged illustrations of this very thing. They will point to certain men and women who have come before their own observation, people who were genuinely and deeply convicted of sin, who earnestly sought relief from a burdened conscience, who eventually believed the Gospel, put their faith in the atoning blood of Christ and found rest unto their souls. They will tell of the bright profession made by these people, of the peace and joy which was theirs, of the radical change made in their lives, and how they united with the church, had blessed fellowship with the saints, lifted up their

voices in praise and petition at the prayer meetings, were diligent in speaking to their companions of their eternal welfare, how they walked in the paths of righteousness and caused the saints to thank God for such transformed lives. But alas these bright meteors in the religious firmament soon faded out.

It is at this point that the Arminian seeks to make capital out of such cases. He tells of how, perhaps in a few months, the religious ardor of these "converts" cooled off. He relates how the temptations of the world and lusts of the flesh proved too strong for them, and how like dogs they returned to their vomit. The Arminian then alleges that such cases are actual examples of men and women who have "fallen from grace," who have apostatized from the faith, and by appealing to such he imagines he has succeeded in overthrowing the doctrine of the final perseverance of the saints. In reality, he has done nothing of the sort. He has merely shown how easily Christians may be mistaken, and thus pointed a warning for us not to be too ready to indulge in wishful thinking and imagining all is gold which glitters. Scripture plainly warns us there is a class whose "goodness is as a morning cloud and as the early dew it goeth away" (Hos. 6:4). Christ has told us of those who received the Word with joy, yet had not root in themselves (Matt. 13:20,21). The foolish virgins carried the lamp of their profession, but they had no oil in their vessels. One may come "near" to the kingdom yet never enter it (Mark 12:34).

In order to make good his objection the Arminian must do something more than point to those who made a credible profession and afterwards falsified and renounced it: he must prove that a person who is truly regenerated, born from above, made a new creature in Christ, then apostatized and died an apostate. This he cannot possibly do, for none such ever existed or ever will. The fact is that while there are many who, in varying degrees, adopt the Christian religion, there are very few indeed who are ever born of the Spirit, and the only way in which we may identify the latter is by their continuance in holiness. He who does not persevere to the end was never begotten by God. Nor is that statement a begging of the question at issue: it is insisting upon the teaching of Holy Writ. "The righteous also shall hold on his way" (Job 17:9): observe that it is not "he ought to" nor merely that "he may do so," but a positive and unqualified "shall." Therefore any one who fails to "hold on his way," be he a religious enthusiast, a professing Christian, or zealous church-member, was never "righteous" in the sight of God.

We will labor this point a little further because it is probably the one which has presented more difficulty to our readers than any other. Yet it should not, for when resolved by the Word all is clear as a sunbeam. "I know that whatsoever God doeth, it shall be forever: nothing can be put to it nor anything taken from it: and God doeth it, that men should fear before Him" (Eccl. 3:14). This is one of the distinctive marks of the Divine handiwork: its indestructibility, its permanency, and therefore it is by this mark we must test both ourselves and our fellows. "The orthodox doctrine does not affirm the certainty of salvation because we once believed, but certainty of perseverance in holiness if we have truly believed, which perseverance in holiness, therefore, in opposition to all weaknesses and temptations, is the only sure evidence of the genuineness of past experience or of the validity of our confidence as to our future salvation" (A. A. Hodge). "Whosoever liveth and believeth in Me shall never die" (John 11:26) said Christ, for the life that He gives is an "eternal" one, which the Devil himself cannot destroy (see Job 2:6!). Thus, unless we acknowledge our mistake in concluding the apostates were once regenerate, we give the lie to the Word of God.

6. By asserting that this doctrine makes all warnings and threatenings pointless. Arminians argue that if the believer be eternally secure in Christ he cannot be in any peril, and that to caution him against danger is a meaningless performance. First, let it be said that we have no quarrel with those who insist that most solemn warnings and awful threatenings are addressed immediately to the children of God, nor have we the least accord with those who seek to blunt the point of those warnings and explain away those threatenings: so far from it, in a previous chapter of this book we have shown that God Himself has safeguarded the truth of the final perseverance of His people by these very measures, and have insisted there are very real dangers they must guard against and genuine threatenings they are required to heed. So long as the Christian is left in this world he is beset by deadly dangers, both from within and from without, and it would be the part of madness to ignore and trifle with them. It is faith's recognition of the same which causes him to cry out "Hold Thou me up, and I shall be safe"(Ps. 119:117).

Yet what we have just admitted above in no way concedes that there is any conflict between the promises and warnings of God: that the one assures of preservation while the other forecasts destruction. For what is it that God has promised unto His people? This: that they "shall not depart from Him" (Jer. 32:40), that they shall "hold on their way" (Job 17:9), and that to this end He will "work in them both to will and to do of His good pleasure" (Phil. 2:13), granting unto them all-sufficient grace (2 Cor. 12:9), and supplying all their need (Phil. 4:19). In perfect accord with these promises are the warnings and threatenings addressed to them, by which God has made known the inseparable connection there is, by His appointment, between a course of evil and the punishment attending the same. Those very threatenings are used by the Spirit to produce in Christians a holy circumspection and caution, so that they are made the means of preventing their apostasy. Those warnings have their proper use, and efficacy in respect of the saints, for they cause them to take heed to their ways, avoid the snares laid for them, and serve to establish their souls in the practice of obedience.

Whether or not we can perceive the consistency between the assurances God has made His people and the grounds He has given them to tremble at His Word, between the comforting promises and the stirring exhortations, between the witnesses to their safety and the warnings of their danger, certain it is that Scripture abounds with the one as much as with the other. If on the one hand the Christian is warranted in being fully persuaded that "neither principalities nor powers" shall be able to separate him from the love of God in Christ Jesus, and that God shall tread Satan under his feet shortly (Rom. 8:38, 39; 16:20): on the other hand, he is bidden to "put on the whole armor of God, that ye may be able to stand against the wiles of the Devil. For we wrestle not against flesh and blood, but against principalities and powers" (Eph. 6:12,13), and "Be sober, be vigilant, because your adversary the Devil, as a roaring lion, walketh about seeking whom he may devour" (1 Pet. 5:8). Yet though the believer is warned "Let him that thinketh he standeth take heed lest he fall," it is immediately followed by the declaration "but God is faithful, who will not suffer you to be tempted above that ye are able" (1 Cor. 10:13, 14). Then let us beware of being wise in our own conceit and charging the Almighty with folly.

Because the enemies of the Christian are inveterate, subtle, and powerful, and the exercise of his graces inconstant, it is salutary that he should live under a continual remembrance of his weakness, fickleness and danger. He needs to be ever watchful and prayerful lest he enter into temptation, recalling what befell the self-confident Peter. Because indwelling corruption remains a part of himself, while he is left in this scene, it behooves him to keep his heart with all diligence, for he who trusteth in his own heart is a fool (Prov. 27:26), unmindful of his best interests. We are only preserved from presumption while a real sense of our own insufficiency is retained. The consciousness of indwelling sin should cause every child of God to bend the suppliant knee with the utmost frequency, humility and fervor. Let not the Christian mistake the field of battle for a bed of rest. Let him not indulge in a slothful profession or carnal delights, while his implacable foes, the flesh, the world, and the devil are ever seeking to encompass his ruin. Let him heed the warnings of a faithful God and he will prove Him to be an unerring Guide and invincible Guard.

7. By drawing a false inference from the Divine righteousness. Arminians are fond of quoting that "God is no respecter of persons," from which they argue that His justice requires Him to apportion the same retribution unto sinning Christians as He does unto non-Christians who transgress; and since our doctrine gives no place to the eternal punishment of a saint, it is said we charge God with partiality and injustice. That the Lord "is righteous in all His ways and holy in all His works" (Ps. 145:17) is contended for as earnestly for by us as by our opponents; but what the Arminian denies is maintained by the Calvinist, and that is, the absolute sovereignty of God. That the Most High is obliged to apportion equal punishment to equal faults and equal rewards to equal deservings, cannot be allowed for a moment. Being above all law, the Framer and not the subject of it, God's will is supreme, and He doeth whatsoever pleaseth Him. If God bestows free grace and pardoning mercy to those in Christ and withholds it from those out of Christ, who shall say unto Him, What doest Thou? Has He not the right to do what He chooses with His own: to give a penny to him who labors all day and the same to him that works but one hour (Matt. 20:12-15)!

To argue that because God is no respecter of persons that therefore He must deal with Christians and non-Christians alike is to ignore the special case of the former. They sustain a nearer relation to Him than do the latter. Shall a parent treat a refractory child as he would an insubordinate employee—he would dismiss the one from his service, must he turn the other out of his home? The Scriptures teach that God the Father is tender to His own dear children, recovering them from their sins and healing their backslidings, while He suffers aliens to lie wallowing in their rebellions and pollutions all their lives. Furthermore a Surety stood for them and endured in their stead the utmost rigor of the Law's sentence, so that God is perfectly righteous in remitting their sins. Nevertheless, so that they may know He does not look lightly upon their disobedience, He "visits their transgressions with the rod and their iniquity with stripes" (Ps. 89:32). Finally, they are brought to sincere repentance, confession, and forsaking of their sins, and thereby they obtain the relief provided for them, which is never the case with the children of the Devil.

8. By alleging our doctrine makes its believers proud and presumptuous. That the carnal may wrest this doctrine, like other portions of the Truth, to their own destruction, is freely admitted (2 Pet. 3:16); but that any article of the Faith which God has delivered unto His saints has the least tendency unto evil, we indignantly deny. In reality, the doctrine of the saints' perseverance in holiness, in humble dependence upon God for supplies of grace, lays the axe at the very root of the proud and presumptuous conceits of men, for it casts down their high thoughts and towering imaginations concerning their own native ability to believe the Gospel, obey its precepts, and continue in the faith and practice thereof. We rest wholly on the goodness and faithfulness of God, the merits of Christ's blood and the efficacy of His intercession, the power and operations of the Spirit, having "no confidence in the flesh" (Phil. 3:3). Only the Day to come will reveal how many who "trusted in themselves" and were persuaded of their inherent power to turn unto God and keep His commandments, were thereby hardened and hastened to their eternal ruin.

Let any candid reader ponder the following question. Which is the more likely to promote pride and presumption: extolling the virtues and sufficiency of man's "freewill," or emphasizing our utter dependence upon God's free grace? Which is more apt to foster self-confidence and self-righteousness: the Arminian tenet that fallen man has the power within himself to turn unto God when he chooses and do those things which are pleasing in His sight, or the Calvinist's insistence upon the declarations of Scripture that even the Christian has no strength of his own, that apart from Christ he can "do nothing" (John 15:5), that we are "not sufficient of ourselves" to so much as "think anything as of ourselves" (2 Cor. 3:5), that "all our springs" are in God (Ps. 87:7), and that because of our felt weakness and acknowledged helplessness, God graciously keeps our feet and preserves us from destruction? It is just because our doctrine is so flesh-abasing and pride-mortifying that it is so bitterly detested and decried by the pharisees.

9. By pretending our doctrine renders the use of means superfluous. If Christians are secure in the hand of God and He empowers them by His Spirit, why should they put forth their energies to preserve themselves? But such reasoning leaves out of account that, throughout, God deals with His people as moral agents and accountable creatures. Rightly did Calvin point out, "He who has fixed the limits of our life, has also entrusted us with the care of it; has furnished us with means and supplies for its preservation; has also made us provident of dangers, and, that they may not oppress us unawares, has furnished us with cautions and remedies. Thus it is evident what is our duty." Grace is not given to render our efforts needless but to make them effectual. To say that assurance of final salvation cuts the nerve of enterprise is contrary to all experience: who will work the harder, the man without hope or even a half-expectation, or one who is sure that success will crown his labors.

10. By arguing that our doctrine makes "rewards" meaningless. If it be God who preserves us, then there is no room left for the recognition of our fidelity or owning of our efforts. If there be no possibility of the saint falling away finally, then is his perseverance

incapable of reward by God. Answer: Heaven is not something which the Christian earns by his obedience or merits by his fidelity, nevertheless, everlasting felicity is held before him as a gracious encouragement, as the goal of his obedience. Let it be recognized that the reward is not a legal one but rather one of bounty, in accord with the tenor of the Covenant of Grace, and all difficulty should vanish. Let this point be decided in the light of our Surety's experience: was it not impossible that Christ should fail of His obedience? yet did not God reward Him (Phil. 2:10, 11)! So, in our tiny measure, because of the "joy set before us" we despise our cross and endure suffering for Christ's sake.

And now a word by way of application. Since this article of Faith be so much criticized and condemned as a thing fraught with evil tendencies, let the Christian make it his studied business that his conduct gives the lie to the Arminians' objections. Let him make it his constant concern to "adorn the doctrine of God our Savior in all things" (Titus 2:10), by taking heed to his ways, giving no license to the flesh, attending to the Divine warnings, and rendering glad and full response to His exhortations. Let him show forth by his daily life that this preservation is a continuance in faith, in obedience, in holiness. Let him see to it that he evidences the reality of his profession and the spirituality of his creed by growing in grace and bringing forth the fruits of righteousness. Let him earnestly endeavor to keep himself in the love of God, and to that end avoid everything calculated to chill the same, and thereby he will most effectually "put to silence the ignorance of foolish men" (1 Pet. 2:15).

In the above discussion we sought to show how pointless is the reasoning of Arminians in the opposition which they make to this blessed article of the Faith: but now in that which follows we shall seek to demonstrate that their use of Scripture is equally unhappy. If the charges they bring against this doctrine be baseless, if the inferences they draw and the conclusions they make upon it are wide of the mark, certainly their interpretations and applications of Holy Writ concerning this subject are quite erroneous. Nevertheless they do appeal directly to God's Word and attempt to prove from its contents that one and another of the saints renounced the Faith, went right back again into the world, and died in their sins; that certain specific cases of such are there set before us of men who not only suffered a grievous fall by the way or entered into a backslidden state, but who totally, finally and irremediably apostatized. In addition to these specific examples, they quote various passages which they contend teach the same fearful thing. It is therefore incumbent upon us to examine attentively the cases they point to and weigh carefully the passages they cite.

Before entering immediately into this task, however, one or two general remarks need to be made that the issue between Calvinists and Arminians may be the more clearly drawn. First, it must be laid down as a broad principle that God's Word cannot contradict itself. It is human to err and the wisest of mortals is incapable of producing that which is without flaw, but it is quite otherwise with the Word of Truth. The Scriptures are not of human origin, but Divine, and though holy men were used in the penning of them, yet so completely were they controlled and moved by the Holy Spirit in their work that there is neither error nor blemish in the Sacred Volume. That affirmation concerns, of course, the original manuscripts: nevertheless we have such confidence in the superintending providence of God, we are fully assured He has guarded His own holy Word with such jealous care, that He has so ordered the translation of the Hebrew and Greek into our mother tongue that all false doctrine has been excluded. Since then the Scriptures are Divinely inspired they cannot teach in one place it is impossible that the child of God should be eternally lost, and in another place that he may be, and in yet another that some have been so.

Second, it has been shown at length in previous sections that God's Word clearly teaches the final perseverance of His saints, and that, not in one or two vague and uncertain verses but in the most positive and unequivocal language of many passages. It has been shown that the eternal security of the Christian rests upon a foundation that "standeth sure," which Satan and his emissaries cannot even shake; that his everlasting felicity depends, ultimately upon nothing in or from himself, but is infallibly secured by the invincibility of the Father's purpose, the immutability of His love, and the certainty of His covenant faithfulness; that it is infallibly secured by the Surety engagements of Christ, by the sufficiency of His atonement, and by the prevalency of His unceasing intercession; that it is infallibly secured by the regenerating work of the Holy Spirit, by His abiding indwelling, and by the efficacy of His keeping power. The very honor, veracity, and glory of the Triune Jehovah is engaged, yea, pledged in this matter. In order "more abundantly to show unto the heirs of promise the immutability of His counsel" the Most High has gone so far as to "confirm it by an oath" (Heb. 6:17). Thus, the indefectibility of the Church is made infallibly certain, and no "special pleading" of men, however subtle and plausible, can have the slightest weight in the balance against it.

Third, in view of what has been pointed out in the last paragraph it should be patent to all honest and impartial minds that the cases cited by Arminians as examples of children of God apostatizing and perishing must be susceptible of being diagnosed quite differently, and that the Scriptures they appeal to in support of their contention must be capable of being interpreted in full harmony with those which clearly affirm the opposite. It is a basic principle of exegesis that no plain passage of the Word is to be neutralized by one whose meaning appears to be doubtful or ambiguous, that no explicit promise is to be set aside by a parable the significance of which is not readily determined, that no doctrinal declaration is to be nullified by the arbitrary interpretation of a figure or type. That which is uncertain must yield to what is simple and obvious, that which is open to argument must be subordinated to what is beyond any debate. True, the Calvinist must not resort to any subterfuges to avoid a difficulty, nor wrest a passage adduced by his opponents so as to make it teach what he wants. If he be unable to explain a verse he must honestly admit it, for no single man has all the light; nevertheless, we must believe there is an explanation, and that, in full accord with the Analogy of Faith, we must humbly wait upon God for further light.

Fourth, in order to disprove the doctrine of the final perseverance of the saints the Arminian is bound to do two things: produce the case of one who was truly born again, and then demonstrate that this person actually died in a state of apostasy, for unless he can do both his example is not to the point. It is not sufficient for him to bring forward one who made a credible profession and then repudiated it, for Scripture itself shows emphatically that such a person was never regenerate: the man who "dureth for a while" only, and then in a season of temptation or persecution is "offended" and falls away, is described by Christ as one "who hath not root in himself" (Matt. 13:21) - had the "root of the matter" (Job 19:28) been in him he had survived the testing. To the same effect the apostle declares of such "they went out from us, but they were not of us; if they had been of us, they would have continued with us"(1 John 2:19). Nor is it sufficient for the Arminian to point to genuine children of God who backslide or meet with a grievous fall: such was the experience of both David and Peter; yet so far from being abandoned of God and suffered to die in that state, each was graciously brought to repentance and restored to communion with the Lord. Let us now look at the examples advanced.

1. The case of Adam. Here is one who was the immediate workmanship of God's own hands, created in His image and likeness, "blessed" by the Lord and pronounced "very good" (Gen. 1:28, 31). Here is one who had no sinful heredity behind him and no corruption within him, instated in the Divine favor, placed in a garden of delights and given dominion over all terrestrial creatures. Yet he abode not in that fair estate, but fell from grace, disobeyed his Maker, and brought upon himself spiritual death. When he heard the voice of the Lord God, instead of fleeing to Him for mercy, he hid himself; when arraigned before Him, instead of penitently confessing his sin he sought to brazen it out, seeking to throw the blame upon Eve and casting the onus upon God for giving her to him. In the sequel his awful doom is plainly intimated, for the Lord God "drove out the man" from Eden and barred his way back to "the tree of life" by stationing around it "cherubim and a flaming sword" (Gen. 3:24). Now, say our opponents, what could be more to the point! Adam certainly had "the root of the matter" within him, and it is equally certain that he apostatized and perished. If sinless Adam fell then obviously a Christian who still has sin indwelling him may fall and be lost.

How, then, is the fatal fall of Adam to be explained consistently with the doctrine of the final perseverance of the saints? By calling attention to the immeasurable difference there was between him and them. What does the case of Adam make manifest? This: the defectibility of man when placed in the most favorable and advantageous circumstances. This: that creaturehood and mutability are correlative terms: "man being in honor abideth not" (Ps. 49:12). This: that if the creature is to be kept from committing spiritual suicide a power outside of himself must preserve him. The case of Adam supplies the dark background which brings out more vividly the riches of Divine grace which it is the glory of the Gospel to exhibit. In other words, it serves to demonstrate beyond any peradventure of a doubt the imperative necessity of Christ if the creature—be he fallen or unfallen—is to be saved from himself. There is the fundamental, tremendous, vital difference between the case of Adam and that of the Christian: he was never in Christ, whereas they are; he was never redeemed by blood of infinite worth, they have been; there was none to intercede for him before God, there is for them.

"Howbeit that was not first which is spiritual, but that which is natural; and afterward that which is spiritual" (1 Cor. 15:46). Though the immediate application of these words be unto the bodies of believers, yet they enunciate a general and basic principle in the ways of God with men, in the manifestation of His purpose concerning them. Adam appears on the earth before Christ: Cain was given to Eve before Abel; Ishmael was born before Isaac and Esau before Jacob: the elect are born naturally before they are born again supernaturally. In like manner, the Covenant of Works took precedence over the Covenant of Grace, so far as its revelation was concerned. Thus Adam was endowed with a natural power, namely, that of his own free will, but the Christian is endowed with a spiritual and supernatural power, even God's working in him "both to will and to do of His own good pleasure." Adam was given no promise of Divine preservation, but the saints are. Adam stood before God in dependence upon his own creature righteousness, and when that was lost, all the blessings and virtues arising from it were lost; whereas the believer's righteousness is in Christ: "in the Lord have I righteousness and strength" (Isa. 45:24) is his joyous confession, and since his righteousness is in Christ it is an unassailable and non-forfeitable one.

Adam was placed under a covenant of works: do this and thou shalt live, fail to do and thou must die. It was a covenant of strict justice, unmixed with mercy, no provision being made for any failure. The grace or strength or power with which Adam was endowed, was entrusted to himself and his own keeping. But with His saints God has made a "better covenant" (Heb. 8:6), of which Jesus is the "Surety" (Heb. 7:22) and in Him are treasured up inexhaustible supplies of grace for them to draw upon. This "better covenant" is one in which justice and mercy harmoniously blend together, wherein "grace reigns through righteousness." In this "better covenant" God has promised to keep the feet of His saints, to put His fear in them so that they "shall not depart from" Him (Jer. 32:40). In this covenant God has made provision for our failures, so that "if we confess our sins He is faithful and just to forgive us our sins and to cleanse us from all unrighteousness" (1 John 1:9). Thus our state by redemption and regeneration is far, far better than was that of our first parents by creation, for we are given what unfallen Adam had not, namely, confirmation of our wills in holiness—though not every act is such—For He "works in us that which is well pleasing in His sight through Jesus Christ" (Heb. 13:21), which He never did in Adam. We may add that most of what has been said above applies to the case of the angels who fell.

2. The case of king Saul. It is affirmed by Arminians that this king of Israel was a regenerate man. In support of this contention they appeal to a number of things recorded about him. First, that the prophet Samuel "took a vial of oil and poured it upon his head and kissed him" (1 Sam. 10:1). Second, because it is said that "God gave him another heart" (v. 9). Third, because we are told "the Spirit of God came upon him and he prophesied" (v. 11). Then it is pointed out that Saul acted in fearful presumption and disobedience (1 Sam. 13:9, 13), thereby displeasing the Lord so that it was announced the kingdom should be taken from him (vv. 13, 14). That because of God's displeasure "the Spirit of the Lord departed from Saul and an evil spirit from the Lord troubled him" (16:14). That later, when menaced by the Philistines, he "enquired of the Lord" but "the Lord answered him not" (28:6). Finally, how that he had recourse to a witch and ultimately fell upon the field of battle sorely wounded, and ended his life by taking a sword and falling upon it (31:4), thereby sealing his doom by the unpardonable act of suicide.

In reply thereto we would say: we grant the conclusion that Saul passed out into an eternity of woe, but we do not accept the inference that he was ever a regenerate man. At the outset it must be remembered that the very installation of Saul upon the throne expressed the Lord's displeasure against Israel, for as He declared to the prophet "I gave thee a king in Mine anger (cf. 1 Sam. 8:5,6) and took him away in My wrath" (Hos. 13:11). Concerning the three things advanced by Arminians to show that Saul was a regenerate man, they are no proofs at all. Samuel's taking of the vial of oil and kissing him were simply symbolic actions, betokening the official status that had been conferred upon Saul: this is quite clear from the remainder of the verse, where the prophet explains his conduct, "Is it not because the Lord hath anointed thee to be captain over His inheritance?" (10:1) — not because "The Lord delighteth in thee" or because thou art "a man after His own heart." It is not said the Lord gave Saul "a new heart," but "another. "Moreover, the Hebrew word (haphak) is never translated "gave" elsewhere, but in the great majority of instances "turned": it simply means the Lord turned his heart from natural timidity (see 1 Sam. 10:21, 22) to boldness (cf. 1 Sam. 11:1-7; 13:1-4). That the Spirit of God came upon him so that he prophesied is no more than is said of Balaam (Num. 22:38; 24:2) and Caiaphas (John 11:51).

3. The case of Solomon. This is admittedly the most difficult one presented in Scripture, and it is our belief that God meant it to be such. His history is such a solemn one, his fall so great, his backsliding so protracted, that had his spiritual recovery and restoration to fellowship with the Lord been made unmistakably plain, a shelter would be provided for the careless and presumptuous. In Solomon the monarchy of Israel reached its zenith of splendor, for he reaped the harvest of glory for which David both toiled and suffered, entering into such a heritage as none else before or since has ever enjoyed. But in Solomon, too, the family of David entered its decline, and for his sins the judgments of God fell heavily on his descendants. Thus he is set before us as an awful warning of the fearful dangers which may surround and then overthrow the loftiest virtues and most dazzling mundane greatness.

That Solomon was a regenerate man we doubt not: that he enjoyed the favor of God to a most marked degree the inspired narrative makes plain. That he suffered a horrible decline in character and conduct is equally evident. Neither the special wisdom with which he was endowed, the responsibilities of the exalted position he occupied, nor the superior privileges which were his, rendered him proof against the temptations he encountered. He fell from his first estate and left his first love. His honor and glory were sadly eclipsed, and so far as the historical account of the books of Kings and Chronicles is concerned, he was buried in shame, the dark shadows of a misspent life and wrecked testimony shrouded his grave. Over the fate of Solomon there rests such a cloud and silence that many good men conclude he was lost: on the other hand there are those who do not believe that he so fell as to lose the favor of God and perish eternally.

With others, it is our own conviction that before the end of his earthly pilgrimage Solomon was made to repent deeply of his waywardness and wickedness. We base this conviction upon three things. First, the fact that he was the writer of the book of Ecclesiastes (1:1) and that it was penned at a later period of his life than the Proverbs and Canticles (see 1 Kings 4:32). Now to us it seems impossible to ponder Ecclesiastes without being struck with its prevailing note of sadness and without feeling that its writer is there expressing the contrition of one who has mournfully returned from the paths of error. In that book he speaks out the bitter experiences he had gone through in pursuing a course of folly and madness and of the resultant "vexation of spirit"—see especially 7:2, 3, 26, 27 which is surely a voicing of his repentance. Second, hereby God made good His express promise to David concerning Solomon: "I will be his Father and he shall be My son. If he commit iniquity, I will chastise him with the rod of men, and with the stripes of the children of men: but My mercy shall not depart away from him, as I took it from Saul" (2 Sam. 7:14, 15). Third, centuries after his death the Spirit declared, "Did not Solomon king of Israel sin by these things? yet among many nations was there no king like him, who was beloved of his God" (Neh. 13:26).

4. The case of Judas. Though his be not nearly so difficult of solution, nevertheless it is admittedly a very mysterious one, and there are features about it which pertain to none other. But that which more immediately concerns us here is to show there is nothing in this awful example which militates in the least against the doctrine for which we are contending. That Judas is eternally lost there is no room to doubt: that he was ever saved there is no evidence whatever to show. Should it be said that the Lord would never have ordained a bad man to be one of His favored apostles, the answer is, that God is not to be measured by our standards of the fitness of things: He is sovereign over all, doing as He pleases and giving no account of His matters. Moreover, He has told us that our thoughts and ways are not as His. The mystery of iniquity is a great deep, yet faith has full confidence in God even where it cannot understand.

That Christ was in nowise deceived by Judas is clear from John 6:64, "For Jesus knew from the beginning who they were that believed not, and who should betray Him." Furthermore, we are told that He declared on this solemn occasion, "Have not I chosen you twelve, and one of you is a devil" (v. 70). Notably and blessedly did that act make manifest the moral excellency of the Savior. When the Son became incarnate He averred "Lo I come to do Thy will, 0 God" (Heb. 10:7), and God's will for Him was revealed "in the volume of the Book." In that Book it was written that a familiar friend should lift up his heel against Him (Ps. 41:9). This was a sore trial, yet the perfect Servant balked not at it, but complied therewith by calling a "devil" to be one of His closest attendants. Christ rendered full obedience to the Father's pleasure though it meant having the son of perdition in most intimate association with Him for three years, constantly dogging His steps even when He retired from His carping critics to be alone with the twelve.

Appeal is made by the Arminians to John 17:12, "While I was with them in the world, I kept them in Thy name: those that Thou gayest Me I have kept, and none of them is lost but the son of perdition, that the Scripture might be fulfilled." Yet there is nothing here which supports their contention. Judas was "given to" Christ and "chosen" by Him as an apostle, but he was never given to Him by a special act of grace, nor "chosen in Him" and united to Him as a member of Him, as the rest of the apostles and as all the election of grace are. This is clear from His words in John 13:19, "I speak not of you all (cf. vv. 10, 11): I know whom I have chosen"; that is chosen unto eternal life, for otherwise He had chosen Judas equally with the others. Let it be carefully noted that in John 17:12

Christ says not "none of them is lost except the son of perdition." In using the disjunctive "but" He sharply contrasted Judas from the rest, showing he belonged to an entirely different class: compare Matt. 12:4; Acts 27:22; Rev. 21:27, where the "but" is in direct opposition to what precedes.

Christ's statement in John 17:12 was designed to show that there had been no failure in the trust committed to Him, but rather that He had complied with His commission to the last detail. It also served to assure the eleven of this, that their faith might not be staggered by the perfidy of their companion. It gave further proof that He had not been deceived by Judas, for before he betrayed Him, He terms him "the son of perdition." Finally, it declared God's hand and counsel in it: Judas perished "that the Scripture might be fulfilled." Among the reasons why God ordered that there should be a Judas in the apostolate, we suggest it was in order that an impartial witness might bear testimony to the moral excellency of Christ: though in the closest possible contact with Him by day and night, he could find no flaw in Him, but confessed "I have betrayed the innocent blood" (Matt. 27:4). It was not from saving grace Judas "fell," but from "ministry, and apostleship" (Acts 1:25).

We turn now to look at some of those Scriptures appealed to by Arminians in support of their contention that those who have been born of the Spirit may fall from grace and eternally perish. We say "some of them," for were we to expound every passage cited and free them from the false meaning attached thereto, this section would be extended to an undue and wearisome length. We shall therefore single Out those verses which our opponents are fondest of quoting, those which they regard as their chief strongholds, for if they be overthrown we need not trouble with their weaker defenses. It is hardly necessary to say that there is not one passage in all the Word of God which expressly states the dogma the Arminians contend for, and therefore they are obliged to select those which abound in figurative expressions, or which treat of national and temporal destruction, or those relating to unregenerate professors, thereby deceiving the unwary by the mere sound of words and wresting the Scriptures by straining fragments divorced from their contexts.

John Wesley in his "Serious Thoughts" on the apostasy of saints framed his first proposition thus: "That one who is holy and righteous in the judgment of God Himself may nevertheless so fall from God as to perish everlastingly." In support of this he quoted, "But when the righteous turneth away from his righteousness and committeth iniquity and doeth according to all the abominations that the wicked man doeth, shall he live? All his righteousness that he hath done shall not be mentioned: in his trespass that he hath trespassed and in his sin that he hath sinned, in these shall he die" (Ezek. 18:24). That the founder of Wesleyan Methodism understood this to refer to eternal death is evident from the purpose for which he adduced it. As this passage is generally regarded by Arminians as "unanswerable and unassailable" we will consider it at more length.

This construing of "shall he die" as "shall perish eternally" is contrary to the entire scope and design of Ezek. 18, for this chapter treats not of the perseverance or apostasy of the saints, neither of their salvation nor damnation. Its sole aim is to vindicate the justice of God from a charge that He was then punishing the Jews (temporally) not for their own sins but for the sins of their forebears, and therefore there was manifest unfairness in His dealings with them. This chapter has nothing whatever to do with the spiritual and eternal welfare of men. The whole context concerns only the house of Israel, the land of Israel, and their conduct in it, according to which they held or lost their tenure of it. Thus it has no relevancy whatever to the matter in hand, no pertinency to the case of individual saints and their eternal destiny.

Again, though the man here spoken of is indeed acknowledged by the Lord to be "righteous," yet that righteousness by which he is denominated only regards him as an inhabitant of the land of Palestine and as giving him a claim to the possession and enjoyment of it, but not as justifying him before God and giving him title to everlasting life and felicity. For this "righteousness" is called "his" (v. 24) and not Another's (Isa. 45:24; Jer. 23:6), that which he had "done" (v. 24 and cf. vv. 5-9) and not what Christ had done for him (Rom. 5:19); it was a righteousness of works and not of faith (Rom. 4:5, Phil. 3:9). This man was "righteous" legally but not evangelically. Thus, if a thousand such cases were adduced it would not militate one iota against the eternal security of all who have been constituted righteous before God on the ground of Christ's perfect obedience being reckoned to their account and who have been inwardly sanctified by the Spirit and grace of God.

Let the reader carefully peruse the whole of chapter 18. The mission of the prophet Ezekiel was to call Israel to repentance. He pointed to the awful calamities which had come upon the nation as proof of their great guilt. They sought to escape that charge by pleading "The fathers have eaten sour grapes and the children's teeth are set on edge." The prophet answers, that, though in His governmental and providential dealing God often visits the father's sin on sinful children, yet the guilt of sinful fathers is never in His theocracy (according to the covenant of Horeb) visited on righteous children. He went further, and reminded them that temporal prosperity was restored to the Nation as soon as an obedient generation succeeded a rebellious, and that as soon as a rebellious individual truly repented he was forgiven, just as when a righteous man became wicked he was plagued in his body or estate.

"Then the Lord of that servant was moved with compassion, and loosed him and forgave him the debt . . . And his lord was wroth and delivered him to the tormentors" (Matt. 18:27, 34). This is quoted to prove that "persons truly regenerated and justified before God, may through high misdemeanors in sinning, turn themselves out of the justifying grace and favor of God, quench the spirit of regeneration, and come to have their portion with hypocrites and unbelievers." Arminians are not the only ones who wrest this passage, for Socinians quote verses 24-27 to disprove the atonement of Christ, arguing therefrom that God freely forgives sins out of His "compassion," without any satisfaction being rendered to His broken Law. Both of these erroneous interpretations are the consequence of ignoring the scope and design of this passage: Christ was not there showing either the ground on which God bestows pardon or the doom of apostates.

The scope and intention of Matt. 18:23-35 is easily perceived if the following details be attended to. 1. Christ is replying to Peter's "how often shall my brother sin against me, and I forgive him? (v. 21). 2. It is a parable or similitude of "the kingdom of heaven" (v.

23), which has to do with a mixed condition of things, the whole sphere of profession, in which the tares grow together with the wheat. 3. From Christ's application in v. 35 we see that He was enforcing Matt. 6:14, 15. On account of the mercy and forgiveness which the Christian has received from God in Christ, he ought to extend forgiveness and kindness to his offending brethren (Eph. 4:32). Failure so to do is threatened with awful vengeance. "IF" I forgive not from my heart those who offend me, then I am only an unregenerate professor. Note how Christ represented this character at the beginning: no quickened soul would boast "I will pay Thee all" (v. 26)!

Luke 11:24-26, appealed to by Arminians, need not detain us, for the last clause of Matt. 12:45 proves it is a parable about the nation of Israel — freedom from the spirit of idolatry since the Babylonian captivity, but possessed by the Devil himself when they rejected Christ and demanded His crucifixion. Nor should John 15:6 occasion any serious difficulty. Without proffering a detailed exposition, it is sufficient to point out that the "Vine" is not a figure of vital relationship (as is "the body": 1 Cor. 12:11; Col. 1:24), but only of external and visible. This is clear from such passages as Psalm 80:8-14; Jeremiah 2:21; Hosea 10:1; Revelation 14:18,19. Thus there are both fruitful and fruitless "branches" (as "good" and "bad" fishes Matt. 13:48): the latter being in Christ only by profession —hence the "as a branch." Confirmatory of this the Father is here designated "the Husbandman" (v. 1) — a term having a much wider scope than "the Dresser" of His vineyard (Luke 13:9).

"For if God spared not the natural branches, take heed lest He also spare not thee" (Rom. 11:21). But such a passage as this (vv. 17-24) is nothing to the purpose. The "natural branches" were the unbelieving portion of the Jews (v. 20), and they were "broken off" from the position of witness for God in the earth, the "kingdom" being taken from them and given to others: Matt. 2 1:43. What analogy is there between these and the supposed case of those united to Christ and later becoming so severed from Him as to perish? None whatever: a much closer parallel would be found in a local church having its candlestick removed" (Rev. 2:5): set aside as Christ's witness on earth. True, from their case the apostle points a solemn warning (v. 22) but that warning is heeded by the truly regenerate, and thus is made a means of their preservation.

"Through thy knowledge shall the weak brother perish for whom Christ died?" (1 Cor. 8:11). 1. It is not affirmed that the weak brother had "perished"! 2. From the standpoint of God's purpose and the sufficiency of His keeping power, the feeblest of His children will not perish. 3. But the strong Christian is here warned of and dehorted from a selfish misuse of his "liberty" (v. 9) by pointing out the horrible tendency of the same. Though Christ will preserve His lambs, that does not warrant me in casting a stumblingstone before them. No thanks were due the Roman soldier that not a bone of Christ's body was broken when he thrust his spear into the Savior's side, and the professing Christian who sets an evil example before babes in Christ is not guiltless because God preserves them from becoming infidels thereby. My duty is to so walk that its influence on others may be good and not bad.

First Corinthians 9:27 simply informs us of what God required from Paul (and all His servants and people), and what, by grace he did in order to escape a possible calamity.

2 Corinthians 6:1 refers not to saving grace but to ministerial as v. 3 shows: as laborers together in Christ's vineyard they are exhorted to employ the gifts bestowed upon them. "Ye are fallen from grace" (Gal. 5:4) is to be interpreted in the light of its setting. The Galatians were being troubled by Judaizers who affirmed that faith in Christ was not sufficient for acceptance with God, that they must also be circumcised. The apostle declares that if they should be circumcised with the object of gaining God's favor then Christ would profit them nothing (v. 2), for they would thereby abandon the platform of grace, descending to fleshly ceremonies; in such case they would leave the ground of free justification for a lower and worthless plane.

"Holding faith and a good conscience, which some having put away, concerning faith have made shipwreck; of whom is Hymeneus and Alexander" (1 Tim. 1:19, 20). So far from these being regenerated men who spiritually deteriorated, Hymeneus was a profane and vain babbler, who increased from one degree of impiety "unto more ungodliness" (2 Tim. 2:16, 17); while Paul said of Alexander that he did him "much harm" and "greatly withstood his preaching" (2 Tim. 4:16, 17). Their "putting away" a good conscience does not necessarily imply they formerly had such, for of the unbelieving Jews who contemptuously refused the Gospel (Acts 13:45, 46) it is said—the same Greek word being used—that they "put it from" them. They made shipwreck of the Christian Faith they professed (cf. Gal. 1:23) for they denied a future resurrection (2 Tim. 2:18), which resulted in overthrowing the doctrinal faith of some of their hearers; but as 2 Tim. 2:19 shows this was no apostasy of real saints.

Hebrews 6:4-8. There are two sorts of "enlightened" persons: those who are savingly illuminated by the Holy Spirit, and those intellectually instructed by the doctrine of the Gospel. In like manner, there are two kinds of "tasting" of the heavenly gift, the good Word of God, and the powers of the world to come: those who under a fleeting impulse merely sample them, and those who from a deep sense of need relish the same. So there are two different classes who become "partakers of the Holy Spirit:" those who only come under His awe-inspiring and sin-convicting influences in a meeting where His power is manifest, and those who receive of His grace and are permanently indwelt by Him. The "repentance" of those viewed here is but that of Cain, Pharaoh and Judas, and those who openly repudiate Christ become hopelessly hardened, given up to a reprobate mind.

The description furnished of the above class at once serves to identify them, for it is so worded as to come far short of the marks of the children of God. They are not spoken of as God's elect, as those redeemed by Christ, as born of the Spirit. They are not said to be justified, forgiven, accepted in the Beloved, or "made meet for the inheritance of the saints in light." Nothing is said of their faith, love or obedience. Yet these are the very things which distinguish the saints from all others! Finally, the description of this class in terms which fall below what pertains to the regenerate is employed again in v. 9: "But (not and'), beloved, we are persuaded better things of you (in contrast from them) and things which (actually) accompany salvation."

Hebrews 10:26-29. The apostle says nothing here positively of any having actually committed this fatal sin, but only supposes such a case, speaking conditionally. This particular "sin" referred to here must be ascertained from the Epistle in which this passage occurs: it is the deliberate repudiation of Christianity after being instructed therein and making a public profession thereof and going back to an effete Judaism—the condition of such would be hopeless. The nearest approach to such sin today would be for one who had been taught the Truth and intelligently professed to the same, renouncing it for, say, Romanism, or Buddhism. To renounce the way of salvation set forth by the Gospel of Christ is to turn the back on the only Mediator between God and men. "There remaineth no more sacrifice for sins" for those who prefer "calves and goats" (Judaism) or "Mary and the saints" (Romanism) rather than the Lamb of God.

"Now the just shall live by faith, but if any man draw back My soul shall have no pleasure in him" (Heb. 10:38). This also is purely hypothetical, as the "if" intimates: it announces what would follow should such a thing occur. To quote what is merely suppositionary rather than positive, shows how weak the Arminian case is. That there is nothing here whatever for them to build upon is clear from the very wording and structure of the sentence: it is not "Now the just shall live by faith and if any man draw back." The "but if any man draw back" places him in opposition to the class spoken of in the first clause. This is further evident in what immediately follows: "But we are not of them that draw back unto perdition, but of them that believe to the saving of the soul" (v. 39). Thus, so far from this passage favoring the total apostasy of real saints, it definitely establishes the doctrine of their final perseverance.

"There shall be false teachers among you, who privily shall bring in damnable heresies, even denying the Lord that bought them" (2 Pet. 2:1). Any seeming difficulty here is at once removed if attention be carefully paid to two things. First, it is not said they were redeemed, but only "bought." The first man was given "dominion" over all things terrestrial (Gen. 1:28), but by his fall lost the same, and Satan took possession by conquest. Christ does not dispossess him by the mere exercise of Divine power, but as the Son of man He secured by right of purchase all that Adam forfeited. He "buyeth that field" (Matt. 13:44) which is "the world" (v. 39)—i.e. the earth and all in it. Second, it is not said they were bought by Christ, but "the Lord," and the Greek word is not the customary "kurios" as in vv. 9, 11, 20, but "Despotes," which signifies dominion and authority — translated "masters" in 1 Tim. 6:1, 2; Titus 2:9; 1 Pet. 2:18. It was as a Master He bought the world and all in it, acquiring thereby an unchallengable title (as God-man) to rule over it. He therefore has the right to demand the submission of every man, and all who deny Him that right, repudiate him as the Despotes.

2 Pet. 2:20-22. There are none of the distinguishing marks of God's children ascribed to the characters mentioned in this passage, nothing whatever about them to show they were ever anything more than formal professors. Attention to the following details will clarify and simplify these verses. 1. The "pollutions of the world" here "escaped" are the gross and outward defilements (in contrast from the inward cleansing of the regenerate), as is clear from the "again entangled therein." 2. It was not "through faith in" but "through the knowledge of the Lord and Savior" that this reformation of conduct and amendment of walk was effected. 3. These are not said to have "loved the way of righteousness" (Ps. 119:47, 77, 159), but merely to have "known" it: there is a twofold knowledge of the Truth: natural and spiritual, theoretical and vital, ineffectual and

transforming — it is only the former the apostates had. The heart of stone was never taken from them. 4. They were never "saints" or "sheep" but "dogs" domesticated and "swine" externally washed.

"These are spots in your feasts of charity, when they feast with you, feeding themselves without fear; clouds they are without water, carried about of winds; trees whose fruit withereth; without fruit, twice dead, plucked up by the roots" (Jude 12). It is the words twice dead which the Arminian fastens upon, but we have quoted the whole verse that the reader may see that it is couched in the language of imagery. A manifestly figurative expression is taken literally: if "twice dead," it is argued they were twice alive — the second time by the new birth, the life from which they had killed. The Epistle in which this expression occurs supplies the key to it. Its theme is Apostasy: of the Israelites (v. 5), angels (v. 6), and lifeless professors in Christendom (vv. 8-19), from which the saints are "preserved" (v. 1) and "kept" (v. 24).Those of v. 12 were dead in sin by nature, and then by apostasy — by defection from the faith, they once professed. "I will not blot out his name" (Rev. 3:5) is a promise to the overcomer, every believer (1 John 5:4).

Chapter 10
Its Benefits

It has been pointed out on a previous occasion that what has been engaging our attention is far more than a subject for theological debate: it is full of practical value. It must be so, for it occupies a prominent place in the Divinely-inspired Scriptures which are "profitable for doctrine" (2 Tim. 3:16), and that, because it is "the doctrine which is according to godliness" (1 Tim. 6:3)—revealing the standard of piety and actually promoting piety in the soul and life of him who receives it by faith. Everything revealed in the Word and all the activities of God have two chief ends in view: His own glory and the good of His people. And as we draw to the close of this book it is fitting that we should seek to set before readers some of the benefits which are conferred by a believing apprehension of this truth, some of the blessed effects it produces and fruits it yields. We somewhat anticipated this aspect of our subject by what we said under its Blessedness (in chap. 6 of this book), yet as we then did little more than generalize it behooves us now to more definitely particularize.

In attempting to describe some of the benefits which this doctrine affords we shall be regulated by whether we are viewing it from the Divine side or the human, for as we have sought to make clear in the preceding sections, the perseverance of the saints in holiness and obedience is the direct effect of the continued operations of Divine grace and power within them, and those operations are guaranteed by the promises of the everlasting covenant. Viewed from the Divine side, perseverance in the faith and in the paths of righteousness is itself a gift, a distinct gift from God: "who shall also confirm you unto the end" (1 Cor. 1:8). Absolutely considered God's preservation of His people turns upon no condition to be fulfilled by them, but depends entirely on the immutability and invincibility of the Divine purpose. Nevertheless, God does not preserve His people by mere physical power and without their concurrence, as He keeps the planets steadfast in their orbits. No, rather does He treat them throughout as moral agents and responsible creatures, drawing them with the cords of love, inclining their hearts unto Himself, rendering effectual the motives He sets before them and the means which He requires them to use.

The infallible certainty of the Divine operations on behalf of and within His saints and the mode of their working cannot be insisted upon too emphatically or repeated too often. On the one hand, the crown of honor and glory must be ascribed to the King Himself; and on the other hand, the response and concurrence or loyalty of His subjects is to be made equally plain. God preserves His people by renewing them in the inner man day by day (2 Cor. 4:16), by quickening them according to His Word, by granting them fresh supplies of grace, and also by moving them to heed His warnings and respond to His exhortations; in a word, by working in them both to will and to do of His good pleasure (Phil. 2:13). Thus our portrayal of some of the benefits and fruits of this doctrine will be governed by our viewpoint: whether we trace Out what follows faith's appropriating of the Divine promises or what follows from faith's appropriation of the Divine precepts. God has promised to carry forward in sanctification and complete in glorification the work begun in regeneration, yet not without requiring us to perform the duties of piety and avoid everything contrary thereto.

1. Here is cause for adoring God. The doctrine set forth in this book most certainly redounds more to the glory of God than does the contrary one, which leaves our everlasting felicity in uncertainty. It exemplifies God's power, whereby He not only restrains our external foes from overthrowing our salvation, but also by fixing the wavering disposition of our wills that we do not cease from the love of and desire after holiness. Also His truth in the promises of the Covenant, on which we securely rely, being assured that He who gave them will certainly make the same good. His goodness, whereby He patiently bears with our weakness and dullness, so that when we fall into sin, He does not cast us off, but by His loving chastenings recovers us through moving us to renewed repentance. His holiness, when because of our folly we trifle with temptation for a season, disregarding His warnings, He makes us conscious of His displeasure by withholding tokens of His favor and declining an answer to our prayers, bringing us to confess and forsake our sins, that fellowship with Him may be restored and that peace and joy may again be our portion.

2. Here is peace for the soul in a world of strife and where men's hearts fail them for fear of the future. This is evident if we consider the opposite. In themselves believers are weak and unstable, unable to do anything as they ought. They have no strength of their own to keep themselves in the love of God, but carry about with them a body of sin and death. They are continually exposed to temptations which ensnare the wisest and overthrow the strongest. Suppose then they had received no guarantee of the unchangeableness of God's purpose, no infallible word of the continuance of His love, no pledge that He will keep and secure them by the working of His mighty power, no declaration that unfailing supplies of His Spirit and grace shall be vouchsafed them, no assurance that He will never leave them nor forsake them, no revelation of an Advocate on high to plead their cause and of the sufficiency of His mediation and the efficacy of His intercession. But rather that they are left to their own fidelity: and in consequence some of the most eminent saints have apostatized from the faith, that thousands have utterly fallen out of God's love and favor, and so been cast from His covenant, from whence few have ever recovered; and all confidence and peace will be at an end, and fear and terror fill their place.

How vastly different is the teaching of the Word from what we have supposed above. There we find God, as it were, saying to His people: I know your weakness and insufficiency, your dullness and darkness, how that without My Son and continual supplies of His Spirit you can do nothing. The power and rage of your indwelling sin is not hidden from Me, and how with violence it brings you into captivity against your desires. I know that though you believe, yet you are frequently made to groan over your unbelief, and that you are then ready to fear the worst. And when in that case Satan assaults and tempts, seeking to devour you; that first he acts like a serpent, attempting to beguile and ensnare, and then as a lion to terrify. But be not ignorant of his devices: resist him steadfast in the faith: take unto you the whole armor of God, watch night and day that ye be not seduced by him, and you shall overcome him by the blood of the Lamb. "Fear thou not, for I am with thee: be not dismayed, for I am thy God: I will strengthen thee, yea I will help thee, yea I will uphold thee with the right hand of My righteousness" (Isa. 41:10). Though you may be tripped up, ye shall not utterly fall. Though you be fearful, My kindness shall not be removed from you. So be of good cheer, and run with patience the race that is set before you.

3. Here is solid comfort for the saints in a day of declension, when there is a great "falling away" of those who once appeared to run well. Though what is termed "organized Christianity" be a demonstrated failure, though corporate Christendom be now in ruins, though ten thousands have apostatized yet let the saints be fully assured that God has and will reserve to Himself a remnant who bow not the knee to Baal; and therefore may those who have the living God for their "refuge" confidently exclaim "Therefore will not we fear though the earth (the most stable and ancient establishments) be removed, and though the mountains (the leaders and most towering professors) be carried (by the winds of false doctrine) into the midst of the sea" — the masses of the wicked: Isa. 5 7:20. When many of the nominal disciples of Christ "sent back and walked no more with Him," He turned to the apostles and said "Will ye also go away?" Whereupon Simon Peter as their spokesman answered "Lord, to whom shall we go? Thou hast the words of eternal life" (John 6:66-68). Thus it was then, has been throughout the centuries, and will be unto the end of time. The sheep are secure, while the goats turn aside and perish.

Observe how Paul emphasizes this very note in 2 Tim. 2. Hymeneus and Philetus eminent men in the church had apostatized, and by their defection and false teaching had overthrown the doctrinal faith of some; yet says the apostle, This is no reason why the real children of God should be made to quake and imagine that their end is uncertain. "Nevertheless the foundation of God standeth sure, having this seal: the Lord knoweth them that are His; and, let everyone that nameth the name of Christ depart from iniquity" (v. 19). Note the two sides of that "seal," preserving the balance of Truth: on the one side there is a cordial—those who are built upon the foundation of God's unchanging purpose and love shall not be prevailed against; on the other there is a warning—trifle not with "iniquity," whether it be doctrinal or practical, but "depart" from it. Similarly John assures believers who might be shaken at seeing certain in their assemblies being seduced by the antichrists of that day, but such were only unregenerate professors (1 John 2:19), and therefore that the regenerate, held in the hand of Christ, shall not be overcome by deceivers.

4. Here is ground for holy confidence. The Lord knows how difficult is the task assigned His people and how deep is the sense of their own insufficiency. He knows too that nothing more enervates their hearts and enfeebles their hands than doubts and fears, and therefore has He made absolute promise to those who hear His voice and follow Him that "they shall never perish" (John 10:29). It was this which armed Joshua to

the battle: "There shall not a man be able to stand before thee all the days of thy life; as I was with Moses, so I will be with thee: I will not fail thee nor forsake thee." And from thence the Lord drew an argument — the very opposite of that which the legalistic Arminian infers —namely, "Be strong and of a good courage" (Josh. 1:5, 6). Such a promise would not make a Joshua reckless or lax, whatever effect it might have upon a self-righteous freewiller. No, rather would it produce a holy confidence, which prompted to the use of lawful means and gave assurance of God's blessing thereon. Such a confidence causes its possessor to trust in the Lord with all his heart and lean not unto his own understanding.

Such encouragement is conveyed and such confidence is engendered by the Divine declaration "the righteous shall hold on his way" (Job 17:9). As the young believer contemplates the likely length of the journey before him and the difficulties of the road which has to be trod, he is apt to give way to despair; but if his faith lays hold of this promise that he shall certainly reach the desired goal, new strength will be imparted to his feeble knees and increased resolution to his fainting heart. It is the confidence that by continuing to plod along the weary traveler will reach home, which causes him to take courage and refuse to give in. It is the assurance of success which is to the right-minded and best stimulus of labor. If the Christian be persuaded that the world shall not overcome him, that sin shall not slay him, that Satan shall not triumph over him, then will he take unto him the shield of faith and the Sword of the Spirit and fight like a man and be more than conqueror. As it has been truly said "This is one of the reasons why British troops have so often won the fight: because the drummer boys know not how to beat a retreat and the soldiers refused to believe in the possibility of defeat."

5. Here is consolation for us in the severest trials. Let us illustrate this point from the case of Job, for it is difficult to conceive one more acute and extreme than his. You know how severe, how many, and how protracted were those afflictions. You know how far Satan was permitted to proceed with him. You know how his wife turned against and his so-called friends tantalized him. His cup of trouble was indeed filled to the brim, yet we find him looking above his afflictions and censorious critics, exclaiming "He knoweth the way that I take: when He hath tried me I shall come forth as gold" (23:10). Weigh well those words and bring to mind the situation of the one who uttered them. Observe that there was no doubt or uncertainty in his mind about the issue of his afflictions: it was not "I fear I shall perish in the furnace," for he refused to allow those fiery trials to turn him into a skeptic. Nor did he merely cherish a flattering hope that things might possibly be well with him at the end, and say "I may come forth as gold." No, there was the undoubting, positive conviction "I shall!"

Ah, my reader, Job saw "the bright light in the cloud" (37:21). He drew comfort from what assured Cowper when he wrote those lines:

> "Judge not the Lord by feeble sense,
> But trust Him for His grace:
> Behind a frowning providence,
> He hides a smiling face."

Job knew that God maketh "all things work together for good to them that love Him, to them who are the called according to His purpose" (Rom. 8:28), and therefore he knew there could be no possibility of his perishing in the fires. And why was there no doubting as to the outcome of his trials? Because he could say "For I know that my Redeemer liveth" and therefore could he add "and though after my skin worms destroy this body, yet in my flesh shall I see God" (19:25, 26). That was the ground of his confidence—nothing in himself. That was what caused him to triumphantly exclaim "I shall come forth as gold." Cheer up fellow believer: the process may be painful, but the end is sure; the path may be rough and you may feel faint, but the prospect is entrancing and certain.

6. Here is cause for praise. Why should I be found still holding on my way when so many who made a bright profession and who appeared to make much faster progress in spiritual things than I did, have long ago dropped out of the race, and have gone right back into the world? Certainly not because I was any better by nature. No, I freely ascribe all the glory unto God who has so graciously ministered unto me and continued to work in me; who has been so longsuffering and recovered me when I strayed. O what thanks are due unto Him. How often have I had occasion to say "He restoreth my soul" (Psa. 23:3)—as He did Abraham's, Jacob's, Peter's. Thus I may say with David "I will sing of the mercies of the Lord forever" (Psa. 89:1). Not today or tomorrow, but for "forever"; not only when I come to the brink of the Jordan, but after I have passed safely through it, the high praises of His faithfulness shall be the theme of my song throughout eternity.

7. Here is a powerful incentive to confirm Christians in their spiritual lives and to spur them unto the duties of piety. This is evident from what regeneration works in them. All the arguments drawn from the possibility of the apostasy of saints are derived from the terror of dreadful threatenings and the fear of eternal punishment; whereas those taken from the assurances conveyed by the everlasting covenant breathe nothing but the sweetness of grace. Since the children of God have received "the spirit of adoption, whereby they cry Father, Father" (Rom. 8:15), they are more powerfully drawn by the cords of love than by the scourge of horror. Moreover since all acceptable obedience springs from gratitude, then that which most effectually promotes gratitude must be the most powerful spring of obedience, and as to whether a grace bestowed by the Lord is perpetual or one which may be lost is likely to inspire the deepest gratitude, we leave to the judgment of our readers. The more firmly be secured the reward of duty, the more diligent shall we be in performing duty.

8. Here is an incentive to practical godliness. If Christian perseverance is one of continuance in the path of obedience and holiness, then will the saints make diligent use of the aids which God has provided for them and eschew the contrary. Especially will they be encouraged to ask for and seek after the grace which God has promised. As it is a sight and sense of Christ's being crucified because of my heinous sins which produces evangelical repentance (Zech. 12:10), so it is a realization of the immutability of God's purpose, the unchangeableness of His love, and the preciousness of His promises which strengthen faith and inflame love to serve and please Him. This twofold doctrine of Divine preservation and perseverance in holiness supplies effectual motives unto pi-

ety. Negatively, it removes discouragements by letting us know that our denials of self, mortifications of the flesh and efforts to resist the Devil, are not in vain (1 Cor. 15:58; Gal. 6:9). Positively, it places upon us the most powerful obligations to live unto God, to show forth His praises, and adorn the doctrine we profess (2 Cor. 7:1).

9. Here we are shown the need of continual diligence in order to persevere unto the end. But, says the Arminian, I would have concluded the very opposite, since final perseverance be guaranteed. That is due to his misconception. God has declared "The righteous shall hold on his way:" not become slack and sit down, still less that he will forsake it for the way of the ungodly. That very promise is the best means of producing the desired result. If a man could be definitely assured that in a certain line of business he would make a fortune, would such assurance cause him to refuse that business or lead him to lie in bed all day? No, rather would it be an incentive to diligence in order to prosper. Napoleon believed he was "the man of destiny:" did that conviction freeze his energies? No, the very opposite. God's promising a thing unto His children causes them to pray for the same with greater confidence, earnestness and importunity. God hath promised to bless our use of lawful means and therefore we employ them with diligence and expectation.

10. Here is a truth to humble us. Admittedly it has been wrested by Antinomians and perverted unto the feeding of a spirit of presumption. But it is "ungodly men" and not the saints who turn the grace of our God into lasciviousness (Jude 4). Different far is the effect of this truth upon the regenerate. It works in them a sense of their own insufficiency, causing them to look outside of themselves for help and strength. So far from rendering them slothful, it deepens their desires after holiness and makes them seek it more earnestly. As the Christian realizes "Thou hast commanded us to keep Thy precepts diligently," he is moved to pray "0 that my ways were directed to keep Thy statutes diligently.. .Make me to go in the path of Thy commandments, for herein do I delight" (Psa. 119:4, 5, 35). The more he is taught of the Spirit the more will he cry "Hold Thou me up, and I shall be safe" (Psa. 119:117).

Chapter 11
Conclusion

It now remains for us to gather up a few loose ends, to summarize what has been before us, make a practical application of the whole, and our present task is completed. Not that we have said anything like all that could be said thereon; yet we have sought to set before the reader the principal aspects of this subject and to preserve a due balance between the Divine and human sides of it—God's operations in connection therewith and the Christian's concurrence therein. Much of the opposition which has been raised against what is termed "the dangerous tendency" of this truth arose from a defective view of the same, through failure to apprehend that the perseverance of the saints exhibited in the Scriptures is their continuance in faith and holiness: that the One who has made infallible promise they shall reach the desired goal has also decreed they shall tread the one path which leads to it, that the means as well as the end are ordained by Him, and that He moves them to make diligent use of those means and blesses and makes effectual their labor in the same.

That for which we have contended throughout these chapters is steadfastness in holiness, constancy in believing, and in bringing forth the fruits of righteousness. Saving faith is something more than an isolated act: it is a spiritual dynamic, a principle of action, which continues to operate in those who are the favored subjects of it. This is brought out very clearly and decisively in the great Faith chapter. In Heb. 11 the Holy Spirit sets before us the faith of Abel, of Enoch, of Noah, of Abraham and Sarah, Isaac and Jacob, and after describing various exercises and fruits of the same, declares "these all died in faith" (v. 13), not one of them apostatized from the same. The "faith" spoken of, as the context shows, was both a justifying and sanctifying one, and those who had received the same from God not only lived by it but died in it. Theirs was a faith which wore and lasted, which overcame obstacles and triumphed over difficulties, which endured to the end. True, the patriarchs had to wrestle against their natural unbelief, and, as the inspired records show, more than once they were tripped up by the same, yet they continued fighting and emerged conquerors.

The Christian is required to continue as he began. He is to daily own his sins to God and he is daily to renew the same acts of faith and trust in Christ and His blood which he exercised at the first. Instead of counting upon some past experience, he is to maintain a present living on Christ. If he continues to cast himself on the Redeemer, putting his salvation wholly in His hands, then He will not, cannot, fail him. But in order to cast myself upon Christ I must be near Him; I cannot do so while following Him "afar off." And to be near Him, I must be in separation from all that is contrary to Him. Communion is based upon an obedient walk (John 15:10): the one cannot be without the other. And for the maintenance of this, I must continue to "show the same diligence" I did when first convicted of my lost estate, when I perceived that sin was my worst enemy, that I was a rebel against God and His wrath upon me, and when I fled to Christ for refuge, surrendering myself to His lordship and trusting entirely to the sufficiency of His sacrifice to save me from my sins — their dominion, their pollution, and their guilt.

"Show the same diligence to the full assurance of hope unto the end" (Heb. 6:11). The selfsame earnestness and pains which actuated my heart and regulated my acts when I first sought Christ must be continued unto the end of my earthly course. This means persevering in a holy life, in the things which are appointed by and are pleasing to God, and unto this the servants of God are to be constantly urging the saints. "Ministerial exhortation unto duty is needful unto those who are sincere in the practice of it, that they may abide and continue therein" (J. Owen). In no other way can the "full assurance of hope" (a confident expectation of the issue or outcome) be Scripturally maintained. The Christian has to be constant in giving "the same diligence" to the things of Cod and the needs of his soul as he did at the outset. "He said, to the end, that they might know they had not reached the goal, and were therefore to think of further progress. He mentioned diligence that they might know they were not to sit down idly, but to strive in earnest." And who think you, my reader, was the author of that quotation? None other than John Calvin! How grievously has Calvinism been perverted and misrepresented.

"That ye be not slothful, but followers of them who through faith and patience inherit the promises" (Heb. 6:12). The apostle here warns against the vice which is the antithesis of the virtue previously enjoined, for slothfulness is the opposite of diligence. The indolence dehorted is in each of us by nature, for spiritual laxity is not something peculiar to those of a lazy disposition. The evil principle of the "flesh" remains in every Christian and that principle hates and therefore is opposed to the things of God. But the flesh must be resisted and the desires of the "spirit" or principle of grace heeded. When conscious of this indisposition unto practical holiness, this native enmity against the same, the believer must pray with renewed earnestness "draw me, we will run after Thee" (Song of Sol. 1:4), "Order my steps in Thy Word, and let not any iniquity have dominion over me" (Ps. 119: 133). It is this which distinguishes the true child of God from the empty professor: his wrestling with the Lord in secret to enable him to press forward in the race set before him.

"But followers of them who through faith and patience inherit the promises." The immediate reference is to the patriarchs who, by continuing steadfast in the faith, persevering in hope amid all the trials to which they were subjected, had no entrance into the promised blessings. Their faith was far more than a notional one: it was influential and practical, causing them to live as "strangers and pilgrims" in this scene (see Heb. 11:13). The word for "patience" here is usually rendered "longsuffering. " It is a grace which makes its possessor refuse to be daunted by the difficulties of the way or be so discouraged by the trials and oppositions encountered as to desert the course or forsake the path of duty. It is just such faith and patience which are required of the saint in every age, for there never has been and never will be any journeying to Heaven on "flowery beds of ease." If the continued exercise of such graces was required of the patriarchs—persons who were so high in the love and favor of God—then let not us imagine they may be dispensed with in our case. The things promised are not obtained "for faith and patience," but they are entered into "through" them.

Assurance of final perseverance neither renders needless wariness and care (1 Cor. 10:12), nor the unwearied use of the appointed means of grace (Gal. 6:9). We must distinguish sharply between confidence in Christ and a weakening of the security of the flesh. The teaching that carnal security and presumption is no bar to eternal glory is a doctrine of the Devil. David prayed "Teach me, O Lord, the way of Thy statutes, and I shall keep it unto the end" (Ps. 119:33). Upon it Spurgeon said, "The end of which David speaks is the end of life, or the fullness of obedience. He trusted in grace to make him faithful to the utmost, never drawing a line and saying to obedience 'Hitherto shalt thou go but no further.' The end of our keeping the Law will come only when we cease to breathe: no good man will think of marking a date and saying, 'It is enough, I may now relax my watch, and live after the manner of men.' As Christ loves us to the end so must we serve Him to the end. The end of Divine teaching is that we may serve to the end" (Treasury of David, Vol. 6). O for more of this well-balanced teaching.

When faith and the spirit of obedience are inoperative the features of the new birth are under a cloud, and when we have no evidence of regeneration we lack any warrant to entertain the assurance of eternal happiness. The man who gives free rein to the flesh and takes his fill of the world gives the lie to his profession that he is journeying to Heaven. It is the glory of the Gospel that while it announces mercy unto the chief of sinners, yet if any be encouraged by this to persist in a course of evil-doing it pronounces his doom. The Gospel encourages hope, but it also promotes holiness; it imparts peace, but it also inculcates godly piety; it cherishes confidence, yet not by looking back to conversion but forward to the desired haven. It justifies the expectation of preservation, but only as we persevere in the path of duty. While it declares emphatically that the believer's continuance in and maintenance of his faith depend wholly on something extraneous to himself or his present case, yet with equal clearness it insists that the believer's perseverance is carried on and perfected by his use of all the appointed means.

It is freely granted that many of the objections which are made against this subject apply most pertinently to the Antinomian perversion of it, for hyper-Calvinists have been guilty of presenting this truth in such an unguarded and one-sided manner as to virtually set a premium on loose walking. They have dwelt to such an extent upon the Divine operations as to quite crowd out human responsibility, picturing the Christian as entirely passive. Others who were quite unqualified to write on such a theme have given much occasion to the enemies of the Truth by their crudities, representing the security of the believer as a mechanical thing, divorcing the end from the means, ignoring the safe-guards by which God Himself has hedged about this doctrine, and prating about "once saved, always saved" no matter what the daily walk may be. Nevertheless such abuses do not warrant anyone in repudiating the doctrine itself and opposing the teaching of Scripture thereon, for there is nothing in the Word of God which has the slightest tendency to make light of sin or countenances loose living, but rather everything to the contrary.

When expressing his hatred of the truth of the eternal security of Christ's sheep, John

Wesley exclaimed "How pleasing is this to flesh and blood," which is the very thing it is not. Such a doctrine can never be agreeable to fallen human nature. Depraved man is essentially proud, and hence any scheme of perseverance accomplished by the strength of man's own will power is pleasing to the vanity of his mind; but a perseverance dependent upon the faithfulness and power of God, a perseverance which is not the result of any human sufficiency but rather of the merits and intercession of Christ, is most unpalatable unto the self-righteous Pharisee. Only the one who has been given to feel the prevailing power of indwelling sin, who has discovered that his own will and resolutions are wholly incompetent to cope with the corruptions of his heart, who has proved by painful experience that he is completely "without strength" and that apart from Christ he can do nothing, will truly rejoice that none cam pluck him out of the Redeemer's hand. As only the consciously sick will welcome the Physician, so none but those who realize their own helplessness will really find the doctrine of Divine preservation acceptable to them.

Moreover, the duties inculcated by this doctrine are most repugnant to flesh and blood. Subjection to Christ's authority and the daily taking of His yoke upon us is a requirement very far from welcome to those who wish to please themselves and follow their own devices. The standard of piety, the spirituality of God's Law, the nature of holiness, the insistence that we must keep ourselves unspotted from this world, are directly contrary to the inclinations of the natural man. That we must discipline our affections, regulate our thoughts, mortify our carnal appetites, cut off a right hand and pluck out a right eye, are certainly not good news to the unregenerate, especially when God insists that such mortification is never to be remitted but continued until mortality be swallowed up of life. No, it is impossible that fallen man will ever be pleased with a doctrine of perseverance in denying self, taking up his cross daily and following a holy Christ who is despised and rejected by this world. Thus it will abundantly appear from all that has been said, how baseless and pointless is the Arminian objection that the preaching of this doctrine encourages laxity and makes for licentiousness.

How can it be supposed that the proclamation of this blessed truth will lead to carelessness and carnality when we lay it down as a fundamental maxim that no one has any shadow of reason to consider himself interested in the blessing of perseverance except as he has and gives clear evidence that he is inwardly conformed to God and outwardly obedient to His commands? Yet it must be allowed, no matter how carefully and proportionately the doctrine of Scripture be set forth by God's servant, there will always be those ready to wrest to their own destruction. If the Lord Jesus was falsely charged with "perverting the nation" (Luke 23:2) His ministers must not expect immunity from similar criminations. If the apostle Paul was slanderously reported of teaching "Let us do evil, that good may come" (Rom. 3:8), we must not be surprised if the enemies of God should falsify our assertions and draw erroneous inferences from them. Yet this must not deter us from proclaiming all the counsel of God or keeping back anything that would be profitable to His people (Acts 20:27, 20). And now to make practical application of all that has been before us.

1. How earnest should sinners be of becoming Christians. In Christ alone is salvation and safety to be found. Security of person and of estate is the principal concern of men

in this world, but security of soul has little or no place in the thoughts of the majority. How fearful to be in imminent danger of death and eternal punishment, and how alarming the condition of those indifferent to their everlasting welfare. Where there is an underground shelter which is out of range of artillery and below the reach of falling bombs, how eagerly will the sane turn thither when the siren sounds. "The name of the Lord is a strong tower, the righteous runneth into it and is safe" (Prov. 18:10). O let every reader who has not yet done so make haste into his closet, fall upon his knees and rise not till he has committed himself wholly unto Christ for time and eternity. Halt no longer between two opinions. The wrath of God is upon thee, and there is but one way of escape: then flee for refuge to the hope set before you in the Gospel (Heb. 6:18). Christ stands ready to receive if you will throw down your weapons of warfare.

2. How diligently you should examine whether or not you are in Christ, the place of eternal security. You should know whether or not you have complied with the requirements of the Gospel, whether or not you have closed with Christ's gracious offer therein, whether spiritual life has come to your soul, whether you have been made a new creature in Christ. These things may be known with definite certainty. Put these questions to your soul. Had I sincere resolution to forsake my wicked way when I came to Christ? Did I relinquish all dependence upon my own works? Did I come to Him empty-handed, resting on His promise "him that cometh to Me I will in no wise cast out?" Then you may upon us is a requirement very far from welcome to those who wish to please themselves and follow their own devices. The standard of piety, the spirituality of God's Law, the nature of holiness, the insistence that we must keep ourselves unspotted from this world, are directly contrary to the inclinations of the natural man. That we must discipline our affections, regulate our thoughts, mortify our carnal appetites, cut off a right hand and pluck out a right eye, are certainly not good news to the unregenerate, especially when God insists that such mortification is never to be remitted but continued until mortality be swallowed up of life. No, it is impossible that fallen man will ever be pleased with a doctrine of perseverance in denying self, taking up his cross daily and following a holy Christ who is despised and rejected by this world. Thus it will abundantly appear from all that has been said, how baseless and pointless is the Arminian objection that the preaching of this doctrine encourages laxity and makes for licentiousness.

How can it be supposed that the proclamation of this blessed truth will lead to carelessness and carnality when we lay it down as a fundamental maxim that no one has any shadow of reason to consider himself interested in the blessing of perseverance except as he has and gives clear evidence that he is inwardly conformed to God and outwardly obedient to His commands? Yet it must be allowed, no matter how carefully and proportionately the doctrine of Scripture be set forth by God's servant, there will always be those ready to wrest . to their own destruction. If the Lord Jesus was falsely charged with "perverting the nation" (Luke 23:2) His ministers must not expect immunity from similar criminations. If the apostle Paul was slanderously reported of teaching "Let us do evil, that good may come" (Rom. 3:8), we must not be surprised if the enemies of God should falsify our assertions and draw erroneous inferences from them. Yet this must not deter us from proclaiming all the counsel of God or keeping back anything that would be profitable to His people (Acts 20:27,20). And now to make practical application of all that has been before us. 1. How earnest should sinners be of becoming Christians. In Christ alone is salvation and safety to be found. Security of person and of estate is the principal concern of men in this world, but security of soul has little or no place in the thoughts of the majority. How fearful to be in imminent danger of death and eternal punishment, and how alarming the condition of those indifferent to their everlasting welfare. Where there is an underground shelter which is out of range of artillery and below the reach of falling bombs, how eagerly will the sane turn thither when the siren sounds. "The name of the Lord is a strong tower, the righteous runneth into it and is safe" (Prov. 18:10). O let every reader who has not yet done so make haste into his closet, fall upon his knees and rise not till he has committed himself wholly unto Christ for time and eternity. Halt no longer between two opinions. The wrath of God is upon thee, and there is but one way of escape: then flee for refuge to the hope set before you in the Gospel (Heb. 6:18). Christ stands ready to receive if you will throw down your weapons of warfare.

2. How diligently you should examine whether or not you are in Christ, the place of eternal security. You should know whether or not you have complied with the requirements of the Gospel, whether or not you have closed with Christ's gracious offer therein, whether spiritual life has come to your soul, whether you have been made a new creature in Christ. These things may be known with definite certainty. Put these questions to your soul. Had I sincere resolution to forsake my wicked way when I came to Christ? Did I relinquish all dependence upon my own works? Did I come to Him empty-handed, resting on His promise "him that cometh to Me I will in no wise cast out?" Then you may be assured on the infallible Word of God that Christ received you, and you are most grievously insulting Him if you doubt it. Do you value Christ above all the world? Do you desire to be conformed more and more to His holy image? Is it your earnest endeavor to please Him in all things, and is it your greatest grief and confession to Him when you have displeased Him? Then these are the sure marks of every one who is a member of His mystical Body.

3. How jealously we should watch over and seek to protect this tree of God's planting, from the winds of false doctrine and the pests which would fain destroy it. If we are to do so then we must give due attention to that injunction, "Keep thy heart with all diligence, for out of it are the issues of life" (Prov. 4:23). We must make conscience of everything which is harmful to godliness. We must walk in separation from the world and have "no fellowship with the unfruitful works of darkness." We must feed daily upon the Word of God, for otherwise growth is impossible. We must have regular recourse to the throne of grace, not only to obtain pardoning mercy for the sins committed but to find grace to help for present needs. We must make constant use of the shield of faith for there is no other defense against the fiery darts of Satan. A good beginning is not sufficient: we must press forward unto the things before. A small leak will eventually sink a ship if it be not attended to: many a noble vessel now lies wrecked upon the rocks.

4. How we should beware of wresting this doctrine. Let none encourage themselves in carelessness and fleshly indulgence through presuming upon their security in Christ. It is those who "hear" (heed) His voice and that "follow Him to whom He has made promise

"they shall never perish" (John 10:27, 28). The ones of whom the Lord has declared "They shall not depart from Me" are those to whom He said "I will put My fear in their hearts" (Jer. 32:40), but He gives no such assurance to those who trifle with Him. God has promised a victory to His people, but that very promise implies a warfare: victories are not gained by neglect and sloth. When Divine grace brings salvation to a soul it teaches him to deny "ungodliness and worldly lusts" and to "live soberly, righteously and godly in this present world" (Titus 2:12), and if it is not so teaching me, then I am a stranger to saving grace. There is nothing which has so much forwarded the Arminian error of apostasy as the scandalous lives of professing Christians: see that your life gives the lie to it.

5. How we must ascribe all the glory unto God. If you have stood firm while others have been swept away, if you have held on your way when many who accompanied you at the beginning have forsaken the paths of righteousness, if you have thrived when others have withered, it is due entirely to the distinguishing mercy and power of God. "Who maketh thee to differ, and what hast thou that thou didst not receive" (1 Cor. 4:7): you have no cause whatever to boast. "But the Lord is faithful, who shall establish you and keep you from evil" (2 Thess. 3:3): if the Lord, then not myself. It is true we "will" and do, but it is God who worketh both in us (Phil. 2:13). Our sufficiency is of Him and not of ourselves, and due acknowledgment should be made of this; and it will be by real saints. "Not unto us, O Lord, not unto us, but unto Thy name give glory, for thy mercy, for Thy truth's sake" (Ps. 115:1).

6. How we should magnify the grace of God. The mind is incompetent to perceive how much we are beholden to the Lord for His interest in and care of us. As His providence is virtually a continual creation, an upholding of all things by His 'power, without which they would lapse back again into nonentity: so the Christian's preservation is like a continual regeneration, a maintenance of the new creation by the operations of the Spirit and the bestowing fresh supplies of grace. It was the realization of this fact that moved David to acknowledge of God, "Which holdeth our soul in life and suffereth not our feet to be moved" (Ps. 66:9). As Charnock well said, "It is a standing miracle in the world that all the floods of temptation shall not be able to quench this little heavenly spark in the heart, that it shall be preserved from being smothered by the streams of sin which arise in us, that a little smoking flax shall burn in spite of all the buckets of water which are poured upon it." Thus God perfects His strength in our weakness. "O give thanks unto the Lord, for His goodness, for His mercy endureth forever" (Ps. 106:1).

7. How compassionate we should be unto weaker brethren. The more you are mindful of the Lord's upholding hand, the more compassionate will you be unto those with feeble knees. "If a man be overtaken in a fault, ye which are spiritual restore such a one in the spirit of meekness, considering thyself lest thou also be tempted" (Gal. 6:1). Call to mind how patiently the Lord has borne with you. Remember how ignorant you were but a short time ago, and expect not too much from babes in Christ. Has not the Lord often recovered you when you did wander? Have not your brethren still occasion to bear with many blemishes in you? If so, will you be hyper-critical and censorious toward them! Despise not small grace in any, but seek to encourage, to counsel, to help. Christ does not break the bruised reed, nor must we.

CPSIA information can be obtained
at www.ICGtesting.com
Printed in the USA
LVHW022353131022
730696LV00012B/563